COMRADES, CONCUBINES AND LOVERS

Graham Hunter

CONTENTS

Acknowledgments

1   A new beginning   1

2   South Africa and Pauline   7

3   Moscow. My first visit   20

4   Sokolniki Park   28

5   First day at exhibition   37

6   Hong Kong and Lolita   46

7   Korea and Ko He-Rang   51

8   South Africa   57

9   Second visit to Moscow   62

10 Mr Pankratov   78

11 Yugoslavia and Zoritsa   85

12 Miss Su 1   91

13 Miss Su 2   103

14 Moscow, third visit   109

15 Moscow, May1986   120

16 Far East, second visit   123

17 Far East and Australia   130

18 Loli in London   141

19 The Proposal   144

20 The next steps   148

21 Zagreb, Belgrade and Far East   150

22   Moscow, October 1986   161

23   Poland, Hungary, Czechoslovakia and Yugoslavia   167

24   Moscow, December 1986   169

25   South Africa and Moscow   174

26   Far East and China   177

27   Moscow, Sri Lanka, Australia and Singapore   185

28   Moscow May 1987   191

29   The Wedding Licence, July 1987   195

30   Kuala Lumpur, Hong Kong and Korea   200

31   The Wedding, September 1987   204

32   First time in Japan, October 1987   212

33   Loy Krathong, December 1987   220

34   Lena's first experience in UK   225

35   Far East & Home, March 1988   233

36   1988 & 1989   238

37   Vilnius & Pskov, August 1989   244

38   The Wall came down   254

39   1991 - 1998   256

40   1998 - 2000   262

ACKNOWLEDGMENTS

I would like to thank the following people for their help in producing this book.

Cerys Pinkman BA for editing my manuscript.

Millie Belding for the beautiful artwork on the cover.

My wife Leah for putting up with me during the months of writing.

The group of friends who proof read my manuscript.

And Elaine who got me started in the first place..

Chapter 1

A new beginning

I had just started a new job as Export Manager for a medical/scientific equipment manufacturing company. After having recently ended a disastrous, loveless marriage I was now free to travel the world. My brief was to increase existing sales in Western Europe and to take on the new territories of Eastern Europe, Africa, India, the Far East and Australasia. I was 34 years old and just entering a phase of my life where most people would be settling down but my life was just beginning. Wow. I am getting paid to visit all these countries! Who wouldn't want that opportunity? With the ending of my marriage, I had no worries about being gone from home for too long. I was excited about what I would see and who I might meet. This would be my time.

I had only joined the company in the January and in February I was sent to Poland with Simon, an engineer, to help install some recently delivered equipment and hopefully sell some more. Neither of us had ever been behind the Iron Curtain before and had not been briefed on any of the culture and customs that would have saved us from some forthcoming embarrassing situations. Apparently the customers had visited the UK before I joined the company and had met Simon.

Warsaw airport was cold and dismal with long queues to get through passport control, which didn't help the nerves. There were uniformed men who wore peaked caps with dark green uniforms and carried guns. Their hard stares further increased my nervousness. I could feel my heart thumping. We had to fill in customs declaration forms, which included listing any money and valuables brought into the country. How naïve of me not to realise what this was for! The

Zloty was a restricted currency and was not allowed outside Poland. All currency exchanges needed to be recorded officially by a bank and all items of value such as gold rings had to be declared in case you sold them during your stay. We were met at the airport by a lady and gentleman from the Institute, Jan and Malgorzheta, who were to drive us to Lodz through a blinding blizzard. It was approximately 135km to Lodz but it seemed to take forever to get there. On the way we went past Frederick Chopin's birth house and were promised a visit there if time permitted. They pointed it out to us but could barely see it through the snow clad trees.

Although I had been warned how cold it might be when we arrived in Lodz nothing could have prepared me for my first experience with temperatures below -25°C. I had come dressed in a business suit and raincoat with no gloves. My moustache had developed icicles and the inside of my nose was freezing solid. I had to squeeze it to break up the ice crystals. On arriving at the hotel I mistakenly pushed the door handle with my ungloved hand, which immediately froze to the bare metal. I was terrified that I might rip some skin off but after a lot of huffing and puffing from both of us, our combined hot breath released me from the door handle.

The following morning we were taken to the Institute for Materials Research where we were to install and train the staff how to use some specialised measuring equipment. The building was very uninviting. The walls were grey and dirty with broken drainpipes detached from their fixings and huge icicles hung from the gutter. The clean white snow from yesterday's blizzard lay untrodden and in stark contrast to the dirty walls. The cars were all fitted with studded tyres and had no difficulty negotiating the frozen roads as I had discovered during my two scary journeys so far. They drove as if there was no difference between normal dry roads and those covered in ice and snow. Not something I was used to coming from a country where everything comes to a standstill if there is a centimetre of snow lying on the road!

Inside the Institute it was very warm and the floor of the entrance hall was awash with dirty melting snow off peoples boots. An old lady wearing what looked her husband's socks rolled down to her ankles was constantly mopping the floor but the influx of people was more than she could keep up with. My feet were very cold as I was wearing leather soled shoes which were not the best thing for coping with these extreme weather conditions.

The morning's work went well and at 12.30pm we were invited to a restaurant for lunch at which point I said that I needed to go via a bank if possible to get some Zlotys.

'No problem,' they said. 'We can change it for you here.'

'Great,' I said handing over US$100 thinking that they must have a staff banking facility here.

When they returned with my money they told me that they had got a "good rate" for me and handed over a large bundle of notes. Little did I realise that I had just used the black market and they had gladly given me 10 times the official exchange rate in order to get their hands on some dollars. Under Communism and in a Command Economy everything was supposed to be supplied for the people but seldom was. The only way that some goods could be obtained was on the black market and only for payment in any hard currency. The American Dollar was always the favourite.

We were taken to a lovely restaurant, a short drive from the Institute. The first course was clear Borscht soup, a highly flavoursome, clear red liquid not dissimilar looking to red wine, in a bowl with two handles. I eagerly started on my mine with a soupspoon only to be told that it was polite to use the handles on the soup bowl as if drinking from a cup. I looked down at the bowl and hesitantly grabbed it with both hands, not sure whether it was a joke. I could see other people doing it so I joined in. This was followed by Polish sausage with cabbage and potatoes, which was surprisingly tasty.

'Would we like to try some speciality Polish vodka?' we were asked.

'Oh yes please,' I said.

Well when the bottle of freezing cold vodka arrived I was horrified to see that there was a dead creature similar to a chameleon inside and the colour of its scaly skin had imparted a colour to the vodka! We just had to drink it neat but after gingerly taking my first reluctant sip I was pleasantly surprised at the taste and drunk it all in one swig as was the custom.

Our hosts were very concerned that we did not have warm clothes or hats so after lunch we were taken to some shops. I was looking forward to this as I was freezing. There was only one clothes shop in town. It was situated on a street corner and appeared to be constructed of horizontal concrete slabs. The door and window together took up no more than eight feet of frontage with dark green painted woodwork, half of which had flaked off years ago. There were two planks of wood acting as shelves in the window front, the top one completely empty and the bottom one had ten very old fashioned looking shirts, stacked vertically on their sides. That was the entire stock of the shop and not a hat in sight. 'Oh well, looks like we will have to stay cold!' I said.

The whole shopping area was stark, covered in dirty snow with very little to buy. However we did come across a camera shop. I had a Russian made Zenith SLR 35mm camera and lo and behold, this shop had a plethora of lenses and accessories for Zenith cameras. The prices seemed very cheap to me especially as I had got a pocket full of Zlotys that I had exchanged at 10x the rate. I bought several telephoto lenses and other accessories that I had not seen in UK camera shops. Of course these were Russian made products in a Soviet country. It was strange to me that the shop that everyone wanted to buy from – the clothes shop – had very little for sale but the shop that had products in – the camera shop – no one needed or had the money to buy. Nevertheless they existed together regardless of demand or profitability as this was a Command Economy.

If you don't know, a Command Economy is where Central Government tells factories how much of their product they need to make to achieve the Central Plan. This is often done with no market research and no regard for profitability. The principal is to make what has been asked for (commanded), whether there be a glut or shortage of said items in the time allocated. If they have achieved their target in less time the workers simply sat around doing nothing. I was in disbelief; surely this system could not work.

As our car pulled in on our return to the Institute I was intrigued to see the bin man collecting the rubbish bins. I had to clear the condensation off the car window to get a good look at him. He was in a wooden sledge, drawn by a white horse, which looked rather dirty against the white snow. He had a hat on. A very warm looking hat at that. It had two ear-flaps hanging either side of his head, bouncing up and down with the rhythm of the horse's footsteps as he had not tied it under his chin.

After further work in the afternoon we were taken back to our hotel in preparation for dinner. On the menu was that lovely Borscht that I had tasted at lunch time so I thought that I would enjoy that again. It arrived in the same bowl with handles which I proceded to pick up and drink.

'NO NO NO,' exclaimed our hosts. 'This is dinner so we eat Borsch with a spoon this time!'

The following morning we completed our work and were taken out for the rest of the day sightseeing. After a brief stop at Frederick Chopin's birth house we continued to the Budowa Mausoleum. I was not prepared for what I was to see there. The Mausoleum was an old concentration camp, used to murder and destroy thousands of people during WW2. The path leading up to the entrance was covered in virginal white snow. The red bricked wall, interspersed with watch towers, was capped in a layer of snow making it look somehow quite beautiful. It had the effect of providing a white picture frame around the building's features in front of a lawn of untouched snow.

Once inside, the feeling of beauty disappeared very quickly and was replaced with a feeling of disgust. The exhibits were mainly old black and white pictures blown up to poster size with the resulting increased grain adding an extra sense of horror to the content. They were pictures of the various ways the Nazis used to kill their prisoners and rows of emaciated people queueing up to meet their fate. The expressions on their faces were unforgettable. The last exhibit that I saw before rushing out in tears was the picture of the vat they used to boil up the bodies and extract the body fat to make soap. After each batch of bodies had been processed the dregs at the bottom of the vat were raked through to find any gold fillings in the mass of teeth that had become detached from the jawbones during boiling. I was sickened and wanted to get out of there as soon as I could. Our hosts were very apologetic about putting us through this experience but obviously wanted to bring to light this awful period of their history and to make sure that it never happened again.

After our visit Jan and Malgorzheta took us back to the airport. During conversation they asked if we had many Zlotys left.

'Quite a few,' I said.

'We can sell you some restaurant receipts if you need some to make your expense claims back at home.'

I was a bit taken aback with this but thought it might be a good idea. I can't remember now how many Zlotys exchanged hands for a selection of undated receipts but thought them very enterprising to do this. Malgorzheta also told us that she was getting married in a few weeks time and these Zlotys would come in handy.

We said our goodbyes and proceded to the Customs check whilst Jan and Malgorzheta waited.

'Customs certificate please,' said a burly officer.

'Any Zlotys left?'

Innocently I took out my wallet and said, 'yes a few.'

He took my wallet from me and started to count.

'You have too many Zlotys here. It is an offence to change money illegally and try to take it out of the country.'

'What do we do now?' I said to Simon who also had some more in his wallet.

'I know. Why don't we give them to Malgorzheta as a wedding present.'

With that I took back my wallet from the Customs Officer and emptied it of Zlotys and added them to Simon's stash. I quickly walked back to where Malgorzheta was still waiting, handed her the cash and wished her a happy wedding day. She was delighted. It was probably more money than she earned in a month.

Chapter 2

South Africa and Pauline

My trip to Poland had taught me a lot. It was essential to research the country's cultures, customs and politics before going on any business trip. It seems so obvious now but naivety and the enthusiasm of youth (if you call thirty four years old young) had clouded my judgement.

I was raring to get to my next destination....South Africa!

Dennis, the Managing Director, had made a trip out there before I joined the company but I was to assist our newly appointed distributors by accompanying them on an extensive demonstration and lecture tour which would take the best part of four weeks.

Image Analysis was still in its infancy and we were discovering more and more applications that it could be used for. The software was the important bit but basically if you could get an image into the system, multiple measurements could be made from simple counts to complex area measurements of irregular shaped objects. The source of the image could be an aerial photograph right down to an electron microscope output. If you could get an image, you could measure it. This meant that anything from a photo from outer space down to organelles of a cell were now measurable. My background in pathology was a great benefit (and was one reason why the company employed me) but applications could be considered in any scientific discipline. My challenge in South Africa was to do a series of lectures on Image Analysis in various Scientific Institutes followed by a live demonstration to the audience. I had told our distributors that when inviting people to attend my lecture they were welcome to bring their own problematical samples and see if I could do anything with them. So no pressure there then!

In the run-up to my departure I had prepared as many 35mm slides as I could, showing different applications in a variety of situations. These included simple bacterial colony counting, area fraction measurement of impurity inclusions in a cut metal surface, counting penguins in the Antarctic and agricultural crop productivity from aerial photographs of fields. A last-minute one I managed to include was measuring the pore size in teabags plus the size of the included tea leaves. When I rehearsed my talk it could take between thirty to forty five minutes depending on how much detail went into it. To keep the attention of the delegates on what could have been a dry scientific talk, I designed my slides to be humorous and rather than show lots of graphs and data, I had pictures of penguins, teabags, farm fields which first caused amusement but more importantly prompted me as to what my next topic to talk about was. I had gathered a wealth of knowledge on my products and could talk at length without notes; just using my pictorial slides as prompts. I prided myself on this as I had worked hard on my presentation skills and was growing in confidence.

My flight to Johannesburg was with Air Zimbabwe via Harare. 'This should be interesting,' I thought. Zimbabwe had only been an independent country since April 1980 (five years ago) when Ian Smith stood down as the last white leader of what was formally Rhodesia. I had read up on South African politics and was very aware that apartheid ruled and Nelson Mandela had been in prison on Robben Island since 1963 – some 22 years! Because of this, South Africa had become a pariah and not a politically correct country to visit. I was advised that once I had a South African Visa in my passport I should obtain a second clean passport. There were countries that would not let you in if you had a South African stamp.

I arrived at Johannesburg airport the following morning after a very long flight. The one saving grace was that there was only one-hour time difference so no jetlag, just tiredness from not sleeping well in a cramped seat. I was met by the Managing Director of the company, Bob, who started to brief me during the journey, first to my hotel to freshen up followed by lunch and then to the office. I was to do a 5000km drive around the whole of South Africa, stopping off at major cities to give a talk and demonstration. He had specially purchased a Volkswagen van and had it sprayed up in the company's colours and logo. His staff would take it in turns to accompany me on different legs of the journey and he had spent a lot of money with us buying a complete set of demonstration equipment. He had even printed a brochure, advertising my visit and the places and times I would be visiting, which he had mailed to his customer base. I began to feel a bit of pressure and knew I had to make a commercial success of my tour to justify Bob's investment.

I was booked into the Rosebank Hotel in Johannesburg for the next two nights, which is where we lunched.

'Do try the bobotie. It's the national dish of South Africa,' said Bob.

It was delicious and very welcome after airline food for the last three meals. It was washed down with very cold Castle beer and seeing that it was still late summer in Johannesburg and a pleasant 24°C, this too hit the spot. In the humidity, the glass bottle had condensation on it with droplets slowly running down, leaving a puddle on the tabletop.

I was now feeling very relaxed and tired but my day was far from over yet. Bob took me to the office where I had to check out all the delivered demonstration equipment and meet the sales guys who would be selling it.

Everything was packed into the company van and I was whisked off to another bar to have drinks with Bob's other director/partner in the business. Then three other members of staff turned up who were going to take me to dinner. By the time I crawled into bed I was shattered. 'Boy, is this going to be a gruelling four weeks,' I thought.

Bright and breezy at 7:30am Bob came to collect me from the hotel. I had just had time to polish off a full South African breakfast, which included among other things a large lump of steak. Our drive today was to Pretoria to visit MEDUNSA, the Medical University of South Africa. It was only 1½ hours travelling but once there, all the equipment had to be taken out of the van and set up in working order. MEDUNSA was an all black university and apparently was the best equipped university in South Africa. Bob had recently sold them 300 microscopes in one order so naturally they were very important to him. I had approximately 30 people come to my lecture and all were keen to see the analysers working. Bob told me afterwards that there would be an order for at least four systems as a result of today's work so I felt as if my tiredness was justified.

We packed up at 2:15pm, got back to the office at 3:15pm in time for a quick cup of coffee and set off again at 3:45pm. We barely had a chance to breathe before setting off for the next talk. The next stop was Bloemfontein, which was 400km away. I thought that we were going to stop but no, Bob wanted to get there that night. I did help out with some of the driving but looming on the horizon was a huge black cloud. We could see from a distance the flashes of lightning and the distant rumble of thunder that was getting nearer. Then the heavens opened, with hailstones the size of ice cubes. The noise in the van was deafening and in order to prevent any damage we sought refuge under a bridge. It only took 10 minutes to pass over but was it scary. On the News that evening they reported that 56mm of rain (or ice cubes) had fallen in that 10 minutes. At last we got to the hotel at 8:45pm had a quick supper and collapsed into bed.

Our visit the next day was the Department of Anatomical Pathology in Bloemfontein University. Bloemfontein is 6000 feet above sea level and now oxygen depletion was adding to my tiredness. I had about thirty visitors, two of which brought specimens for me to look at. One involved measuring different areas in a bone section, which had been stained red and green and was relatively easy with the increased contrast. The second sample was an acetate filter on which were trapped asbestos fibres from an air sample. This was a bit more difficult but eventually we cracked it. Another two sales were promised. Sorry to give exact timing details again but you will begin to see just how hard I was being worked. Bob wanted to get as much out of me as possible during my visit. We left Bloemfontein at 2:40pm and drove another 543km to Beaufort West where we found a motel at 8:15pm. Today was Friday. Surely I had no work to do tomorrow so could have a lie in.

9

No way! 7:15am and Bob was knocking at my door. We were now going to drive 230 km to Matjiesfontein for breakfast, and what a drive. Through the Great Karoo Desert. 230km of nothing but desert, sand, stones and boulders, prickly pear cactuses and balls of tumbleweed blowing down the road. No garages, no habitation and very few other vehicles. You had to be prepared for this drive and fill up with fuel before starting. Emergency rations were also essential and ours were bottled water and dried biltong. Biltong is a South African delicacy and is basically dried meat. This can be made out of any meat and commercially available types include ostrich, kudu, gazelle, antelope, wildebeest, zebra et cetera. When you put it in your mouth at first all you got was the dry texture of the meat but as you chewed it, the flavour of the spices exploded in your mouth.

Matjiesfontein was an oasis in the Karoo. One road in and one road out. It was a leftover from the old colonial era and is preserved exactly as it was built. The single road through it was lined with beautiful old buildings along one side behind a long white painted brick wall with ornate wrought iron work between square brick pillars. The buildings included a post office, a bank, a Masonic Hall, resplendent in a bold green and white striped corrugated roof, a bar and right in the middle, the Lord Milner hotel. This beautiful colonial style building had a balcony all around the upper floor, again with wrought iron work all along. On top of the balcony was a castellated roof with three towers, one in the middle and one on each front corner. It was an iconic reminder of an age gone by. A Union flag still fluttered on the flagpole on the roof, a constant reminder of the town's past.

The bar was a real jewel. Once inside you were transported back to the 1800s. The beautiful oak panelling interspersed with mirrors reflected the sparkle from the glasses and optics. The central wooden feature behind the bar concealed the door down to the cellar. Above the door was a mantelpiece, which held two soda siphons, reminiscent of the Kipps apparatus in chemistry lessons for making hydrogen sulphide gas. Between the siphons was a large picture of Queen Victoria, staring down on the drinkers with a stern look, haunting them with her stare from a time gone by when she ruled.

The other side of the single road was completely taken up with the railway station with a platform large enough to take 20 carriages or more. It was a single-track railway with some passing places to allow trains to pass in opposite directions. A large forecourt, lined with palm trees, looked like a big car park, now empty. An old red London Transport double decker bus was parked by the exit from the platform. This did seem superfluous as you could walk the whole length of Matjiesfontein in five minutes.

We breakfasted in the Lord Milner hotel and then headed back to the van. As soon as we left Matjiesfontein we were back in the Karoo desert. It was now 238 km to get to Cape Town but we were stopping in Paarl in the wine region for a wine tasting. About 50km out of Cape Town the scenery changed dramatically. Rolling hills covered in lush green vineyards - miles and miles of them. After nearly 500km of nothing but desert it provided a welcome relief to the traveller. The four wines we tasted, chilled perfectly, were nice but not being a wine connoisseur I couldn't taste what we were supposed to taste. Freshly mown grass, elderflower with a hint of gooseberries! Tasted like wine to me!

We arrived in Cape Town at 2.00pm. During the journey Bob had sworn me to secrecy and told me that he had a girlfriend in Cape Town. After a wash and brush up in the hotel we were off again round to Megan's flat. At Megan's we swapped the company van for her car and Bob drove us around Devils Peak. The central district of Cape Town is nestled in a mountainous backdrop somewhat like half an amphitheatre. Looking at the mountains from the harbour Devil's Peak is on the left of Table Mountain and Lions head is on the right. The view over Cape Town was stunning but I was told it was even better from the top of Table Mountain and we might find time to go up if the weather stayed clear. I had to pinch myself, to witness the glory of this mountain for myself. What a sight to behold.

Back at sea level we dined at the Harbour Café having had to go through a customs check as the restaurant was in a bonded warehouse area. Finally we had an Irish coffee with one of Megan's friends and I eventually got to bed at 1.00am.

Sunday was just as frantic. Bob and I left the hotel at 8:30am and drove down to the Cape. This is often referred to as the most southerly point but actually it is not. It is however where the warm waters of the Indian Ocean and the cold Atlantic meet and a visible line of currents on the surface of the sea can be seen going out from the tip of the peninsula. You could see the line stretching out to sea as the two oceans met. Baboons freely frolic around the rocks while signs warned visitors from getting too near them, especially if you were carrying food. On the drive back we had to stop for a troop of baboons to cross the road when a female jumped up onto the bonnet of the car, closely followed by a big male and proceeded to fornicate vigorously just on the other side of our windscreen. I was slightly embarrassed, not knowing what to say but we were both amused as we waited for our unexpected guests to finish!

The last stop of the day was to visit the company's Cape Town salesman, Kieren, just on the periphery of the city. His family were very welcoming and had organised a fish braai for me. (Braai is South African for barbecue). Kieren offered to give me a lift back to my hotel as Bob was going to stay with Megan. He was a very large, bearded man with a hard Afrikaans accent. We discussed the problem of apartheid and whether it was dangerous to drive around the city at night. He put his hand under the driver's seat and pulled out a handgun. 'If I get stopped at night by a black (he did use a more derogatory term) I shoot first and ask questions later.' I didn't know quite what to say to this, I was stunned and somewhat scared at his frankness.

At last I got to bed at a reasonable time and was told that I could have the morning off and would be picked up for lunch.

The following morning was bliss. The hotel had a pool, Jacuzzi and sauna which I relished until I looked like a wrinkled prune. I tucked into a hearty South African breakfast and set out for the shops. I had not got any short-sleeved shirts and thought I would feel more comfortable in the humidity, dressed like the locals did.

My next venue was the Medical School attached to Groote Schuur Hospital, famous for the world's first heart transplant carried out by Dr Christian Barnard on the 3rd December 1967. He was no longer operating as he had bad arthritis in his fingers but had opened up a restaurant in town where we were going to eat that night. I gave my talk and demonstration to about 60 people and felt exhilarated that I was standing on the podium that Chris Barnard would have lectured his medical students from. One of the delegates had heard that penguin counting was one of my applications and had brought along some of his photographs. He wanted to count seal populations on rocks from aerial photos. Unfortunately brown seals on rocks had little contrast compared with black penguins on white snow so I had to reluctantly admit defeat on this one. No immediate sales would transpire from this venue as they had no money left in this year's budget but said they would put in for a system in the next financial year. Oh well, you can't win them all.

After packing up, Kieren and Bob took me to two English pubs. Why I should want to visit English pubs in South Africa I don't know but that was their idea of hospitality. Bob had booked a table at Chris Barnard's restaurant, La Vita. Megan was coming and bringing a friend for me. That would be nice. Kieren was bringing his wife so I realised that they too were party to Bob's little secret as well.

La Vita was a lovely restaurant offering haute cuisine and specialising in seafood. Megan turned up with her friend Pauline who was to be my companion for the evening. Pauline was slim with short medium brown hair. Her face looked kind and very pretty. She was thirty eight years old compared with my thirty four. She was married and had two teenage children but her marriage had gone stale and they were contemplating divorce. She still lived in the family home but led a separate life from her husband. Interesting combination of people I thought. Kieren and his wife happily married, Bob cheating on his wife, me waiting for my divorce to be finalised and Pauline leading another life, with her husband's knowledge and presumably approval.

The speciality of the day was a fish stew with whole crayfish served in a cauldron to share at the table. Chris Barnard must have had a big ego as all the plates, cups, saucers etc. had his autograph under the glaze plus the words La Vita with a rose on the top. They were white with a maroon halo on the rim. A simple yet bold design.

The conversation flowed effortlessly and I got on very well with Pauline. We talked about food, fish especially as they were always on the menu in a coastal city. Some I hadn't heard of before such as "Snoek." When we had finished Bob suggested that I should lick my plate clean and stuff it down my trousers as a souvenir. It was a bit difficult fitting it in as my tummy was now a bit swollen from all the over indulgence and no exercise for the past seven days. As we left our table and went to pay, who should be sitting in reception signing autographs was the great man himself, Christian Barnard. We stopped and chatted for a while but conscious of the fact that I had one of his plates stuffed down my trousers I made a speedy exit.

Once outside Kieren and his wife said they had to go home to the children but Bob suggested that as it was such a lovely clear night with thousands of stars twinkling, we should have a drive up to the Rhodes Memorial, which was part way up to Devil's Peak.

Bob was driving Megan's car while Pauline and I jumped into the back seat. She took my arm and snuggled up to me. I had not had any female attention for a long time and this felt amazing. I kept telling myself how lucky I was to get this job where I was paid to travel the world and now to get a bit of female companionship as well.

The Rhodes Memorial was built to honour Cecil Rhodes, the diamond magnate, and was a monstrous edifice looking more like a Greek temple, with four lions on either side of the twenty five stone steps leading from his statue on horseback to the multi pillared temple. Bob parked up and we decided to walk up the steps to admire the magnificent view under this star lit sky. Pauline took my arm and held me close as we went up the huge stone steps. At the top we paused, turning towards each other and it just seemed right to kiss her. She returned my kiss with equal affection as she must also have been deprived of attention for some while. We held that embrace for I don't know how long but felt like an eternity until eventually Bob called over, 'are you two coming down now?'

We dropped Pauline off at her home when I asked if I could see her again. I was staying in Cape Town for three nights and suggested that she had a dinner with me at my hotel the following night. Bob thought that this was a good idea as it meant he didn't have to look after me and could stay with Megan.

The next morning started with a swim, sauna and Jacuzzi at 7 o'clock in an attempt to try to get rid of some of the weight that I must have put on. Another busy day followed but I will spare you the details of that.

After we had finished work Bob said, 'right, the weather is still clear. Let's go up Table Mountain.'

I am frightened of heights but I was excited at the thought of going up this iconic mountain. There were some fluffy clouds hanging around the top of the mountain but the cable car was still running. Great...

At the cable car base station I was beginning to wonder whether it was such a good idea as I looked upwards to the top station. At one point the cables went nearly vertically as they approached the top. The cars had large glass windows to enable a good view all round so there was nowhere that I could hide. What an adrenaline rush that ride was for me particularly as we approach the top. But it was worth it, the view was spectacular and we were actually above the level of the clouds. I managed to pose for one photograph looking out from the observation platform but I didn't hang around there long. It was beginning to get dark so after only 10 minutes on the top we decided to come down.

Bob dropped me off back at my hotel where I had arranged to meet Pauline. He zoomed off to spend the night with Megan. Pauline arrived bang on time at 7:30pm by taxi and we went into the hotel bar for a pre-dinner drink. The menu in the hotel restaurant was not brilliant but served a purpose for our meeting. To this day I cannot remember what we had to eat but I do remember that after we had finished I suggested that we took coffee in my room. Pauline instantly agreed. My heart raced.

I felt a little bit nervous taking her up to my room but there was no one around in reception to see me so we quickly ran up the stairs. The only coffee I had to offer her in my room was the little sachet of instant coffee and a plastic pot of sterilised milk but that didn't matter. After only a few sips of coffee Pauline turned to me and said,

'Will you make love to me?'

I hadn't been intimate with a woman for such a long time I was beginning to worry how I would manage with a lady I had only met the night before.

I shouldn't have worried. It was magic. We made love with an intensity that I had never known before. Wow, what had I been missing all these years. It all exploded in a massive orgasm for both of us and we collapsed panting in each other's arms. It was what I needed but hadn't expected.

Within half an hour (and not wishing to brag) I was ready for more, which culminated in similar joint satisfaction. It was as if we both knew each other's bodies and how to stimulate them. I glanced at my watch. It was 01.00am. 'I'll have to go soon,' said Pauline, 'but just one more time.' I didn't know I had it in me but I managed to perform a third time.

By now it was 2.30am and the night porter had locked up for the night. Pauline and I crept down the stairs and were confronted by a very large, black security guard. I had a lot of explaining to do as to why Pauline, an unregistered guest, was with me in my room until such a late hour. Eventually he gave in, telephoned for a taxi for Pauline and opened the front door so we could wait outside for it to arrive. It didn't take long and after agreeing to meet again that evening, Pauline went home and I walked quickly past the security guard with a cheerful, 'Thank you. Good night.' Back in my room I collapsed into a deep, contented sleep.

7.00am came all too quickly. I managed to get my swim and sauna plus breakfast before Bob came to collect me.

'How did you get on last night?' he said with a massive grin.

'Very nicely thank you,' I replied. 'I will be seeing her again tonight if that's OK with you.'

'That's fine by me but just remember we have a 6.00am start tomorrow morning so make sure you are ready.'

That evening Pauline took me to her favourite pizza restaurant in Seapoint. After eating our fill we went for a walk along the seafront, which was a popular place for young lovers. We were not alone walking along the promenade holding hands. We shared a lot of details about our lives and how we had both come to the same conclusion that our current partners were not for us.

A quick taxi ride got us back to my hotel where by now, the night security guard had already come on duty. He gave me a knowing look and said, 'will madam be requiring a taxi again tonight boss?'

'Yes please,' I said as we quickly ran up the stairs into the safety of my room.

We made love another two times before going down to confront the security guard again. Before Pauline left, we tried to arrange another meeting but as I did not know my exact itinerary for the next couple of weeks I suggested that Bob could organise something for us. She agreed and drove off into the night hoping that we would meet again.

The next morning we left Cape Town at 6.00am en route for the Houw Hoek Hotel, the oldest licenced establishment in South Africa, where we had breakfast. In the grounds of the hotel was the largest blue gum tree in South Africa. The next leg of our drive was to take us to Plettenburg Bay where we could enjoy a swim. I don't remember any of the route as I was out cold in the van and slept for nearly 4 hours, so Bob told me.

Plettenburg Bay was beautiful with a small peninsula at one end where a luxury hotel now stood. 'Come on,' said Kieren, 'let's go for a swim.' There were only three people on the beach, which I found strange as the weather for swimming was perfect. I ran in through the waves like a child who had never

15

seen the sea before. The waves were perfect for body surfing, which I enjoyed for about 10 minutes until Bob shouted at me,

'Graham come out quick NOW!'

I looked behind me and not 50 yards away from me was the dorsal fin of a shark gliding through the water towards me. A sense of terror came over me and I struck out for the shore faster than I have ever swum before. Needless to say, because you are reading this book, I made it safely to shore before the shark reached me. Now I knew why there were only three people on the beach.

After drying down we drove over to the Beacon Island Hotel and had afternoon tea. 'How quaint,' I thought. The restaurant was right at the sea end of the building and had water around three sides. I looked out for my shark but couldn't see him. He must have gone off seeking an easier prey! Off we went again. The final destination for today was Port Elizabeth. This time I stayed awake to see the scenery with the occasional stop for a photo. We crossed Storms River Gorge on a single span bridge and through Nature Valley. It was beautiful. Occasionally a troop of baboons would cross the road in front of us often sitting in the middle and forcing us to stop. 'Keep your windows wound up,' said Bob. 'This is a trick of theirs to make you stop and then hijack your car looking for food.' We eventually arrived at the Beach Hotel in Port Elizabeth at 8:00pm and enjoyed a dinner of several varieties (species) of steak in their Bell Restaurant.

Friday morning gave us plenty of time to set up a demonstration in Port Elizabeth Technikon followed by my talk in the afternoon. Two delegates had brought samples that were new to me but we had a go. A research scientist from Ford Motor Company had brought some brake linings on which he wanted to measure some stress patterns. I nearly cracked it but to work really well it needed some special illumination techniques on the microscope. No worries, Bob could sort that out at a later date but it looked like another sale. The second person with a sample was a lady from the Wool Bureau who wanted to measure the length and diameters of wool fibres. Easy Peasy. She went away happy also promising to place an order.

While we were packing up Bob gave me a massive compliment. 'I've got to hand it to you. The way you deal with the audiences and confidently take the samples that you have never seen before is amazing. You certainly know your stuff and I am so pleased to have you working with us.' I felt incredibly good upon hearing this, all the nerves had long gone and were replaced with a sense of confidence.

Bob was a personal friend of Rod, a Senior Lecturer from the Department of Biological Sciences who asked us to join him for drinks. After a few very welcome cold Castle beers we went back to his house to pick his wife up and off to dinner at a steakhouse called "the Hungry I". I ordered the ribs but when they came I was sure I would never be able to finish them. They were huge and fell off the sides of the plate. I did manage them but felt extremely uncomfortable. The South Africans are great meat eaters and I couldn't let my hosts down by not finishing it. My poor stomach was getting bigger and I noticed that I was now using one hole larger on my belt!

On Saturday morning Bob flew back to Johannesburg leaving me in Kieren's capable hands for the weekend. Konnor was flying down on Monday to take over allowing Kieren to go back home to Cape Town. At last a free weekend with nothing to do except touristy things and relax. First off Kieren took me to a dolphinarium followed by a snake park. After a modest lunch we went to Seaview Game Reserve where we saw lions, cheetahs, zebra, rhino and wildebeest. It seemed strange going "on Safari" in the company van, loaded with thousands of pounds worth of equipment and microscopes.

Back to the Beach House hotel. This was the third night in the same hotel bed but with no female company. We ate in a curry house, one of Kieren's favourites and I ordered my usual vindaloo.

'Are you sure?' asked Kieren.

'Yes no problem. I love hot curries.'

Well I wished I had heeded Kieren's warning. Was it hot! Determined not to be a wimp I ate it all but by the last mouthful. I could no longer feel my lips and my tongue was on fire. Then on to Lilies bar in the Holiday Inn to listen to an Irish duo singing. It took several pints of cold draught Guinness before my mouth started to come back to life.

Sunday morning was quite relaxed. We went to Addo Elephant Park and drove around in the company van in search of the herd of elephants that were resident there. A leisurely lunch in the park and then a drive to Grahamstown where we arrived at 4:00pm. We were booked into the 1812 Settlers Motel where Konnor was waiting for us. We were all knackered and after an early supper we all retired to bed at 8:45pm.

The morning set up was in the department of Ichthyology in the University of Grahamstown. We had to be ready for a 9:30am start. About 20 people turned up, freely admitting that they knew nothing about Image Analysis and wanted to learn. I was complimented on how interesting my talk was and got them thinking how they could use Image Analysis to solve their measuring problems. A couple of the University lecturers insisted that we stay for lunch at the University but Kieren had to leave to get back to Cape Town and left Konnor and me to it.

After lunch we drove through the Ciskei where the weather turned very misty with rain. We arrived at the King's Hotel for the night at 5:30pm with a gale blowing and whipping the sea up into a frenzy with large white horses on the waves. I went to bed at 9:45pm with the sound of distant waves crashing sending me into a dreamy sleep.

We left the hotel at 7:30am and drove all day through the Ciskei, arriving at the Blue Waters Hotel in Durban at 5:15pm. This was quite a change from previous venues as Durban is a big, sprawling, high-rise city and we had rooms on the 17th floor of the hotel.

Wednesday morning's set up was at the University of Natal where I had an audience of 30 due in at 9:00am. After I had finished at 11:00am Professor Berzac asked if I could do the lecture again if he brought in a new audience. 'Of course,' I agreed and somehow he got together another 70 attendees comprising students and lecturers. Professor Berzac insisted we joined him for lunch as a thank you for my services.

In the afternoon there was nothing booked for me so I went with Konnor to the local technical college to help him set up some microscopes he had sold. Konnor had a brother who was an ophthalmologist in town and said that we should go and visit him and share a couple of beers. We then went out for dinner at the Pick & Shovel, another carnivore restaurant where I went for the ribs again. After dinner drinks were at the London Town pub, which had an actual London bus inside.

Thursday was another early start. Breakfast at 6:30am and left the hotel at 7:00 am, destination Pietermaritzburg. Only three people turned up at the venue so we left at 12:00midday and arrived back at Konnor's home in Johannesburg at 6:30pm. We had a couple of beers and dinner with Konnor and his family and then back to the Rosebank Hotel where I was booked in for the next week. It had been 14 days since I was last here but it seemed like an eternity. So much had happened in those two weeks.

I was picked up by Bob at 8:00am and spent the morning in the office doing a debriefing on the tour. Bob and David took me to lunch and then up the Carlton Tower to the 50th floor to get a good view over Johannesburg. Then back to the office for beers with the lads and then to Bob's house. Dinner was at the Chinese restaurant in the Rosebank hotel after which Bob and Christine left me to recover from the last 16 days activity.

The weekend was going to be action packed. On Saturday we went to Sun City, a Las Vegas style entertainment centre which took nearly three hours to drive there. Fortunately we were staying overnight as we went to a variety show followed by a late supper. Three hours driving back to Joburg the following morning and then a family Braai at Bob's house. Taking me aside, Bob told me that he arranged through Megan to get Pauline to fly up from Cape Town and stay with me at the Rosebank for a couple of nights. I couldn't wait.

The next couple of days were taken up doing personal customer visits around Johannesburg until Wednesday afternoon when we had to go to Jan Smuts Airport where Pauline was arriving at 2:30pm.

'What are you going to tell your wife?' I asked.

'I just told her that she was a friend of a friend that you had met in Cape Town and hit it off straight away.'

I was so excited to see Pauline get off the plane. I had only known her for three nights in Cape Town and now I had the opportunity for her to stay with me for two more nights, officially checked in to the Rosebank Hotel.

Bob dropped us off at the hotel and said, 'I just need you in the office for a couple of hours in the morning and the rest of Thursday is yours. On Friday we are having a lunch time braai at my house with all the guys from the office coming plus of course Pauline. It will be a fitting celebration for all the hard work you have done and a very successful sales tour around the country. I need to get you to the Airport by 4:00pm to catch your flight home.'

The next two nights where sheer bliss. I don't know whether it was because we had both come from disastrous relationships and hadn't had a caring physical relationship for years or whether there was some definite chemistry between us, which was worthy of following up. Either way I felt on top of the world. Our successful tour meant that there would be a lot of new sales, which would need installation and training so I should be coming back very soon.

The lunchtime braai at Bob's house went off very well although I did feel awkward introducing Pauline to Bob's wife. Kieren had flown up from Cape Town for a sales meeting but also to see me off. All the other sales guys were there which really made me feel quite important. All too soon Bob said, 'okay Graham it's time to go to the airport now.' Sadly I said my farewells but as Pauline had got a return flight to Cape Town at a time very close to my departure she was able to come with me. With just the three of us in the car Bob said that he was very pleased with what we had achieved over the last four weeks and would definitely want me back again not just for business but it also because it gave him a reason to travel to Cape Town with me.

At the airport, Pauline and I went our separate ways after an emotional goodbye. I agreed that I would telephone her whenever I could but my forthcoming schedule would be taking me out of the UK frequently. She was happy with Bob's comments knowing that she would see me again in the not too distant future.

I sat on the plane contemplating my new life. I was only three months into my new job and what an amazing time this had been. Who knows what the future might hold.

Chapter 3

Moscow, my first visit

The next Eastern European venue on my schedule was Moscow, USSR. After all the mistakes and faux pas I had made in Poland, Dennis had decided that I should have some comprehensive training on how to work and survive behind the Iron Curtain. I was much relieved to hear this. We took on a Consultant who had many years experience of trading in Eastern Europe and he was to be my mentor.

My first meeting with Terry filled me with confidence. He was larger than life, a very jovial character and seemed to have an endless supply of amusing anecdotes gained from his years of traveling. His swept back, silvery grey hair belied his years but gave him an air of authority. 'I am going to enjoy working with him', I thought. We went through my brief and put together a list of all the forthcoming Medical and Scientific Exhibitions coming up over the next few years in all the countries I had been charged with. Exhibitions were always good venues to base your activities from and even more so in Eastern Europe as I was about to learn.

There was a large exhibition coming up in Moscow in May which was now only a few months away. This was being held in Sokolniki Park, one of Moscow's largest exhibition sites but on the periphery of the City. As Terry had several companies in his portfolio he had booked a stand in his name and allocated a share of the space to the participants. Not all companies sent their representatives but relied on Terry's activities to get their business. Not so with me. I was keen to get as much experience as I could and was exhilarated at the thought of a trip to Moscow.

Organising an exhibition in the USSR was totally different from any Western European exhibition I had participated in. Firstly the stand would be divided in two halves. The front half was the display area but the rear half was the office, meeting room, storeroom and kitchen. YES A KITCHEN. As there were no cafes, restaurants or drink dispensers in Sokolniki we had to take everything including the kitchen sink! This back area was much more important than displays in the front as this was where the business was done, out of sight of prying eyes. It was also the place where we would cook and eat during the day and offer our customers copious alcoholic drinks that were denied them under Communism.

Packing the first crate with demonstration equipment was easy. The next crate was to include pots and pans, electric kettle, cutlery and crockery for as many attendees as were booked on the stand. Then came the food. I joke not – we had to pack as much dried and tinned food as we thought necessary for the 10 day exhibition including such delicacies as Vesta Dried curries, Pot Noodles, baked beans, tinned meats and fish, pasta and plenty of bars of chocolate. We hired a specialist transport company to collect the crates and drive them all the way to Moscow. They also organised crates of duty-free spirits, beer and soft drinks, vital for doing business in Moscow, as you will see later. All this had to be done at least 2 weeks before the start of the exhibition to allow the lorry driver plenty of time to get to Moscow and complete all the necessary formalities.

Russian visas were obtained through a specialist company, as to apply personally to the Russian Embassy in London would take a day out of your life and needed a great deal of patience queueing outside the high walls in Kensington High Street. The queue normally started to form at around 7.00am to guarantee entry to the Visa Section that day. People were called in one at a time from the queue in the street but the doors were closed at midday so anyone left standing outside at that time would have to come back the next day. Travel arrangements were booked through another specialist travel company but the final details of where we were to stay in Moscow and how to get there from the airport were organised by the Russian travel company INTOURIST. Nothing was easy or straight forward and I was beginning to wonder what I had let myself in for.

Next came my personal training. Terry was going out to Moscow two days ahead of me so I had to have enough information to be able to get through the airport and to the hotel.

'Let us deal with your luggage first', Terry said.

'Your bags will all be X-rayed on arrival and opened for inspection. Do not take any religious material or girly magazines as these will be confiscated and render you liable to a more thorough search. Do not take any items of value that are not necessary. Wedding rings, watches, bracelets and any other items of value will have to be declared to customs and will be checked again on departure to make sure you have not sold them. Take currency in US dollars and make sure you have an exchange receipt for them. Take a few packs of ladies tights and use your duty-free allowance of spirits plus a carton of 200 Marlboro cigarettes of which you always need to keep a packet of 20 in your pocket. Take a few cheap ballpoint pens and any plastic carrier bags you can get your hands on. Most importantly of all – bring a Universal bath plug.'

I was flabbergasted at the list but it was sound advice as I was soon to learn.

He continued.....

'On the plane you will be given an immigration form and a customs declaration form, both of which have to be given to the Customs officer on arrival. Your visa (which was issued as a separate sheet of paper) should be kept in your passport and will be stamped on arrival. DO NOT LOSE IT. When you are served your lunch on the plane ask for extra rolls but don't eat them. Bring them with you because you can't be sure that you will eat when you get to the hotel. Do not leave anything edible on the serving tray – bring it all with you.'

As he rambled on I noticed Terry's face become more and more serious, he wasn't joking anymore.

'It is a good idea to take some reading material with you to while away the time in the queue for Passport Control. War and Peace is a good choice,' Terry said. I thought he was joking but he wasn't. 'I have known it take up to 4 hours to get through so just be patient. There is nothing you can do about it.'

'After Passport Control retrieve your luggage and queue up again to have your bags X-rayed before opening them for inspection. Then make your way into the Arrival Hall.' I was getting more and more anxious about all these formalities that had to be completed. Now I was really worried about what I had let myself in for.

'What do I have to do to get a taxi to the hotel?' I interrupted.

'Nothing,' said Terry. 'Your taxi driver will find you'.

"What?'

'I have been told that we are staying at the Mezhdunarodnaya Hotel,' said Terry, 'so once you have checked in, make your way to the Hard Currency Bar and I will meet you there.

All this information...

I had so many questions...

The day of my departure came quickly. Terry had already gone to Moscow two days earlier so I really was on my own. I had packed my suitcase with all the necessary extras, checked and double checked my paperwork and waited for my taxi to Heathrow. I was really feeling apprehensive now but there was no going back. Check-in at Terminal 2 was easy enough; my visa was in order so off I went to Duty-Free. I felt strange buying 200 Marlboro cigarettes as I was a passionate non-smoker but I had to follow instructions.

The three and a half hour flight to Moscow was on British Airways with most of the passengers on business like myself. The atmosphere was cheerful with plenty of alcohol being served. Lunch was served and I duly grabbed several bread rolls when offered, carefully wrapping them in a serviette and secreting them in my hand baggage. About one hour before our arrival time the Captain came on the PA system saying that we were now in Russian airspace and under their control. The atmosphere on board immediately changed and people became quiet and sombre. This only added to my already heightened anxiety.

Looking out of the window, the countryside looked drab and uninspiring. I could see grey, high-rise blocks of flats in the distance as we circled round Sheremetyevo Airport, waiting for permission to land. Down we came with a thump and taxied over to our allocated stand. Well I made it.

Sheremetyevo Airport was equally drab and depressing. My first observation inside the terminal building was the ceiling was covered in what looked like bronze coloured, non-stick cake tins in irregular, upside down piles resembling mini stalactites. 'How odd,' I thought as I joined an enormous queue for Passport Control. Terry was certainly right about that.

After what seemed like several hours of waiting I was eventually called over to the next vacant booth where I was met by a pair of steely blue/grey eyes peering out of a small slit. I slid my passport and visa through the slit when it was grabbed and disappeared out of my sight. The steely blue/grey eyes continued to stare at me, unblinking. I didn't know whether to return the stare, looking defiant or to look around nervously, looking shifty. In the end I went for a combination of the two. This went on for at least ten minutes with me standing there, wondering what on earth was happening and what to do. At last I heard the thud of the official stamp on the ink pad and the softer thud as my visa was endorsed. I was through.

The next hurdle was to get through the melee at the baggage carousel to find my luggage. It had been such a long time getting to this point that my bags must have done the circuit hundreds of times but they were not there. The carousel was empty. A sense of fear overcame me thinking that someone had made off with my luggage and I would be stuck here with nothing other than what I stood up in. I frantically looked around, weaving in and out of the crowd and eventually saw a row of suitcases that had been taken off the carousel. 'There's mine,' I thought with a great sense of relief and pushed my way through to retrieve it.

With a firm grip on my suitcase I looked around wondering what I should do now when there was a tap on my shoulder. 'Mr Hunter', said a gruff voice with a thick Russian accent. 'You want to go to Mezhdunarodnaya Hotel?' I was staggered. How did he know who I was and where I wanted to go to. Nevertheless I had no choice but to follow him outside to the huge row of cars with engines running and their drivers aimlessly hanging around, cigarettes gripped in the corner of their mouths and occasionally grunting to each other. All the cars were the same except for small differences in colour. They were remarkably clean but I subsequently learnt that it was illegal to drive a dirty car around the city.

It was a good forty-minute drive to the hotel. The standard of driving was the same for taxi drivers all around the world. I sat in the back, nervously watching the endless blocks of grey, high-rise apartment blocks go past. As we neared the city the roads got wider and wider, eventually turning into sixteen lane highways, eight lanes either side with what turned out to be a VIP lane in the centre. I was glad I was not driving. My level of anxiety was reaching a crescendo.

Eventually we reached the Mezhdunarodnaya Hotel. I took my bags and made my way over to the hotel entrance, which was guarded by a bunch of thugs who demanded to see my passport.

'How many bags?' one grunted in English.

'Two,' I said.

I was handed a scrap of paper with the figure 2 scrawled on it and told to take it to reception. After pushing my way past the unyielding thugs and squashing into the revolving doors, I made my way to the reception desk feeling absolutely drained.

My passport and scrap of paper were taken from me and another piece of paper handed over. 'Take this to Level 8,' said the receptionist. 'The lady outside the lift will take you to your room.'

The Mezdunarodnaya Hotel had been built in the 1960s in preparation for the Olympic Games. It was much cleaner and newer than any of the buildings we had passed on the journey from the airport. The Reception Desk was at the edge of an eight-story Atrium, the central feature of which was a huge metallic column with an equally huge clock on the top. Perched on the top of the clock was the largest cockerel I had ever seen. This cockerel crowed on the hour and half hour much to the amusement of the people below. On the opposite side of the Atrium was a Japanese restaurant, which was restocked daily from the Japanese Airlines flight from Tokyo to London, which stopped over in Moscow. I could see rows of open balconies around each floor with well-kept plants cascading out of large window boxes. Each floor was served by four, all glass lifts which were busily running up and down their wall mounted rails. 'That's my next hurdle to overcome,' I thought, as I am terrified of heights and going up and down in this glass box to the eighth floor would surely cure me of it, surely?

I got into the lift, pressed button 8, pushed my back against the doors and shut my eyes. Fortunately there was no one else in the lift so we went straight up to the eighth floor at great speed. As the doors opened I spun around quickly and jumped out much to the amusement of the lady sitting behind the desk immediately in front of the lifts. This was the Floor Lady or Dezhurnaya, the much-feared controller on every floor. She ruled the roost, knew everyone's comings and goings and was the sole custodian of the keys to every room on her floor. I handed her my scrap of paper and she retrieved my room key from her locked desk drawer. She indicated that I should follow her to my room, which she unlocked and proceeded to make a handwritten inventory of how many sheets, blankets and pillows I had, which I had to sign for. As she left she told me in poor English that if I wanted to leave the floor to go down to the restaurant or bars I should return the key to her in exchange for another scrap of paper.

Phew. After what seemed an eternity travelling I had made it to my room. Not a particularly well-appointed room but it would do. Glancing around the bathroom I was glad I had heeded everything that Terry had told me as there was no bath plug! How could this be? Why would anyone steal a bath plug? Anyway, it didn't appear on the Dezhurnaya's inventory and I had brought my own so I was alright.

Quickly depositing my luggage I remembered I had to meet up with Terry in the Hard Currency Bar on the ground floor so I started the reverse procedure up to the Floor Lady to exchange my key for a scrap of paper and back down in the scary glass lift to the ground floor. The Hard Currency Bar was a popular venue for all visitors in the hotel and I was relieved to see Terry sitting in a corner seat.

He could detect my worried look and anxious voice and welcomed me to Moscow. 'Calm down,' he said, 'and have a drink. I hope you have brought some food from the plane because the restaurants are now closed and all we can do is drink.' He ordered two Vodkas with orange juice and as soon as it came I gulped it down. It didn't touch the sides.

'Just remember you are still training so just sit tight, observe everything that happens and let me handle any conversations that might occur. Only speak when you are spoken to and listen to what I say,' said Terry.

This made me feel better. The country itself seemed so tense so how could I not be? A country full of secrets and desperate to know yours.

The vodka was just beginning to relax me when a gorgeous young blonde approached our corner table and asked if she could join us. 'Of course,' said Terry casting me a sideways glance, which acted as a reminder to me to observe his earlier instructions.

'Can I get you guys a drink?' said the blonde who introduced herself as Olga.

'Thank you,' said Terry. 'We are drinking Vodka Sok.'

Off she went to the bar and returned with three glasses, ice cubes chinking invitingly. Olga was indeed very attractive although very heavily made up. She sat with her long legs carefully crossed, allowing just a tantalising area of thigh to be exposed. Polite conversation followed for some while with several questions aimed at me, which Terry fended off, saying it was my first night in Moscow. A third Vodka followed by which time I was feeling normal again until Olga made a surprising suggestion.

'If you like, you boys could come back to my flat with me and I will do the both of you for $100!' I was flabbergasted.

'Well,' said Terry, 'tempting as it may be, Graham is a bit tired and we haven't eaten so we will decline your offer tonight. Thanks all the same.' With that she said her goodbyes and left to return to a distant barstool.

After she was out of earshot Terry turned to me and said, 'what have you learned from that?'

'There are some gorgeous girls in Moscow,' I said.

'And what else? What did she pay for the drinks with?'

'American dollars,' I replied.

'Exactly,' said Terry. 'Firstly normal Russians are not allowed in this hotel and would not get past the thugs on the door. Secondly, they are certainly not allowed to have foreign currency in their possession and would be imprisoned if caught. She was definitely KGB approved and after you as the new boy on the block. The invitation was her way of setting the honey pot trap to get as much information out of you as possible during pillow talk.' Terry looked at me with a stern face, forcing me to realise the seriousness of the situation.

My knees went to jelly and my anxiety levels returned to critical. 'How on earth do I cope with all this,' I stammered.

'Just do as I say and remember that you are being watched all the time. There will be a bug in your room and have you noticed that there is a big mirror above the bed head. There will be a camera behind there so don't do anything in your room that you don't want to be recorded.' He paused for a moment, looked at his watch and decided we should call it a night.

'We have a busy day tomorrow completing the exhibition stand so I suggest we go to bed now and you can eat your British Airways rolls as that is all you are going to get tonight,' said Terry. 'We'll get a good breakfast in the morning. See you down here at seven.'

Up I went again in the scary glass lift, handed my scrap of paper to the Dezhurnaya in return for my room key. Once inside I devoured my two bread rolls now conscious that someone could be looking at me with the camera behind the mirror.

Surely all the rooms couldn't be bugged?

But Terry had been spot on so far. Just in case, I turned out all the lights before stripping off for bed. Sleep was not far away as I drifted off with images of Olga in my mind.

Chapter 4

Sokolniki Park

Breakfast at the Mezdunarodnaya Hotel was interesting to say the least. A help yourself buffet including osetrina (cold sturgeon slices), beetroot, overdone hard boiled eggs, grated carrot, apple juice, kefir and black bread. Having only had two bread rolls for supper I was ravenous and had a bit of everything. We had to fill up as we did not know when we would be able to eat again. Today we were completing the set up of our exhibition stand at Sokolniki Park, which was right on the opposite side of the city and would either involve a long taxi ride or three changes on the Metro.

Terry opted to take a taxi as we had several bulky items to carry. 'This is the next part of your training,' he said. 'Don't forget that there is a taxi somewhere that has been assigned to you but you don't know where it is. Somehow the taxi driver will make himself known to you.' This was all alien to me but so far Terry had been right about everything so I went along with him. Outside the hotel there was a large collection of taxis and the procedure was to start at the beginning of the row and go along all the drivers stating your destination.

'Sokolniki?'

'Nyet'

'Sokolniki?'

'Nyet'

'Sokolniki?'

'Nyet'

'Sokolniki?'

'Tooda' (over there) said one driver at last, pointing to another driver two cars away.

'Sokolniki?'

'Da'

'Skolka?' (how much) said Terry.

'Thirty roubles' said the driver.

'How about two packets of Marlboro,' said Terry.

'And two ballpoint pens,' said the driver.

'OK,' said Terry and we were off.

'Let me explain what has just happened,' said Terry. 'All the taxi drivers had been pre-assigned a customer and destination. They were not being awkward in saying no because you were not their fare. If your trip was only a short one they might have slipped you in quickly, pocketed the fare and got back to the Hotel before their assigned fare came out. Ours is right on the other side of town so we had to take our assigned man. The fare of thirty roubles at the normal 1:1 exchange rate would be thirty pounds or at the black market rate of 10:1 would be three pounds. We have purchased 200 Marlboro for five pounds so two packets have cost one pound. He can sell one packet to his mates on the black market, smoke one packet himself and still pay the fare to the taxi company plus he has two ballpoint pens. We have all won and have simply oiled the wheels of the black economy.' I was in total disbelief at this system.

Terry was hoping that we could complete our set up in the morning, leaving the afternoon free for a bit of sightseeing for me in Red Square. The taxi pulled up outside our Hall and the driver was duly paid.

'You want later?' said the taxi driver in broken English.

'Maybe,' said Terry. 'Let's say 3:00pm here' and passed over a third packet of Marlboro.

'OK,' said the driver and zoomed off.

I couldn't believe it. 'You have paid him in advance but we might never see him again,' I said. 'There don't seem to be any taxi ranks here so if he doesn't turn up we are stuck', a bit confused with how this system worked.

'He will,' said Terry with a knowing smile. 'Effectively we have given him permission to go off and earn a few extra fares which he will pocket and be back on time to complete his official assignation for the day. It's all about trust. He now trusts us not to report him to his bosses and we trust him to turn up when required. It is an unusual system but it works. Hopefully you are beginning to learn that working in the Soviet Union is not something you can teach in textbooks and lectures. You have to live it and experience it.'

I agreed wholeheartedly with Terry as I could never have envisaged these situations, even if he had prepared me at the briefings.

We made our way into the exhibition hall and found our stand where numerous crated pallets were strewn across the floor. The back room was appropriately equipped with a fridge, cooker and sink plus meeting table and chairs with some storage cupboards. Now that we were in attendance the delivery company delivered our drinks supply, which Terry transferred to the fridge or the lockable cupboard. The crate containing our kitchen supplies was unpacked and distributed around the kitchen. I busied myself setting up my equipment on the display area.

The other important item that Terry had brought was a portable typewriter with a supply of carbon paper. In the Soviet Union photocopiers were only allowed in Government Offices and were regarded as a means of distributing propaganda so they were prohibited elsewhere. If we were asked for a quote or a proforma invoice we had to produce it there and then with only carbon paper to make copies. I found it strange that photocopiers were banned but Rank Xerox had a high profile office in the centre of Moscow as did IBM, computers being another tightly controlled item. It took me years out find out the reason for this. Essentially it was a way of covertly obtaining "Intelligence."

Lunchtime was looming and as I had finished my part of the set up I volunteered to prepare it.

'What do you fancy today,' I asked Terry.

'I think a Vesta Chicken curry would be nice,' he replied.

I rummaged around the food store cupboard and found a packet serving two people (allegedly). The cooker worked and water supply was connected to the sink so all was well. It felt so strange cooking in the middle of an exhibition hall and not being able to pop over to the nearest cafeteria, as there was none.

'We will go into town this afternoon for some sightseeing and will drop into the Beriozka shop on the way to get some supplies,' said Terry.

'Beriozka shop?' I said quizzically.

'Yes it is a shop that stocks lots of imported foods, drinks, cigarettes etc. but is only open to foreigners with hard currency. Russians are not allowed in as it is illegal for them to have foreign currency and Roubles are not accepted,' he explained.

I found it very strange that there could be a shop selling everything that is in short supply in all other shops and that resident Russians were not allowed in. How on earth did Russians cope with this knowing that there was a shop with lots of lovely food in that they couldn't access and would have to walk past enviously to join a queue for a single loaf of bread?

It was 3:00pm and we were all done so we walked outside to see if we could find our taxi. There he was as promised and waved us over.

'Red Square please but first the nearest Beriozka shop,' said Terry as we climbed into the back seat. The driver's ears pricked up at the mention of a Beriozka shop. He turned around and very sheepishly asked if we could get him some cigarettes if he gave us some money. 'Certainly,' said Terry 'but in return can you look after our shopping while I show Graham around Red Square?'

'Konechno,' (of course) replied the taxi driver while furtively removing a twenty-dollar note from under the dashboard. While we were driving Terry explained that he had probably done another job during the morning for which he was given dollars and needed to get rid of it quickly before he was caught. He needed us as much as we needed him and hence the element of mutual trust was strengthened.

We pulled up outside what looked like a shop but all the windows were blanked out. The only clue was the red neon sign above the door saying Beriozka. I would not have known what it was if Terry hadn't shown me. Inside was what looked like a normal supermarket to me with fridges stocked with delicatessen foods, rows of wines, spirits and beers and of course cigarettes. We bought cold meats, tomatoes and the driver's cigarettes. 'I'll get our driver some Doktorskaya sausage,' said Terry. 'That will cover our fare and waiting time this afternoon.'

Needless to say, our driver was over the moon with Terry's purchases. He had food for his family tonight and a carton of Marlboro cigarettes. He sped off towards Red Square and pulled up in the taxi rank outside the National Hotel, which is right in front of the Kremlin. Indicating that he would wait for us here and to leave our shopping in the back, he went off to talk to his mates while we took our lives in our hands to cross the huge expanse of road between the National and the Kremlin.

Seeing Red Square for the first time is an experience which I will never forget. It is huge. I had seen it on the television during the Mayday parade when the Russians paraded their weaponry in front of the Big Wigs watching from the balcony above Lenin's Tomb. Being here for real was breathtaking.

As you enter Red Square past the Nikolskaya Tower, the first thing that hits you is St Basil's Cathedral with its brightly coloured and gold Cupolas which looked like giant onions. To our right was the Kremlin Wall with all the gravestones of famous people embedded in it. Standing out from the wall was Lenin's Mausoleum, a huge square block of polished marble with enormous bronze double doors, one of which was always left ajar. Two sentries stood either side of the doors, completely motionless as if they were statues. The open door was symbolic of Lenin always being available to his people and the sentries guarded the entrance 24/7. During the day a queue would build up of people wanting to see Lenin and pay their respects to him. The queue would snake around into Alexandra Park and could be up to a kilometre long. It did keep moving slowly and once in the queue you were guaranteed a sighting of Lenin before it closed for the night.

To the left was a department store called GUM (Glavnyi Universalnyi Magazin). It sold all manner of Russian made goods and lots of tourist memorabilia. High on the list was always the sets of brightly painted Matrioshka Dolls that fitted snugly one inside the other.

Turning round to face where we had come from we saw the Lenin Museum (now renamed to The State Historical Museum) which housed a lot of artefacts from Lenin's life including his Rolls Royce!

Terry had timed our visit so that I could witness the changing of the guard outside the Mausoleum. This happened every hour, on the hour and was timed to military perfection. It was just coming up to 5:00pm and crowds were gathering, jostling to get a good view. The changeover was synchronised to the chimes in the clock tower. With about sixty seconds to go, three soldiers appeared from the top gate of the Kremlin, the Spasskaya Tower, goose-stepping with high kicks, a rifle precariously balanced on their white-gloved left hands and the right arm swinging to and fro across the front of their bodies. It sent a shiver down my spine. Their uniform was a sage green colour, trimmed with yellow braid and a bright yellow belt around their waists. Their knee length, highly polished leather boots made synchronised stamps on the tiled walkway. On reaching the steps in front of the Mausoleum they halted briefly, executed a perfectly timed left turn and marched up the steps in time with initial chimes of the clock. The two new soldiers positioned themselves in front of the motionless guards and exactly on the first bong of five o'clock carried out a neatly executed sidestepping manoeuvre to change places. They had to achieve a comfortable standing position during this quick changeover, as that was the position they had to maintain, motionless, for the next hour. Twitching or movement of any kind was simply not allowed. The relieved soldiers then marched down the steps, did a right turn and goose-stepped back to the barracks inside the Kremlin Wall. It was a spectacle to behold. Apparently this procedure was even carried out in the depths of winter, the guards having to stand motionless in blizzards and temperatures that could go down to minus thirty degrees.

I had been warned to be careful where I took photographs. Changing of the guard was a tourist attraction but pointing the camera the other way at road junctions, stations or Government Buildings was a definite NO NO.

'How do I know what is allowed and what isn't,' I asked Terry.

'Most forbidden subjects are fairly obvious but if you overstep the mark usually someone will correct you.'

'I don't believe it. You mean someone is watching me all the time?'

'That's right,' said Terry 'and don't forget it. If you don't believe me walk over to the bridge and start to take some photos of the traffic lights at the road junction.'

'I will,' I said with an air of defiant bravado.

We walked past St Basil's Cathedral and over to the bridge crossing the Moscow River. There was a large crossroad controlled by traffic lights. I raised my camera and started to focus on the view beyond the traffic lights. To my surprise, a man standing a few metres away from me who, up until now, I hadn't noticed, was starting to get visibly agitated. When I made eye contact with him he raised his hand and shook it in a negative wave. I put my lens cap back on and covered the camera with the case and when I looked up the man had gone.

'Told you so,' said Terry with a smug grin on his face. 'Just listen to me and you won't go wrong.'

Another cold shiver went down my spine. 'I really have a lot to learn in order to survive out here,' I thought.

We made our way back to the National Hotel and by now I was not surprised to see our taxi driver waiting for us.

'Back to the Mezhdunarodnaya Hotel please,' said Terry. Our shopping was still safely stored in the back of the taxi.

'See you in the morning,' he said to the driver as we got out at the hotel.

He nodded acceptance

Now we had to go through the charade again of exchanging bits of paper with the thugs on the door, reception and finally the Floor Lady to get our keys. At reception the lady behind the counter told me I could have my passport back now as all the formalities had been completed. I was glad to have it back safely.

'See you down here at seven thirty,' said Terry as we got in the lifts.

Back in my room I nervously glanced around, now fully aware that there really could be a camera looking at me from behind the mirror. I walked into the bathroom and to my surprise, there was a bathplug hanging on a chain in the bath. I don't know what came over me but in a loud voice I said, 'thanks for the bath plug!'

Terry was waiting for me back in the foyer and we agreed to go straight to eat as we had missed out the night before. The Japanese restaurant was always full but very pricy and only payable in US dollars or a credit card so we went to the Russian restaurant. The waiter, dressed all in black was hovering at the door. There weren't many people eating so we thought we would be alright.

'A table for two please,' Terry said to the man in black.

'Nyet,' came the reply.

'But I see you have tables free.'

'Reserved,' said the man in black.

'Ah I see,' said Terry reaching for a packet of Marlboro in his pocket.

'Will this get us a reserved table?' He inched the packet out slowly with his head tilted slightly as if he was daring him to be tempted.

'Da,' and with that, we were allowed in.

I couldn't believe that I had only been in Moscow for 24 hours and already I had learnt many useful lessons in survival that you could not teach in a classroom.

We were shown over to a table with a grubby red checked tablecloth and a single flower in a vase that would be have been better off on the compost heap. The salt and pepper pots had long been empty. The man in black hovered as we looked at the menu. Terry had suggested that I try the stewed pig's knuckle and cabbage so he asked the waiter for it.

'Nyet,' came the reply.

'OK what about the steak?'

'Nyet.'

'And the carp with mushrooms?'

'Nyet.'

'OK you tell us what you have,' said Terry now sounding slightly frustrated. After all, he had taken our packet of cigarettes as an entry bribe and now couldn't offer us anything off the menu.

'Caviar and black bread,' the waiter gruffly replied.

'That will do nicely. We will have two please.'

'Could we also have two beers please?'

'Nyet,' came the reply again.

'Well what can we drink?' Terry said now sounding quite annoyed.

'Russian champagne.'

'That will do nicely. A bottle and two glasses please.'

The champagne came first and was remarkably tasty but a bit on the sweet side. I didn't know that the Russians made Champagne. Then came the Beluga caviar on a silver platter, balanced carefully on a dish of ice. Two tiny spoons were perched on the edge of the platter. A second plate contained square slices of black bread with pats of very white butter. It was extremely tasty and my first experience of Beluga caviar.

After we had finished the lot plus a second bottle of champagne Terry asked for the bill. I don't remember how much it was in Roubles but Terry just turned to me and said,

'How much do you think that meal was worth?'

'Why do you ask? You have the bill.'

'I think it was worth five dollars each, don't you?'

I was flabbergasted as Terry took out a ten-dollar note. The waiter took it willingly. After he had disappeared into the kitchen Terry explained that the waiter has to buy the food from the kitchen. He then has to get the money from the diner to compensate himself. He now has ten US dollars that he can use on the black market and be in profit after he has paid the kitchen, plus he has got 20 Marlboro for himself. 'Don't worry. Everyone is happy.' I had just dined out on Beluga caviar, black bread and a bottle of champagne for US$5. It is crazy out here. The simple things in life are difficult to get but champagne and caviar – no problem.

Feeling good with ourselves we went off to the Hard Currency Bar for a Vodka or two. There were several newcomers in the bar tonight and guess who else was there. Yes, our very attractive blonde Olga from last night

'Sit quietly and observe,' Terry instructed me.

It wasn't too long before Olga had selected her next victim, a young, fresh-faced guy who, like me, was probably on his first foray into the USSR but with no mentor and all alone. She made her way over to his table and sat down next to him. You could tell how the conversation was going and could see from his glances that he was admiring her long legs.

'Look,' whispered Terry. 'She has hooked him. They are off to her flat'.

The next morning at breakfast there he was, sitting alone and looking rather worried.

'Can we join you?' asked Terry.

'Oh please do,' he replied, his face changing to a smile.

After a few bits of polite conversation, Terry blurted out,

'We couldn't help noticing that you went off with that lovely blonde in the bar last night. How was it?'

'I was really taken with her and flattered that she wanted my company. I had a lovely time back at her flat. About midnight I thought I had better come back to my hotel so went downstairs to look for a taxi. Not five yards from the door was a taxi with the engine running.

'Mr Smith,' the driver called. 'You want to go back to Hotel Mezhdunarodnaya?

'He knew exactly where I was, when I was ready to come home and where I was going to. I felt really shaken by it,' said the young man.

'Don't worry too much,' said Terry trying to give words of comfort. 'They will probably have photos of you now but as long as you don't put a foot out of place they won't need them.'

How was this comforting? I barely knew how to get around this country but realised that the best way to stay safe was to keep my head down.

He went on to tell the story of one guy he met who kept flaunting the system and trying to get more than the allowed one or two cans of caviar out of the country. The 'officials' got so fed up with him that they set him up with a lovely lady who called at his bedroom one night. It didn't take much enticing to get him into bed and various photos were taken in a series of compromising positions. When he returned home he was confronted by his boss, who had received copies of said photos with a note saying,

'We do not want this member of your staff visiting Moscow any more'. Needless to say, he lost his job and probably his marriage as well.

I don't know whether that gave comfort to our new friend but we didn't see him again all week and could not ask him.

Chapter 5

First day of exhibition

It was the first day of our exhibition at Sokolniki Park. Terry and I got in bright and early and gave our taxi driver the rest of the day off. There was one new visitor on the stand from another company that Terry helped out. All we were waiting for was the arrival of our official interpreter who was crucial to not only a successful show but an interesting social life as well.

Brian (the other new boy) and I were briefed by Terry on what to expect from our interpreter. All interpreters reported back to the KGB regularly so we were not to say anything that we did not want repeating. However, with the clout that they had, they could arrange meetings, get the occasional photocopy but most importantly could get otherwise unobtainable tickets for the ballet or circus and get us into decent restaurants out of town. They were chosen for us and could be male or female.

Ours turned up just before the exhibition opened apologising profusely for his lateness but his car had a flat tyre. His name was Vladimir, he was single, had a girlfriend and liked to play tennis. He was tall and slim and possessed those steely blue-grey eyes that could stare right through you. Brian and I started off by teaching him a little bit about our exhibits so he could translate more easily when visitors arrived. Terry gave him a list of all the companies he wanted to see and sat Vladimir next to our phone to call as many as possible. I should mention here about the Russian telephone system. All subscribers had a seven-digit number with the first three as an area code and the second three the unique number. We had a number allocated to us that anyone in Russia could call directly. Even our hotel rooms had a unique number that anyone could call. International calls were different. They had to be booked through the International operator, 24 hours in advance. All other urgent communication was by telex.

The doors were opened and the public came flooding in.

'Just remember that not everyone is a potential customer,' warned Terry. 'The majority are general public who have to see what freebies they can grab.'

In one of Terry's packing cases were a few hundred carrier bags, normally used to put genuine customer's brochures in.

'Here you are Graham,' he said, giving me a handful of carrier bags. 'Go and see if you can attract some customers.'

I should have guessed from his wicked smile that he was up to something. As soon as I emerged from the back of the stand with carrier bags I was besieged by a crowd clambering towards me shouting 'packet please.' The twenty or so that he given me had disappeared in a flash.

'What's the thing with carrier bags here,' I asked, seeking shelter in our back room.

'They don't have them so are desperate for any they can grab. If it has foreign text on it, all the better because they can show off to their friends.'

'The same with ballpoint pens but don't give them away willy nilly as they are part of our currency.'

Soon Vladimir was in great demand as customers that he had telephoned earlier were beginning to turn up. They would push forward to the barrier ropes around the front of the stand and ask if they could come in for a meeting. This normally meant that they wanted to drink some alcohol while discussing business but out of sight. The whisky was very popular and after our second meeting we had already got through a bottle.

There was no let up to the crowd. Even school kids were coming in now asking for pens or carrier bags. Terry would occasionally give one a chocolate bar but this only encouraged more to start begging.

During a short break in the crowds Vladimir asked us what we wanted to do this week. The choices were Bolshoi ballet, Moscow State Circus or a nice restaurant that he knew. Including Vladimir, there were only four of us so he was happy to take us anywhere in his little Lada car. I had never been to a ballet before and didn't give it much thought until Vladimir explained that tomorrow was the last performance ever of Moscow's equivalent to Dame Margot Fonteyn, namely Maya Plesetskaya and tickets would be in great demand. She was a Russian Prima Ballerina and had danced many times with Rudolph Nureyev during her international tours.

'OK,' I thought. 'It is in the Bolshoi Theatre which is a tourist attraction as a building let alone seeing a full-blown production there.'

'I'll see if I can get four tickets,' he said. 'So tonight we will go to a nice restaurant. You have all got your passports back haven't you? Please bring them with you.'

After an exhausting and challenging day, we returned to the hotel to change out of suits and into something more comfortable for the evening. Vladimir had arranged to pick us up at seven o'clock in the hotel foyer. While we were waiting for him Terry took the opportunity to run through a few things with us.

'OK Guys, what have you learnt about Vladimir?' Terry asked.

'Nothing other than what he has told us,' I said.

'Wrong,' said Terry.

'Point number one. He has a car. Private car ownership in Russia is not common. There are no bank accounts in Russia so everything has to be paid for with cash. Having enough cash to pay for a car usually means that some irregular dealings on the black market have been done. This would normally arouse the attention of the KGB so some bribery must also have taken place.

'Point number two. He plays tennis so has access to a tennis court. This is only something afforded to officials, especially KGB.'

'Point number three. He was able to pick up the phone and straight away get four tickets to the ballet for Maya Plesetskaya's final performance. KGB.'

'Point number four. Did you notice how he could talk very knowledgeably about a lot of things in the UK? He has not travelled outside the USSR but has been trained and probably has had access to International newspapers and magazines. KGB.' He took a deep breath in for his grand finale....

'Finally I bet you that he comes striding through the hotel door unchallenged by the thugs outside. KGB.'

Seeing our worried faces Terry finished by saying, 'don't be put off by this because we need Vladimir but just remember that everything you say may be noted.' I gulped!

At seven o'clock precisely, (I know because the cockerel was noisily crowing) Vladimir came marching unchallenged through the door into the foyer.

'Told you so,' whispered Terry, slightly smugly.

'Are you all ready? Have you got your passports?' Vladimir asked. 'Then let's go.'

We squeezed ourselves into Vladimir's Lada and off we went. Vladimir explained that the restaurant was out of town, in a Dacha in the middle of a silver birch forest. Our journey entailed going through the "ring of steel" which is one of the check-points on the city boundaries. This was designed to stop non-Moscow passport holders from getting into the City and to prevent people like us from travelling outside the City. Apparently our business Visas did not allow us to travel outside the City.

'When we reach the checkpoint just sit quietly and let me do the talking,' said Vladimir.

Although he said nothing I could hear Terry thinking – 'KGB'.

I could see the checkpoint in the distance. An air of nervousness pervaded the car. Even Vladimir looked a bit worried but confidently drew up to the machine gun toting guard, wound his window down and passed out his papers. A few words of Russian were exchanged and the guard bent down and put his head through the window to look at all of us. I can genuinely say I was scared. No, more than that, I was terrified. It was a very intimidating situation to be in, not knowing whether we were going to be let through or carted off to the guard-house for trying to attempt an illegal crossing. After being scrutinised by the guards piercing steel blue eyes he stepped back from the car, raised the red and white striped pole and let us through.

'Well done,' said Terry.

'It was easy,' Vladimir said. 'I knew his brother. We were at school together.'

'KGB,' thought Terry.

We continued up a silver birch-lined road with not another car or person in sight. After a few kilometres Vladimir turned onto a narrow track. In a clearing ahead stood a magnificent log cabin made out of silver birch logs.

'Here we are,' said Vladimir, pulling up alongside a large black Zil with darkened windows. There were other cars in the car park, some empty and some with drivers waiting patiently, puffing on smelly Russian cigarettes.

Inside the building was just as beautiful with everything possible made of wood. There were quite a few diners with bottles of ice cold Vodka on the tables. An air of merriment permeated the room.

Vladimir had reserved a table, which was conveniently tucked in the corner. We must have stood out like a sore thumb but we did not want to look too much like we didn't belong there. Silly me – we were talking in English so how could we not stand out!

The waitress was dressed in traditional Russian costume. She brought some menus over to the table but as they were in Russian, we had to rely on Vladimir to translate them. Even the menus were bound in a wooden frame. Here they only took Roubles but luckily Terry had a supply. He had done a little bit of wheeling and dealing and unseen by Brian and I had changed money with someone at 10 times the official exchange rate. It was an opportunity for him to spend them before going back through Customs at the Airport. For all I know it might have been with Vladimir but *I didn't need to know*. This meant that we could dine in style for a tenth of the price.

I should mention here that the banks had a way of helping customs find out if someone had changed money illegally. When you changed money at a bank or official exchange bureau the maximum sized note they would issue was twenty Roubles. You would also get a stamp on your customs declaration document to say how much money you had exchanged. The Rouble is a restricted currency and cannot be taken out of the country so you have to get rid of any excess. The one anomaly which always amused me was that to hire a baggage trolley on the way in or out of the airport required a one Rouble note and you weren't allowed to have any. They did cast a blind eye to up to five Roubles in your wallet but no more. If you were caught with notes of a denomination higher than a twenty then you were in trouble. The official exchange rate was always one Rouble for one Pound.

The food was all traditional Russian fare with of course Beluga Caviar. The Vodka was drunk neat and down in one, straight out of the freezer, which gave it a syrupy consistency. Everyone was having a good time. Once the Vodka had worked its magic everyone started talking to us and many toasts were raised. I remember Vladimir's toast very well as his command of the English language was impressive.

'Gentlemen, here's to all the kisses we have snatched and vice versa,' said Vladimir, standing up and knocking his Vodka back in one.

Everyone agreed with that one and more Vodka was tossed back.

Time flew by as it always does when you are enjoying yourself and now, unfortunately, it was time to go back to the hotel. We made our way back to Vladimir's car, a little concerned about his ability to drive but he assured us he was all right.

Back at the "ring of steel" barrier the guards had changed. This time Vladimir had no connection to the men with guns and a lot more questions were asked. They peered through the window menacingly and we were all expecting to be dragged out and interrogated. Eventually to our relief we were let through.

'See you in the morning,' said Vladimir as he let us out of his car. The thugs at the door gave us a disinterested look and let us in without any challenge. They obviously knew us now and the company we kept.

The Dezhurnaya had changed too. She gave me a look which said, 'what have you been up to until this time of night?' and handed over my key.

'Breakfast as normal,' I said as Terry and I went our separate ways down the corridor.

'Good night,' I said to my mirror as I turned out the light and fell into a deep, alcohol-induced sleep.

The next day at the exhibition was equally manic but now we had to contend with the hangovers from the previous night's Vodka drinking. Terry sat in the backroom office, tapping away on his portable typewriter. One of yesterday's visitors had telephoned asking for a proforma invoice to be prepared which he wanted to collect at lunchtime. The keys had to be tapped much harder than normal to make an impression through the three sheets of paper and interspersed carbon paper. At Terry's request, I had had a company stamp made up which I had in my suit jacket pocket. The Russians liked official stamps as it made the documents more important.

Vladimir had got the tickets for the ballet and was pleased with himself that he had got quite good seats for us. The seats were not expensive, much to my surprise, but were always in short supply. He was not coming but would drive us there, leaving us to get a taxi back. He suggested that it would make sense to go straight from the exhibition to the Bolshoi Theatre as it was across town.

Our customers arrived at about 12:00md, pushed their way to the ropes and let themselves through. Vladimir sprang into action and brought them into the meeting room, which had been appropriately prepared with glasses at the ready and chocolates in bowls. We went through the social pleasantries and then got the paperwork on the table. Everything had been made easy for them. Delivery and installation were included and there was enough allowed for me to come back with an engineer to do the installation and training. The only issue was timing. They obviously wanted it as soon as possible but I explained that as I had to apply for an export licence, I was at the mercy of the Department of Trade and Industry in Victoria Street to issue this. The three of them added their signatures to the documents and I followed by adding the company stamp and signing over the top of it. Deal done. My attendance at this exhibition had been justified just with this one contract and my return visit assured

Out came the drinks. Whisky seemed to be the most popular so far as I imagined vodka was easier to obtain. More toasts ensued (but not Vladimir's special one). Lunchtime merged into teatime and ultimately closing time. We cleared up the leftovers from our successful meeting and prepared our minds for the ballet. Vladimir drove us to the Bolshoi Theatre, handed over the tickets and left us with, 'see you in the morning. Enjoy.'

The Bolshoi Theatre was an iconic building that featured on the 100 Rouble note. The front canopy was supported by 16 pillars on top of which was a chariot pulled by four horses. The huge semi-circular forecourt sported a large, multi spurting fountain. I couldn't believe I was here. It felt like a huge achievement. Vladimir had really pulled all the stops out for this experience. In the foyer, crowds of people queued to leave their coats, bags etc. at the cloakroom. Young girls, dressed in their finest, with ribbons and bows in their hair, chattered excitedly.

Our tickets not only had our seat and row numbers but helpfully, the door to go through from the foyer. The first time in the large auditorium is breath-taking. Surrounding the tiered floor-level seating area were five balconies, each being divided into individual compartments, separated by white pillars capped with gold and lavish red curtains. The fronts of the balconies were also white with ornate gold embellishment. At the back in dead centre was the 'Royal Box' where countless dignitaries must have sat. It spanned three balcony levels in height and was almost like a mini version of the stage, with full-length red curtains draped back and decorated with thick gold braid.

Up in the brightly painted ceiling hung a huge chandelier, which was divided into eight smaller chandeliers. Around the balconies were also chandeliers, spaced in alternate compartments. There were fourteen per semicircle making seventy in total. I must confess that while waiting for the performance to start I sat looking around for any bulbs that had blown and hence my intimate knowledge of these chandeliers! All the bulbs appeared to be working. I found this intriguing as light bulbs are difficult to buy in the shops but there must be thousands of them all glowing brightly in this theatre. I suppose that was because it is a well-publicised tourist attraction, it had to be maintained in pristine condition and was a symbol of Russian culture.

The performance began and boy was it brilliant, even to me with no knowledge or experience of ballet. The ballet that she was performing was a modern one that I did not know but the emotion that she put into it was enthralling. You felt it with every move of her body, muscles pulled tight and sinews stretched. What was even more amazing were the encores Maya Plesetskaya got. The thronging audience, demanding further dances and tossed flowers on to the stage. This went on for one and a half hours and only stopped when she disappeared behind a mountain of bouquets. That was it. Her last performance ever and I was privileged to have seen it.

I didn't stay for the whole of the 10 day exhibition as I was on a tight schedule. I had to get back to Heathrow in time to meet up with my boss who was going to the Far East with me and I only had a short time after landing to check into the long haul flight to Hong Kong.

I bade my farewells and found my taxi driver who took me to the airport. The check-in procedure at Sheremetyevo was very different. First of all, you queued up to have your baggage X-rayed and opened for inspection. The customs officer took your currency declaration document and checked for official money change transactions. He asked me to show him the contents of my wallet which I happily did as I had not done any black market deals and had spent any Roubles I had except a couple of small denomination notes I had saved for the baggage trolley hire on the next trip out. Then there was a walk across a large open space to the check-in desks where cheery British Airways staff were allocating the seats and tagging suitcases. Then came a walk through a metal detector and over to passport control. I thought that this was not very secure as I could have had something in my pocket when my luggage was scanned and then transferred it to the case during the walk over to the check-in desk.

The same procedure as before at passport control. The man with steely-blue, piercing eyes staring out of a slit in the kiosk took my passport and separate paper visa, stamped it and handed back the passport. I was disappointed as there was no record of my visit behind the Iron Curtain left in it.

At last I was through and made my way to the Duty Free shop. This was a welcoming sight, seeing all the usual array of drinks and cigarettes at very good prices, such a change from the near empty shops in the streets of the City. I was still bemused by the upside down cake tins in the ceiling and couldn't work out whether they were for decorative purposes or something more sinister.

Looking through the glass panels I could see that our plane had not yet arrived from Heathrow. There were no announcements of delays so I assumed it would arrive soon. I could detect a sense of relief from other passengers when it finally touched down on the runway with a puff of smoke from the tyres. It didn't take them long to turn the plane around and soon we were boarding, being greeted by more cheery faces. They say that it is always better to fly back on the returning country's national carrier, as the crew are always happy at the thought of going home. The atmosphere on board was definitely that of relief, having got through all the trials and tribulations of working in the USSR. As soon as we were airborne the drinks trolley came round much to everyone's delight. After about an hour of flight, the captain came on the PA system to announce that we were now leaving

Russian airspace and a huge cheer went up.

As I sat drinking my Vodka and orange juice my mind went through everything that happened and how much I had learnt in a short time. I felt much more confident about a return visit and even began to look forward to it. What stories I had to tell now when I got home.

Chapter 6

Hong Kong & Lolita

I had been in Moscow for a week and flew back into Heathrow to join Dennis, my Managing Director, before flying straight out with him to Hong Kong. It was my first visit to the Far East and after the difficulties of getting even basic necessities in Moscow I was really looking forward to enjoying the more lavish and glamorous lifestyle of Hong Kong. But before all this, I had to experience the landing at Kai Tak airport. For those of you who have not had this experience let me try to describe it.

The plane descended through the clouds and suddenly you were confronted by the curve of the mountains going round the island. The plane followed the periphery of these mountains in a sweeping curve, descending rapidly until you were flying through a built-up area of high-rise apartment blocks. You could see washing strung between balconies. You could see people in their bedrooms. And if this wasn't nerve wracking enough just as you thought the plane was near enough to touch the ground the pilot did an abrupt right turn and to the uninitiated it felt as if the right wingtip was going to touch the ground. No sooner did the plane level out then the wheels touched down with a shuddering thud and the pilot slammed the brakes on as the runway ended abruptly in the sea. The experienced Hong Kong travellers were still casually reading their papers while the new boys like me, white knuckled and queasy, were thanking their lucky stars that they had survived.

Our baggage was handled as deftly as the pilot handled the landing and within some 30 minutes of my weak kneed yet exhilarated exit from the plane we had found a taxi and were heading to our hotel.

Hong Kong was an assault on the senses. It was 31°C when we arrived with a relative humidity of 95% which seemed to exaggerate the smells to an intoxicating intensity. Those of you who have been there will agree that you could recognise this aroma instantly - a heady mix of ladies' perfume, Chinese food and open sewers! You would know you were in Hong Kong with your eyes shut.

We stepped into the hotel foyer and found instant relief from the intense heat of the streets and our sweat soaked shirts were soon clinging coldly to our bodies in the air-conditioning. The combination of high humidity and air conditioning gave the hotel corridors a unique smell of perfume and damp carpets but the bedrooms were different, a complete joy. Appointed to the sort of luxury I was quite unaccustomed to, I immediately felt very special and privileged.

After unpacking showering and changing we decided to explore the city. The front porter told us that Kowloon was where all the action was. On his advice we took a taxi across the city, under the harbour tunnel and over to Kowloon Side as it is known. This was where we made our first mistake. In their front windows, taxis display a sign in Chinese announcing whether they are registered in the Hong Kong side of the tunnel or the Kowloon side. If you flag down the wrong taxi, the fare is hiked up by the return tunnel toll to get the taxi back to base. The initiated will always look for a taxi returning to its own side of the city knowing that the return toll has already been paid by the previous passenger.

Kowloon was yet another attack on the senses. There were bright glowing neon lights of every imaginable colour amid the tangle of wires straddling the narrow streets above our heads. Adverts enticed people to buy cameras, electrical goods and food. Thousands of people pushed and shoved their way through, carrying an assortment of strange items under their arms including live chickens and suckling pigs. Rickshaw peddlers, often laden to extreme heights, also jostled for position, frantically tinkling their bells, all adding to the sense of chaos.

We were now feeling very thirsty and decided to find a suitable watering hole. One particular doorway looked very inviting and was advertised as the Playboy Club. The burly bouncer at the top of the red carpeted stairway stepped aside to let us descend into the incandescently lit depths.

Sitting at the bar we were bemused to see two pricelists, one labelled standard drinks and the other labelled executive drinks. They must see newcomers coming a mile off! We ordered our drinks. The Barman asked whether we would like standard or executive and when we hesitated he said with a conspiratory smile that of course we should have executive drinks. Well why not we thought. The drinks arrived with two ladies who took us from the bar to sofa seats where they could sit beside us and get comfortable.

Having been starved of female attention for some while I naturally quickly grew attached to my companion and I have to say that one of her most endearing attributes was a beautiful pert bum on which perched a fluffy cotton bobtail. She told me that she had been photographed for several Hong Kong tourist brochures because, as she described it, she had the most photogenic arse in town.

Under Chinese naming custom, Chinese people have three names but tend to adopt an English name, which can be more easily pronounced by non-Chinese speakers. My newly found friend introduced herself as Lolita, or just

Loli to her friends.

As the evening went on and the number of drinks we consumed increased the barman suggested that it would be a good idea if I left my credit card in his charge. 'Of course,' I said. My MD and I had come to an agreement that if I paid for everything on my card, he would sign my expense claim when we got back home.

The girls were getting very friendly and suggested we took them out of the bar and back to our hotel. At this point they raised the issue of a bar fine. A bar fine we discovered was the amount the girls would have brought in if they stayed in the bar with us all evening persuading us to buy lots more drinks. At this point we both thought that as we had to come this far, why not. I was apprehensive at first as I settled the bar bill, which came to several hundreds of pounds, but anticipated a good time with these lovely ladies.

We hailed a taxi and this time, having Chinese girls with us who knew which ones to stop, we didn't have to pay the tunnel toll.

When we entered our hotel it was blatantly obvious that we were two English guys with two Chinese girls in tow, intent on the obvious. A security guard jumped into the lift with us looking all innocent and nonchalant. 'Which floor sir?' he said, offering to press the button. He was going there too apparently. He accompanied us up the corridor to our rooms and indicated that he would open the doors for us if we gave him our room keys. 'Have a nice evening,' he said with a knowing smile as the door swung closed behind me.

Once inside the subject of money was brought up which was a bit of a surprise to me as I thought I had paid for everything. Loli said she charged HK$1000 which was approximately £100 or HK$2000 if she stayed all night. I couldn't help hoping that Dennis, who was in the next-door room was going to honour his agreement with my expenses. The receipt from the Playboy Club was very discreet, mentioning something innocuous, but how was I going to explain HK$1000 in cash for a "Lady of the Night".

Not only did Loli have a beautiful, curvaceous bum but she also had nipples that you could hang your coat on. Her skin was silky soft thanks to the high humidity. She wore a Jade necklace which, when she had her head between my thighs, dangled teasingly against my swollen parts and intensified the eroticism of what she was doing.

After several hours of passion she asked me what my first thoughts were about Hong Kong girls and naturally I was very complimentary. 'You certainly know how to make a man feel good,' I said. I also told her that I was travelling on to Korea in two days time.

'Be careful,' she said, 'the girls are very attractive.'

As I was returning to Hong Kong from Korea she asked me if I would visit her again and tell her what I had got up. Of course I was not going to turn down such an invitation.

On my return to Hong Kong a week later I went back to the Playboy Club and specifically asked for Lolita who was very happy to see me again. She came bounding over to my table with her fluffy tail wiggling behind her. After a couple of drinks she asked if I was going to take her out. Of course I agreed only this time I knew full well what the expenses would be. Loli inevitably asked me for my opinion of Korean girls.

'Sexier and even softer than Hong Kong girls,' I told her.

She was taken aback with this.

'We can't have this. I will have to do something to change your mind.'

With this she picked up the house phone and had an animated conversation in Chinese. Putting the phone down she said that if I waited fifteen minutes she would try to change my mind.

In short while another lovely girl joined us introducing herself as Jenny. She worked in the Bottoms Up Club (as featured in the James Bond film, The Man With The Golden Gun), which was just up the road. She asked me if I had ever had two girls before. I hadn't and told her so. My heart was thumping, not with worries that I couldn't perform with two girls but with concerns for my expenses. There was now the bar fine for the Playboy Club and the Bottoms Up Club plus the night's expenses for two girls….! What was Dennis going to say?

Arriving back at my hotel I was beside myself with worry as to how to get past hotel security with two Chinese girls, both of whom were dressed very conspicuously. I was in luck. The security guard was not there – probably wishing someone else a goodnight! We moved swiftly across the foyer, jumped into the lift and walked quickly up the corridor into the safety of my room.

The both the girls stripped off and started to caress me. 'I am in heaven,' I thought. Incredibly, Jenny's skin was even softer and silkier than Loli's and I couldn't help but to keep stroking it. I don't remember how much time we all spent together but I was wishing it would never end. Ultimately it had to and on leaving I was flattered that Jenny also asked me to look her up next time I was in Hong Kong. This conceit was however short lived.

The following night Dennis and I decided to go and have a drink in the Bottoms Up Club which turned out to be another new experience. Instead of having one bar along a wall they had a collection of islands of circular bars with a pedestal in the middle. On the pedestal was a scantily clad young lady with an almost non-existent G-string disappearing between her cheeks. The idea was that you went in with a friend and sat on opposite sides of the island bar. You then took it in turns to buy your friend a drink, which would be poured by the young lady with her hindquarters right in your face. We were at Jenny's island.

'Hi Jenny,' I said. 'Remember me?'

I was greeted with a blank nonchalant look, which really put me down. I thought that having made love to this girl the night before she might at least remember me, which apparently she didn't. What a blow to my ego.

Before we left Hong Kong I spent another night with Loli by which time we were both feeling a mutual attraction. I knew I wasn't deceiving myself this time because when I said I was returning in a few months, she gave me her home phone number and address and asked me to call her as soon as I knew my travel plans so she could take time off work to be with me and not have to pay for executive drinks and bar fines.

Chapter 7

Korea & Ko He-Rang

The next port of call on our Far Eastern tour was South Korea. Neither of us had been there before and did not know what to expect. Landing at Kimpo Airport in Seoul was not as challenging as Hong Kong but as soon as the aircraft doors were opened we were hit with the high temperature and humidity plus the most overpowering smell of garlic. On the flight path coming in to land we had seen lots of fields with piles of harvested vegetables waiting for collection. Now we knew what they were – **GARLIC**. Garlic was eaten at every meal in Korea in one form or another and everyone's breath stank of it. The only way to stop smelling it I was told was to eat it yourself.

We were taken by taxi through very noisy streets where every driver seemed to indicate his intentions in morse code with the hooter. Back at home I only used my hooter a couple of times a year but here it was part of every day driving. It was impossible to tell who was hooting at whom. Beep Beep – I am turning left. Beep Beep Beep - I am turning right. Long Beep – I am overtaking you. The noise was dreadful.

The taxi stank of garlic breath and we were glad to get out at our hotel. 'Wow', I thought looking up at the canopy over the entrance. "The Hilton Hotel". As far as I was concerned, being able to stay in a Hilton Hotel said something about your status in life and here I was staying in one for the first time.

It was our first evening in Seoul and we were on our own as our agents weren't meeting us until the morning. We wanted to take a stroll around the city but had no idea where or what to eat. We asked the doorman who suggested a very good "hands free" restaurant.

'What's a hands free restaurant?' I asked.

'You will find out,' he replied with a smile.

'What shall we eat?' asked Dennis.

'Don't worry,' said the doorman. 'They will suggest something.'

We eventually found the restaurant and went in with some trepidation.

It didn't look like a usual kind of restaurant. There was a long corridor with doors on either side. There was no sign of a kitchen, waiters or fellow diners. It was unnerving. We were eventually greeted by a cheery lady in full traditional costume who introduced herself as the Mama-San. She showed us through one of the doors into a cubicle where we were asked to take our shoes off and sit cross legged on the floor in front of an oblong table.

Within minutes drinks were brought into us by two very pretty ladies, again in full national costume which I found very attractive. In their limited English they explained that they were our companions for the night. We were not allowed to use our hands for anything and the best thing to do was to sit on them. The girls would do everything for us. They proceded to wash us with hot towels then pour the drinks which they held to our mouths while we sipped.

'What is this we are drinking?' I asked.

'Soju,' replied one of the girls. 'It is the most popular Korean spirit, a bit like sweet vodka. Normally it is the custom to drink each glass down in one.'

I should mention at this point that understanding their English was made worse by their mixing up of not only their L's and R's as the Chinese do but also their F's and P's. Rice soup for example became "lice souf". Never mind, it became easier to understand them as more Soju was poured down our throats.

The next shock we had was the man with the Karaoke machine, which he wheeled into our cubicle. 'Time for singing,' said the girls gleefully as they went first with melodic renditions of some popular Korean songs.

'Your turn now,' they said.

'But I don't sing,' I protested.

'You have to,' they chorused.

Dennis and I decided that our best chance was some British pop song that we knew the words to so we went for "We all live in a Yellow Submarine" by the Beatles. We shared the only microphone and got a rapturous applause from the girls for what we thought was an awful cacophonic rendition.

The man with the Kareoke machine joined us for a couple of glasses of Soju, sang a song and went on his way to the next cubicle.

Food was brought in in dribs and drabs, accompanied by lots of Kimchi – a Korean delicacy of pickled fermented cabbage and garlic. Boy was it strongly flavoured but at least now we were immune to other peoples bad breath. Not only did you eat the solid material but you drank the juice as well. The girls were tucking in to it like there was no tomorrow.

After a while the Mama-San came in to clear the table, announcing that the meal was over and we would be left in peace. 'This sounds ominous,' I thought. With that my girl whispered in my ear what her price was and we were now expected to have sex with them on either side of the table. Dennis and I looked at each and with only a second's hesitation he said,

'Usual rules apply....'

This trip was turning out to be a real eye opener for me. First a threesome with two lovely girls in Hong Kong and now a foursome with two lovely girls and my boss in a restaurant of all places. Good job we had eaten the kimchi!

It was awesome but after a while came a discreet knock on the door announcing that our time was up. I was presented with the bill for food and drinks having settled up with the girls for cash.

It was getting rather late but we eventually found a taxi to take us back to the Hilton.

'Did you have a nice meal?' said the cheeky doorman as we came through the door.

'It was great. Thank you for the recommendation,' I replied nonplussed.

I figured that he must be getting a tip for everyone he sent but got great pleasure in seeing their faces on their return.

The following morning we were taken to the offices of our distributors to discuss business and to meet their staff. We were familiarised with the etiquette of peoples' names and how to address them. In Korean there are five common surnames of which the top three are Lee, Park and Kim and we should use the title of Mr or Miss plus the surname when addressing someone. Only family and very close friends got to use their two given names, which always followed the surname. So in the office when someone called out, 'Miss Lee,' three people responded much to my amusement. There were multiples of each surname working in the office and to this day I don't know how they differentiated each other.

Mr Im was the Sales Manager and would be working closely with me. At the end of the day he and the Managing Director invited us to dinner and suggested that we went to the disco in the basement of the Hilton afterwards. More Kimchi was served up with dinner but now we were to be taught the niceties of drinking with Koreans. It was frowned upon to pour your own drink, which made drinking on your own difficult unless you could find someone to pour for you. Soju was served ice cold from a flagon but only came with one glass. The correct procedure was to pour the drink for the person sitting next to you. You held the glass with your free hand placed at right angles to the wrist of the hand holding the glass. The aliquot of liquor was then knocked back in one and the glass passed to the next person. So it meant that you had to finish your glass before anyone else could have a drink so they set the pace. After several drunken evenings like this, I learnt that if I chose a seat in the restaurant near to a potted plant I could cause a small distraction and while the others were looking away I tossed my drink into the plant pot. It was the only way I could keep up without getting trollied.

After many Sojus we made our way down to the disco where we had our next cultural shocks. After a couple more drinks our two (male) hosts asked Dennis and me to dance with them. What!!! I had never danced with a man before but apparently it was commonplace in Korean circles. We were led energetically around the dance floor much to our embarrassment, hoping that there were no other Brits there to witness this. Eventually I needed the loo and asked where it was. 'I will take you,' said Mr Im, taking me firmly by the hand and lead me to the toilet. It was a mixed toilet, the like of which I had never seen before. Whilst the gents were standing peeing into the urinals, the ladies were crouched behind us, peeing down little holes in the floor. When I had finished Mr Im took my hand again and lead me back through the crouching ladies to my seat.

During my machinations around the dance floor I had noticed a very pretty little girl sitting in the side-lines, who was watching me intently. Mr Im also noticed this and suggested that I should go and talk to her. She spoke very good English and told me her name was Ko He-Rang or Miss Ko to me. After a few more drinks she asked me if I would like her to spend the night with me. This was totally unexpected and not the sort of thing you thought would happen in the basement of the Hilton Hotel.

How could I refuse – she was gorgeous!

'Give me your room card and I will go and check in,' she said.

I followed her upstairs to reception where she duly checked in to my room. The receptionist handed my key card back to me saying that Miss Ko was now registered and she had her own key card.

'Have a good night sir,' he said.

My head was reeling. This situation was so unreal but it was happening to me. Miss Ko made herself at home in my room and proceded to do things to me that I couldn't possibly write about in this book. I was in seventh heaven. We went down to breakfast together in the morning where the waiting staff treated her normally as my guest. After the events with the night security guard in the Hong Kong hotel this was unbelievable. I had to keep pinching myself to see if I was dreaming.

'Would you like me to stay with you tonight as well?' she asked.

'Silly question,' I thought.

'That would be wonderful if you could,' I said.

She now had her own key card so could come and go as she pleased and was in my room waiting for me when I got back from work. This continued every night for the week I was in Korea. I was getting very attached to her, as she was with me a lot of the time. All good things must come to an end as at the end of the week I had to return to Hong Kong. We exchanged phone numbers and I promised her I would contact her as soon as I returned to Korea, which would probably be in a couple of months.

Two months passed and I was planning my next trip to Korea. I had contacted my distributors to confirm my travel arrangements and they responded by asking if I would like Miss Ko again. On arrival to my hotel there she was, already booked in and eagerly waiting for me. I still couldn't believe my luck that I had a job that took me all around the world and paid me to share my life with some of the most beautiful girls in the world. One night during this trip the men asked me out for the evening so I told He-Rang (as I was now allowed to call her) that she might as well go home. Off she went with her final comment being,

'Enjoy yourself but don't misbehave.'

The "lads" took me on a pub crawl around several "escort bars" where Mr Im insisted on getting a girl for me and one for himself. My girl had some European features accentuated by her hair being tied back in a bun and wearing big glasses. After a very boozy and gropy evening Mr Im said,

'Can I come back to your hotel with you two as I want to make love to this girl and I can't take her home because my wife is there?'

Fortunately my room was twin bedded so we had enough space. During a trip to the bathroom my phone rang which my partner answered for me. It was He-Rang checking to see if I was home safely!! Oh my, now I would be in trouble.

The following night after work I returned to my hotel and there was He-Rang waiting for me.

'That's the last time I let you out of my sight,' she said wagging a finger at me.

This is getting a bit serious I thought, as I really felt bad having two-timed her. She quickly forgave me and out of the blue suggested that it was silly to spend money on a hotel so why didn't I move in with her for the rest of the week. By now I was getting used to surprises but this one really caught me off guard.

'Why not though,' I thought.

With that I packed my bags, checked out of the hotel and took a taxi to her flat.

The flat was small and sparsely furnished. The floor was highly polished with mats around the short legged table, obviously for sitting on while eating. The bedroom was very different. The bed was huge with a beautifully carved dark wood headboard. I was told to put my clothes in the equally ornate wooden wardrobe.

We went out shopping in the backstreets that I had never ventured down before to get the ingredients for tonight's supper. She had invited five of her girlfriends round to meet me, all of them "working girls" from the Hilton. They all apparently knew that I was more than just your average client to He-Rang; I was someone special.

He-Rang was busy in the small kitchen when the girls arrived. I was tasked with letting them in, greeting them all. They all took a place sitting cross legged on the floor in front of the table, chatting and giggling amongst themselves while trying to talk to me in their limited English. I would forgive you dear reader at this point to think that I must be making all this up. Believe me I am not – it all happened.

'I must be the luckiest guy in the world right now,' I thought, 'to be surrounded by six of the most beautiful girls I have ever met.' I would be the envy of all my male friends back home.

The week flew by and sadly I had to leave He-Rang. I had become very fond of her and was deeply saddened at leaving her.

'I will be back in a few months,' I said as I tried to comfort her.

Little did I know how things would change in my life and I would not see her again for a long time.

Chapter 8

South Africa, September 1985

My first year in my new job had already exceeded expectations as I had visited two countries behind the Iron Curtain, spent a month in South Africa plus two long trips to the Far East and it was still only August. For September I had another visit to South Africa planned, as Bob had been very successful in sales after my first lecture tour. This meant that there were some orders being delivered that I could install and train the customers in their use. There was also a big scientific exhibition in Johannesburg that Bob wanted my help with and knowing that I had been in contact with Pauline several times since my last visit, he came up with a plan.

'If you were to fly out to Cape Town on Wednesday 18th of September you could do two installations on the Thursday and Friday and then hire a car. Pauline could meet you whenever she is free and spend the weekend with you driving up the Garden Route. You could also do another installation in Port Elizabeth on Monday, leave the car there and fly on to Johannesburg in time for helping with the exhibition set-up on Tuesday. I will book the Rosebank for you and Pauline can stay with you as long as she likes. I'm sure she would be happy going around Johannesburg while you are working during the day and fly back to Cape Town whenever convenient for her.'

'What a fantastic arrangement,' I thought.

Bob was obviously well used to organising his working life around his social activities and had thought this out well. My travel agents had got me a good deal on my flights, using Air Zimbabwe via Harare again. On boarding the plane at Heathrow, my first observation was that unlike the Far Eastern airlines where the lady flight attendants were all petite, the cabin crew here were all large ladies. There was little room for manoeuvre as they walked up and down the aisle during boarding. I wondered how they would manage the food and drinks trolleys, especially if someone wanted to pass to get to the toilet.

As it happened, the flights were very good and although there were a few reversings up-and-down the aisle with the food trolleys, all went smoothly. We had a couple of hours stop over in Harare and then on to Cape Town. When I had told Pauline of my travel plans she was very excited and agreed to meet me on the Friday afternoon after I had finished the installation. We went to collect the hire car and I was a bit surprised when she turned up without any luggage. After a very affectionate greeting she told me that we were going to drive to her house to pick up her suitcase and I could meet her husband and kids! I must say I felt a bit nervous about this meeting to start with, but my worries were unfounded.

As I mentioned in the first chapter on South Africa, Pauline was estranged from her husband but continued to live in the family house for convenience. The house was quite large and she had something akin to a Granny Annex on the side. Her husband greeted me amicably enough and introduced me to the children while Pauline went off to get her luggage. It felt so surreal and I was glad when Pauline re-joined us.

'I'll be back sometime next week,' she told her husband as we left. 'I'll give you a call and you can come and fetch me from the airport.'

We were booked into the Houw Hoek Inn in Grabouw for the first night, which was just 80km out of Cape Town and a short distance from Hermanus, on the coast of False Bay. This very scenic bay is flanked on the western end by Cape Peninsula and to the east is Cape Hangklip. The bay is home to a large variety of marine mammals including four species of whales.

The Houw Hoek Inn dated back several hundred years and was a delightful Olde Worlde Inn. We had a beautiful room with a large four-poster bed which was put to immediate use on our arrival, even before the bags were unpacked. It had been five months since I last saw Pauline but all the affection was still there.

Eventually hunger got the better of us so we showered and changed ready to go down to supper. As an inveterate carnivore the South African diet suited me just fine. Meat, meat and even more meat. Steaks so big I could hardly finish them and portions of ribs that fell off the edges of the plate. Huge sausages neatly wound into coils were fresh off the hot coals and vied for position on the already overcrowded plate.

We had the whole weekend to ourselves so long as I was in Port Elizabeth on Monday. After a night of passion and a leisurely breakfast in the morning we stopped off in a coffee shop on the beach at Hermanus and sat looking out to sea, hoping to see a whale or two. We were not disappointed as before long we spotted the classic whale sighting of a huge tailfin coming out of the water in a graceful curve before re-entering with a large splash. There was no mistaking that it was a whale, even at a distance. I managed to get a few photos using my zoom lens but it was very difficult to predict where the creature was surfacing next and by the time you had focused on the tail, it was already disappearing underwater.

We took our time driving along the Wine Route until we came to a winery with accommodation in classic Cape Dutch style housing. Perfect. We would be able to spend the afternoon doing a wine tasting and then chill out before another meat fest supper.

After our tasting we went up to our room, which had a Juliet style balcony with double doors opening up onto it. The sun was just setting and the cicadas had just started their incessant chirping. I personally found this to be a very romantic sound and with your eyes shut you could imagine you were in the jungle. Pauline drew her chair up close to mine and handed me another glass of wine. We sat transfixed to the view of the setting sun and the sound of the chirping insects, both enjoying each other's company. I know I have said it before but I considered what a lucky person I was to have such a job and to meet such lovely ladies in different parts of the world.

After another night of unbridled passion and a leisurely breakfast in the morning, we idled our way along the Coast Road, eventually reaching Port Elizabeth in the afternoon. I had one job to do in the Technical University in the morning and then we were catching a flight to Johannesburg where we were staying the rest of the week in the Rosebank Hotel. Pauline was happy to stay with me until Saturday and then felt she ought to go back home, not for her husband's sake but for the children. That would make eight days and nights that we would have been together and I was enjoying every minute of it.

We were greeted with familiarity when we checked in to the Rosebank, which was sort of nice. Pauline was going to do some shopping and catch up with an old school friend so she would have plenty to do while I was working. Tuesday was set-up day at the exhibition followed by three days of activity. We had a lot of visitors to our stand, some producing samples from their pockets for me to try to analyse. The week went far too quickly and after dismantling the exhibition on Saturday morning, Bob and I took Pauline back to Jan Smuts Airport for her flight back to Cape Town. I had to confess that I was very fond of her but contemplated how we could keep up a long-distance relationship as we said our goodbyes.

Knowing that I would be feeling a bit down now, Bob suggested that we went back to his house for a sauna and swim followed by a few beers. His wife had booked a table for the three of us at the Manchurian restaurant for supper, returning to his house for drinks which went on until 1:30am. As I left in a taxi for the Rosebank he told me that two of the lads and a sister would look after me on Sunday and would take me waterskiing on the river Waal. They would pick me up at about 10:00am so I should be ready with a towel and my swimming trunks and a change of clothes.

I wished I had more warning as I would have gone to bed a lot earlier but as I had never waterskied before I was quite excited and I woke quite early. Philip and his sister Christine plus Wyndham turned up in a big 4x4 towing a large boat with 175hp motor on the back of it. Wyndham was the junior skiing champion and frequently practised on a stretch of the river Waal. It was perfect for waterskiing as it was perfectly flat, unlike trying to ski on the sea. We headed for a particular stretch of the river where it was very wide and had a slipway down to the water where we could launch the boat. The weather was fine and reasonably warm, being the start of their spring but wetsuits were necessary and they had bought a collection of half-suits to see which one fitted me the best. I found one that just fitted but was a bit loose around the short legs. No worries, it wasn't a fashion show. It was worn for warmth and some cushioning from heavy awkward landings on the water at speed. It took a little time to reverse the large boat down the slipway and get it off the trailer but once we had parked the car we waded into the water and hopped on-board.

The rear of the boat had a special frame around the huge black outboard motor, a Mercury I believe, which kept the tow rope from fouling up on it. Philip had a couple of pairs of skis and a mono ski on-board. He went first with Christine driving and Wyndham acting as a rear lookout, to keep an eye open on the skier to see if and when they fell over. He made it look so easy. The procedure was to position yourself in the seating position with the ski tips sticking upwards out of the water and the rope running between them. The boat would move slowly to take up the slack in the rope and then keeping your arms straight and braced, hold firmly the bar handle, as the boat would accelerate quickly. As you rose out of the water you had to lean back to angle your skis so that they started to plane. If you didn't do this quick enough, the pressure of the rushing water on the flat surface of the ski would make you do the splits and fall over. Do this too quickly and you would go head over heels, bouncing along the surface of the water.

We went up and down the river for a couple of miles each way with Philip performing a variety of manoeuvres, swinging from side to side to gain extra speed. When he got tired we hauled him back into the boat and then it was his sister's turn to don the skis. She was equally as good as her brother and made it look so graceful. When she tired they suggested that I went next.

I slipped over the side of the boat and clumsily tried to put the skis on. The skis wanted to float upwards but I had to keep them under the water to get my feet into the rubber straps. I didn't realise how difficult this first manoeuvre was as I bobbed from side to side. Eventually I managed it and Philip brought the boat round, skilfully dragging the floating handle close enough for me to be able to grab it. I positioned the rope between the ski tips and indicated that I was as ready as I could be. The boat accelerated, the rope went taught and I was jerked straight out of the water and somersaulted with a large splash. They told me that it would take a few goes before I could stand up so we tried again. This time I knew what the pull on the rope felt like so I lent backwards a bit more. This time the water came rushing through my legs and up the front of my body and I had to let go falling over backwards. On the third go I didn't keep my legs straight enough ended up bouncing along on my bum. On the fourth go I did it. I stood up but not for long. I didn't keep my skis at the right angle and went over forwards in a series of spectacular somersaults. Now I knew how it felt to stand up, I indicated that I was ready to try again. This time I got it right and managed to stay up for about 500 yards, but my downfall was I let my arms bend and immediately fell over. Philip turned the boat round and I had one more go. It felt fantastic as I zoomed up the river, this time for about a mile, managing to do a couple of side to side swings before my arms were so tired that I had to let go.

They hauled me back into the boat, absolutely exhausted but exhilarated. Now it was Wyndham's turn on the mono ski. Boy could he ski. He even performed some controlled somersaults, landing back on the water perfectly balanced. No wonder he was junior champion. After they had all had enough we made our way back to the slipway where Philip jumped out to go and reverse the trailer into the water. I stayed seated in the boat as it was hauled up the slipway and clambered out once it had stopped. They told me to take off my wetsuit but I wondered why they were looking at me with grins on their faces. I soon found out. All beginners suffer from this same problem. When you are dragged along the surface of the water on your bum, the water gets forced up the inside of the legs of your wetsuit and some of it gets forced up your back passage. As soon as you remove your wetsuit and stand up straight you get a sense of something warm running down your legs. The expression on my face brought my hosts into fits of laughter. It was as if I had just had an enema, the results of which were now running down my legs. The bastards hadn't warned me about this little "inconvenience" and had a great joke at my expense. I rushed back down the slipway into the water to wash myself off and once the laughter had subsided they apologised saying that this happened to most beginners, especially if like me you had loose fitting legs on the wetsuit.

We towed the boat back to Christine's house where they kept it on her drive. I had a much welcomed shower followed by a few beers and the compulsory braii. I got back to the Rosebank relatively early but being absolutely shattered, quickly fell into a deep sleep.

Monday, my last day, was spent in the office having a debriefing session and of course a few more beers in the evening. Bob again thanked me for my sterling work and for my support. Not many of his suppliers gave him the same amount of time as I had done but it did pay dividends. On the way back to the airport Bob asked me about my friendship with Pauline. Megan had told him that she was very attracted to me and enjoyed our times together. I told him that I had telephoned her from home but didn't think that anything more than a nice friendship would come of it. Her kids were in Cape Town and I wouldn't move to South Africa so we would have to content ourselves with occasional meetings whenever I visited the country. Bob was more than happy to have me as a visitor whenever I wanted to come, so it was all up to me.

Chapter 9

Second visit to Moscow

M y second visit to Moscow was coming up soon, some six months after the first. During the interval I had done two trips to the Far East, a second lecture tour of South Africa, my first tour of India and another tour of Yugoslavia and Bulgaria. It was a punishing schedule but I was enjoying it very much and looking forward to being in Moscow again. This time it would be winter and the conditions are very different from my last visit. I had purchased all the necessary thermal underwear but I still did not have a very warm hat. Terry had suggested it might be a good idea to buy one in a Beriozka shop as soon as I arrived in Moscow as Russian furs were very warm and cheap.

Terry and I were flying out together on British Airways and this time my boss David wanted to come and see what doing business was like behind the Iron Curtain. Naturally I had told him of my experiences back in May and he was intrigued. He could not spare the full twelve days that I was doing but opted to come for the last three days of the exhibition. He managed to get a seat on the Japan Airlines flight to Tokyo, which stops off in Moscow.

The exhibition was going to be held in Sokolniki Park again but this time we had been put into the Cosmos Hotel, which was conveniently nearer but way out of town. It was affectionately known by regulars as the Cock mock Hotel due to the Cyrillic spelling of 'Kocmoc'. In the Russian language a letter "C" is their letter "S".

Everything had been crated up a lot earlier than last time as our lorry driver now had to battle through snow storms and temperatures that could dip down to minus 30 degrees at night. When he picked up our goods he told me that several times in bad winters the diesel in his fuel tank had frozen up and he had to find kindling wood in the forest and light a fire right underneath the tank to thaw it out. After they had unloaded their goods at Sokolniki they were allocated a lorry parking space where the driver lived in the cab for the duration of the exhibition. He kept the engine running all day to stop it from freezing up and to provide some warmth in the cab. Often they had to dig it out before the return run but it was easier if they cleared the snow regularly. As soon as they crossed the border into Russia they were monitored all the way to Moscow. They were not allowed to deviate off the main road and were timed through various checkpoints to make sure they didn't.

Going through all the procedures at Sheremetyevo Airport was not so daunting this time, as I knew what was coming. Nevertheless it took just as long. Terry explained that the long wait in front of the passport inspection booth was simply because their computer link was very slow. After they had typed in your passport details into the system they had to wait for a positive response before they could let you in. There was nothing else to do in the interim hence they stared at you. Their threatening looks still managed to arouse a sense of fear in me.

The Cosmos Hotel was something to behold. It was 23 storeys high including the tall Atrium and was in the shape of a very large crescent. Before going in out the cold Terry said, 'one quick lesson for you. Count how many floors there are.'

So I Did.

'One...two...three..seven...ten...fourteen,' I counted silently as my finger guided me.

'Twenty three,' I said.

'Right. Now remember that and when we are checked in and get in a lift, count how many floor buttons there are'.

It was so cold, much colder than I had ever experienced, and my knitted woolly hat that I had brought was no barrier to the frost. The wind had penetrated straight through the stitching. My ears were freezing. I was so glad to get into the warm. Once we had checked in we got into one of the many lifts and after the doors had closed behind us Terry said, 'now count the number of floors.'

'Twenty two,' I said quizzically. 'Why is that?'

'Because one floor is completely given over to surveillance and unless you are authorised, no one can get access to it. Only those who work there know which floor it is on,' said Terry. 'All rooms have cameras and microphones so you will be monitored. Don't forget that.'

Getting in and out of the Cosmos was easier than the Mezhdunarodnaya but there was still the stern looking Dezhurnaya sitting at her desk as the lift doors opened. 'Oh this procedure again,' I groaned to myself.

I had noticed that there was a Beriozka shop in the hotel so while waiting for Terry to come down for dinner, I ventured in on my own. There were some beautiful fur coats and hats, some silver fox, some mink and even some made out of grey squirrel. I asked for a hat to which the lady shop assistant said, 'Balshoy,' which I now knew meant large. 'Da,' I responded confidently only to be faced with a barrage of Russian which I could not understand.

'English please,' I asked, to which she replied, 'try this one on.'

It was too small. I tried several on until we found one that fitted me. It was made of fox and looked like a big ginger puffball siting on my head. I had no other choice as their stock was limited so I took it. I was a bit shocked at the price of 250 Roubles, which would be 250 pounds at normal exchange rates but I thought that Terry might be able to help me with some unofficial dealings.

I was very pleased with my purchase and found it much warmer than my woolly hat. I did get some funny looks but I thought that it was my being very obviously British and besides I felt warm now.

When we got to Sokolniki we discovered that we were in Pavilion 4, Stand 48 which unfortunately was the last one in a blind ending row and facing a wall. Not very inspiring but our customers knew where to find us. Our interpreter arrived and much to our pleasure it was Vladimir again. 'Great,' I thought, 'that means we will have some nice evenings out again.'

Still feeling very pleased with my hat I pulled it on again and said 'look what I have bought' to Vladimir. He gave a little laugh and said, 'you do realise that it is a woman's hat!' My heart sank. That is why I had been getting funny looks.

'Never mind for now. The important thing is to keep warm in these penetrating Russian frosts. If you like we could look for another shop and get you something more appropriate and cheaper.'

I agreed. I can always give the fox fur hat to my mother when I get home. She would love it. Taking me aside Vladimir said in a quiet voice, 'if you need some roubles I can change some dollars for you.' Wow. Vladimir had just put himself on the line. Obviously he trusted us now and probably wanted to buy something that roubles would not. I gave him US$50 to which he gave me 500 roubles – that's 10:1. Fantastic. That would cover the cost of my fox fur hat, which now came in at only $25 and I would be able to buy another.

When I had finished setting up my part of the exhibition stand Vladimir suggested that if Terry agreed, we could walk out of the park and go to some shops that he knew. Terry was happy as he still had quite a bit to do so off we set into the cold. I was determined to keep warm by wearing my woman's hat and who cares if I get funny looks.

We came to a shop, which was a bit dingy but had some hats in the window. 'There,' said Vladimir, pointing in the window 'that's what you need. It's made from grey squirrel and has earflaps which will really keep your head warm and yes it definitely is a man's hat. It's what the police and army wear when out on the streets in the cold.' Vladimir waited outside while I went in and tried some on. Success. I found one that fitted me perfectly. It cost 50 roubles so now with my black market money in my pocket this would only cost me US$5. I bought it, put it on my head and walked out to Vladimir who fell about laughing again.

'What's wrong now?' I asked.

'Just pull the earflaps down and see what happens' he said.

I undid the little grey bow on the top, which holds the earflaps up neatly, folded them down but they were connected to a neck flap which also came down - over my eyes! I had got it on back to front. Oh dear. Thank heavens Vladimir corrected me before I walked down the street attracting more funny looks.

As we walked back we chatted and I explained that my boss was coming out in a few days to see what doing business is like out here. 'It would be great if you could organise a few outings to impress him. I personally would love to go back to the Russ restaurant but what else can we do this week?'

'Well there is the Moscow State Circus that is performing this week but I don't think that there are any ballets on. You could take him to eat in the restaurant in the National Hotel which is right opposite the Kremlin and has a lovely view from the first floor window. I can see if I can book a table for you but I won't be able to accompany you.'

Back at the stand, Terry had just finished setting up and had been joined by new visitor from another company that he represented. He had also bumped into an ex-colleague from a company he worked for in the past, a guy called Barry, who lived not far from me back home. Terry thought it would be great if Vladimir could get us all into the Russ restaurant that night and asked him to make some calls.

Just a few phone calls later Vladimir appeared with a smile on his face. Yes we can go to Russ and to make it easier, a friend of mine has agreed to lend me his bigger car so we can all get in it,' he said. I could just imagine what Terry was thinking -'KGB.'

'Don't forget your passport guys,' he said.

Vladimir arrived punctually as usual at the Cosmos hotel to pick us four guys up. 'The drive is going to be a bit different to last time as we have had a lot of snow recently,' he said. We all piled in and off we went. It amazed me that although there been significant snowfall, the roads had been cleared and with piles on the pavement about 3 feet high. I was a bit scared at the speed Vladimir was driving but he explained that it was compulsory in Moscow to fit studded tyres during the winter months and these gave you excellent grip in the snow. Regardless, I was still clenching my fists in fear. As we approached the "ring of steel" checkpoint on the outskirts of Moscow. Vladimir reiterated his instructions on how to behave, particularly for the benefit of the new boy. As before, after a little heated conversation, the barrier was lifted and we were through.

The Russ restaurant looked really inviting in the headlights of Vladimir's car as we pulled into the car park. The surrounding silver birch trees were decked in snow and the ground was covered with at least 3 feet, which was now sparkling in these frosty temperatures. The roof of the log cabin style building was piled high with snow, with icicles of varying lengths, some 2 to 3 feet, hanging off the eaves. Light streamed out of the net curtained windows made it a very welcoming sight.

Inside the merrymaking had already started with another group of six making toasts with ice cold vodka shots. As I walked past the table I noticed a very pretty girl whose eyes followed me round to my seat. She had short dark brown hair brushed back from her forehead, which emphasised her beautiful green eyes.

'She's gorgeous,' I thought as I took my seat.

Our food came in fits and starts, interspersed with much vodka swilling. We had fried spatchcocked chicken with much garlic, gherkins with honey, Russian vegetable salad, cold sturgeon (osetrina) and of course Beluga caviar with black bread. There was obviously no shortage here. I was very conscious of the fact that every time I looked over to the next table that the lovely brown haired girl was looking back at me. Vladimir had picked this up to.

'Do you like her?' he asked me.

'Corr yes,' I replied.

'Would you like me to introduce you to her? She is with a friend of mine and often accompanies him on these social gatherings.'

He walked me over to her table and said,

'Graham, this is Lena. She speaks very good English and I can see that you're going to get on.'

She invited me to sit down next to her as Vladimir walked back to the others.

'Where are you from?' she asked.

'What are you doing in Moscow?

66

'What are your hobbies?'

The questions kept coming and whilst I was really smitten with her I was mindful of Terry's first lesson to me in the Hard Currency Bar and the lovely blonde Olga.

'She can't be KGB,' I hoped.

I fired some questions back and discovered that she was 24 years old, had a degree in hydrometeorology from Moscow State University, played the piano, loved the ballet both dancing herself and going to performances. She said that she had made friends with Alexei, who was the interpreter for his group, as he could get access to these places, as could our Vladimir. She lived in a small flat with her mother in the elite district of Fruzenskaya, where a lot of government officials also lived.

I couldn't help it but I was falling for her hook, line and sinker. It was getting late and I didn't want to leave her.

'If I can get a car, would you look after me and take me home?' she asked.

My heart leapt with joy.

'Have you got any Marlboro on you?'

Yes I had.

I went back to Vladimir to ask if this was OK. All the other guys on the table were teasing me as to how obviously I had fallen for her. He came back over to Lena with me and asked a few questions in Russian which I didn't understand.

'Yes you can go with her. She has promised to get a taxi in the city to get you back to your hotel. Just be very careful at the checkpoint.'

I accompanied Lena to the cloakroom where she put on a most gorgeous silver fox fur coat and hat whilst I donned my Russian army issue grey squirrel hat and my sheepskin jacket. She took my arm and led me out to the car park where she proceeded to go up to several of the parked cars, asking the waiting drivers if they could give us a lift. She found one who agreed to take us for 40 Marlboro plus US$10.

Once in the back of the car she snuggled up to me and I could feel the warmth of her breath on my face. I hadn't experienced a feeling like this for a long time. My heart was racing and I kept pinching myself to see if I was dreaming. I couldn't bear it any longer and moved my head round to face her and kissed her. All my emotions exploded at once. Could this really be love at first sight? Could it really be happening to me? She returned my kiss with genuine emotions.

'Would you like to stay with me tonight?' she whispered in my ear. 'I will make sure you get a taxi back to your hotel in the morning.'

'I would love to,' I replied.

I was still worried about how she was going to cope with getting through the city perimeter checkpoint so I asked her. She explained that her grandfather used to work as a chauffeur in the Kremlin and as such got some perks with the job including a family Dacha (which was essentially a log cabin style summer house) in the country, outside the ring of steel. This meant that she had permission to travel outside Moscow to visit the Dacha and had a stamp in her domestic passport to this effect. Although we were not on the road to where the Dacha was, she would be able to sweet-talk the guards to let her through and hence her ability to have travelled to the Russ restaurant. This began to quell my worry that she might be KGB and was simply a normal girl with some privileges. A saying came to mind, "under Communism everyone is equal but there are some more equal than others!" This seemed to fit her situation nicely.

As she rightly said she was able to get through the ring of steel guards without much trouble, with me sitting nervously and very quietly by her side, trying to be as inconspicuous as possible.

In Moscow it was commonplace for people to flag cars down and ask for a lift for a small payment. Car owners (or users) were only too willing to do this to earn a bit extra on the side and if it was a foreigner with hard-currency or cigarettes then all the better. Our driver had given someone a lift to the restaurant and had sat patiently outside hoping that he would get a fare back into the city. There was still so much more for me to learn and as I had said previously, there is no way you could learn this in the classroom or by reading books. You just had to live it.

Before we got out of the car Lena had told me to stay quiet until we got inside as one of the neighbouring apartment blocks housed many government VIPs. Their thuggish drivers were often parked outside in their big black Zils or Chaikas with the tinted windows making it difficult to see if there was anyone inside, other than for the occasional puff of smoke coming out of the slightly opened window. I don't think my heart rate had gone back to normal since I had met this lovely lady but it went even faster now and I felt a bit like James Bond trying to avoid the bad guys!

Once inside her flat, which was on the ground floor, I could relax a bit. We took our shoes and coats off and embraced passionately in the hallway. Lena lived with her Mum, being the only child of a single parent, her father having left her Mum when she was only one year old so didn't remember him. We made our way quietly down the corridor to her bedroom at the end and there I stayed all night.

When I awoke in the morning I couldn't believe how quiet it was. More snow had fallen during the night, which muffled any noises. Lena telephoned a cab company and they said my car would be here in about 20 minutes. Apparently they ring back five minutes before arrival to give you the registration number. I asked Lena if I could see her again during the coming week which she readily agreed to.

'Here's my phone number,' she said. 'What's yours?'

I gave her my hotel room phone number and agreed that I would call her probably tomorrow.

The phone rang. It was my taxi and he would be outside in a minute or two. Lena quickly dressed and took me out into the cold to find him. Sure enough he was there. She gave him instructions in Russian which I didn't understand but assured me that he would take me back to my hotel. By now I had used up my supply of Marlboro so I said I would have to pay in roubles.

We embraced passionately in the frosty air, the snow flakes beginning to come down again, settling on her hair. The taxi sped off along the snowy road but by now I have got used to the fact that they all had studded tyres. It felt completely normal, like they were driving on a dry road, but that didn't ease my anxiety of getting into a skid. I couldn't believe my luck in meeting such a lovely girl and longed to see her again but knowing full well that this may not be allowed to happen if the "Authorities'"objected to it.

It was about 7:00am when the taxi pulled up outside the hotel. The driver asked for 20 roubles, which I gave him.

Smiling wryly he said, 'and a ballpoint pen?'

Fortunately I had some of these in my jacket pocket so I was able to give him one. The thugs at the door gave me a stern look but let me in. I quickly moved over to the escalators and jumped in, hoping that not too many people had seen me coming home at this hour. But there was the Floor Lady outside the lift as the doors opened on my floor. She said something in Russian with a disapproving look on her face but I walked quickly past her with a greeting of, 'Good Morning '.

I had made it back on my own and was feeling quite proud of myself. I quickly rang Terry's room to tell him that I was back okay and would meet him and the others for breakfast. Boy was I interrogated.

'What was she like?'

'How much did she charge you?'

'Where did she live?'

'Listen guys,' I said, getting very protective of Lena, 'she is a normal girl living a normal life with her mother, not KGB and certainly not a prostitute! I like her very much and want to see her again this week if I can.'

'Just be careful,' said Terry in a very fatherly manner. 'I don't want you to get hurt.'

At the exhibition that day I couldn't help but keep thinking about Lena. Dennis, my boss, was arriving today so I couldn't go out and leave him tonight. Terry had sent him an urgent Telex the day before to say that our provisions were getting low and could he bring out some more Vesta packet meals. As many as he could manage! He was on the JAL flight which got into Moscow a bit earlier than the British Airways flight. Terry had given him exact instructions on how to get straight to the exhibition hall but I am sure the taxi driver would have known where he wanted to go.

The day dragged by with my mind fixated on Lena. We had several business meetings with the usual alcoholic content and crowds of people asking for carrier bags and ballpoint pens. Two girls kept coming to our stand and making head movements as if to say 'come over here and talk to us.' I thought that they were just after the usual giveaways and tried to ignore them.

Vladimir had been off the stand for a while but reappeared with a smile on his face.

'Good news guys. I've got five tickets for the circus tonight. I won't come with you but you four can take Dennis with you when he arrives. You will have to go in directly after the exhibition closes and won't have time to eat anything so make sure you have something here.'

At about 4:00pm Dennis arrived on the stand, exhausted and shell-shocked from his first experience of Sheremetyevo airport. 'Come in the back and relax,' said Terry. Have a drink. Have you got the Vesta packet meals?' He had, much to Terry's relief but he also handed me a duty-free carrier bag. 'A little something for you,' he said. 'Seeing as it is coming up for Christmas there is a Christmas cake and a bottle of gin.' I loved Christmas cake and readily accepted the unusual present.

'Dennis,' I said. 'Vladimir has got tickets for the circus tonight. Do you want to come?'

'Not really,' he replied, 'I am knackered and I could do with a quiet night. You go with the other two guys and Terry will take me back to the hotel.'

'But we've got five tickets,' I said.

Terry being a bit of a tease and a joker noticed that the two girls had reappeared and were making gestures to encourage me out to the front.

'Why don't you ask the girls if they will go with you to the circus?'

'I can't do that,' I said.

'Oh yes you can. Come with me,' and with that led me over to where the girls were standing.

'You look very nice young ladies,' he said to them in English. 'Would you like to go to the circus with the guys tonight?'

They did speak some English and said they would love to go.

'Done,' said Terry handing me the tickets. 'You make the arrangement with the girls.'

It took me quite by surprise but not wanting to miss out on some possible fun I started chatting. One girl was very slim with long brown hair was the other was quite plain looking but both spoke some English. Their names were Larissa and Svetlana and they were students at the University. The circus started at 7:00pm but as it was now 4:30pm and as the exhibition shut at six, the girls agreed that they would meet us in the foyer of the circus at 6:45pm and off they went.

Terry explained that although the authorities frown on it, Russian girls know that if they befriend visiting foreign businessmen it is a means of getting otherwise unobtainable goods from the West. I was beginning to understand a bit more about how people survive in a regime where there is censorship, a crumbling economy and no goods in the shops.

Promptly at 6:00pm the other two guys and I found a taxi outside and armed with my carrier bag with the Christmas cake and bottle of gin plus pockets replenished with packets of Marlboro and ballpoint pens we set off for the circus. Moscow State Circus is famous all around the world and as it is one of the USSR's showpieces they are allowed to tour outside the country, showing off the best of what Russia can produce.

Inside the foyer people queued at the cloakroom whilst excited children chattered loudly. There were several entertainers dressed as clowns walking around the crowd and playing with the children. In one alcove a man was holding a tiger cub and invited anyone to come and stroke it. I left my coat and carrier bag with the cloakroom attendant and hoped that no one would steal the contents.

'There are the girls,' I said pointing to the other side of the tiger cub. It was a strange feeling like going on a blind date with two people you had never met before.

We took our seats, boy, girl, boy, girl, boy, with me in the middle. The other two guys didn't seem that interested in our new friends, so the girls spent much of their time talking to me. As the lights dimmed and the audience grew quiet with anticipation the two girls snuggled up to me and took a hand each.

Latterly I have been on a couple of safaris in Africa and pledged that I would never go to a zoo or circus again. However at this time I did enjoy the animal acts and marvelled at how they trained them. The act that still sticks in my mind was an illusionist with a fully-grown tiger. A cage was wheeled into the arena containing this magnificent animal, roaring loudly and pawing at the bars of the cage. The handler, dressed in a bright red double-breasted tunic with two rows of brass buttons was holding a whip, which, as he walked around the cage, poked it underneath from all sides to show that there was nothing hidden underneath. A rope was lowered from the ceiling, which he grabbed with one hand and was hoisted into the air and onto the top of the tiger's cage. He walked around the top of the cage waving his whip around each side so that we could see that there were no mirrors and you could see through the cage from each side. A bright burgundy coloured curtain suspended on a rectangular frame came down, covering both the tiger's cage and the man on top but leaving the space under the cage completely visible. A roll of drums sounded out from the orchestra pit and only a few seconds after coming down, the curtain was whisked up again to reveal the tiger gone and the man in the red uniform now in the cage. Loud applause followed. The curtain came down again and whisked back up quickly at which point the man had now gone. After the second round of applause had died down there was another roll of drums and spotlight was directed at the top of an aisle between two sections of seating. There in the bright ring of illumination stood the man in red, holding the tiger on a lead and proceded to walk down the stairs and back into the arena. The applause was deafening as the cage was folded down and wheeled out followed by the tiger and handler. I knew it was an illusion but I was dumbfounded….how on earth did they do it?

The lights dimmed, there was the sound of engines whirring and after about five minutes the standard circus ring had been replaced with an aquarium. A seal act followed and I was glad that I was not in the front rows as water splashed everywhere as the seals dived in and out performing a variety of tricks with balls and hoops. They dived through the hoops, catching a fish in mid air as a reward. One of them came out of the tank and hopped around the edge of the ring with a ball balanced precariously on its nose.

More whirring noises as the aquarium was lowered into the bowels of the building only to be replaced by an ice rink. I would have loved to see the equipment under the arena as I couldn't visualise how they moved such heavyweights so quickly.

We sat enthralled, not noticing that three hours had passed. My enjoyment was enhanced by the girls holding me tighter as the suspense increased in the high wire and trapeze acts....no safety nets at all! We made our way out to retrieve our coats and my carrier bag. The girls were intrigued to know what was in the carrier bag and when I showed them they suggested that we should go back to their flat and share the cake and gin.

'Okay guys who is coming with the girls and me?' Neither of them showed any interest so I said, 'looks like I will have to look after both of them then.'

There were hundreds of people outside the building looking for taxis. The two guys found one to take them back to the hotel and bade their farewells with, 'see you at breakfast then!'

Hugging the girls close to me to keep us all warm, we eventually got our taxi. I had no idea where we were going to or how to find my way back to my hotel but I had to trust the girls to arrange something for me. The flat was a small single bedroom apartment with a large double bed. It was cold when we got in so Larissa lit all the burners on the gas stove in the kitchen.

'That will warm us a bit,' she said.

Russians had no conception of wastage or costs as all of their household utilities were supplied free of charge. If you got too hot you opened the windows, too cold and you turned the cooker on as well. No thermostats! Svetlana cut some large slices of Christmas cake and poured out three large neat gins.

'Na zdorovie,' she said chinking the glass against mine and downing all in one.

I didn't realise just how hungry I was as we had not had time to have dinner before the circus. I had barely finished my cake when as if on cue, they both took hold of my hands and led me into the bedroom where we all stripped off. Larissa, the prettier one, had a lovely figure with long hair cascading over her shoulders. Svetlana was rather plain compared with her friend and a bit more chunky, but I couldn't help but notice that she had inverted nipples which intrigued me. There was just enough room in the bed for the three of us, with me in the middle. Larissa got to work on me with her mouth and hand and it didn't take long before I reached my climax. Svetlana rolled over towards her demanding some action from me. It wasn't long before I was ready again and although we were making a lot of noise and motion, Larissa had gone to sleep.

Svetlana drained me twice before I was exhausted and also fell asleep sandwiched between the two naked girls. I had just had amazing sex with two girls in exchange for a Christmas cake and a bottle of gin.

Larissa shook me and said, 'it's 7:00am and we have to go to university. I will telephone for a taxi for you.'

It didn't take long for him to arrive and after saying goodbye with no exchange of telephone numbers, I was taken back to my hotel. The thugs on the door were getting used to my early morning arrivals and gave me an almost smile as I push the revolving door around.

As I walked through the foyer I saw Terry and the guys going for breakfast…talk about getting caught out!

'I'll just have a quick shower and change and I'll join you,' I said.

The floor lady was not there when I got out of the lift so I quickly went to my room and closed the door without being seen. In order to give the impression that I had been in my room all night I ruffled up the sheets which I had not slept in for two nights.

'Stupid me, 'I thought. 'What about the camera behind the mirror. They will know that I've not been in and worse still probably know where I've been.'

The next few days were totally filled with business meetings and drinking and eating when we could. Vladimir had managed to get a table in the restaurant of the National Hotel so Terry and I took Dennis there after a quick trip around Red Square. Despite my little dalliance with the two girls at the circus the other night I couldn't stop thinking about Lena. I had looked up Fruzenskaya on the Metro map and it was only three stops from Biblioteka Imeni Lenina (Lenin Library), the nearest station to the National Hotel, which was only five minutes walk away. After we had finished eating Terry and Dennis wanted to go back to the Cosmos hotel and have a drink in the bar.

'Do you mind if I don't join you? '

'Why, where are you going?' enquired Terry, his eyebrows raised.

'Thought I might give Lena a ring.'

'OK,' he said cheekily and winked.

There was a public telephone in the foyer although not very private. Three kopecs were required to make a call. I called the number with trepidation and a beating heart. There was an answer. I didn't recognise the voice so I guessed it was Lena's mother.

'Can I speak to Lena please?'

'No English, no English,' came the reply plus something else in Russian.

'Lena – Lena,' I said but the phone had gone silent. I didn't know whether she had hung up or put the phone down to go and get Lena, so I hung on. Fortunately the latter was true and after what seemed an eternity to me, Lena's voice came on the phone.

'Allo?!' she said gruffly.

'Hello Lena, it's Graham here.'

'Ah Graham.' Her voice sweetened. 'Where are you?'

'I have just finished dinner in the National Hotel and would love to see you again.'

'I was in the shower but give me 30 minutes and I will come and get you. Wait for me outside the hotel.'

I went back to our table and told the guys I was fixed up for the night and would see them at breakfast in the morning.

I waited nervously on the steps outside the hotel. The wind was cold so I kept going back inside to warm up. When I saw her coming up the street in her Arctic Fox fur coat and hat and my heart skipped with joy. As she reached the hotel I went to give her a hug but she stopped me abruptly saying, 'no not here.'

I was a bit taken aback but she later explained that there would be people around possibly watching me and it was not good to be seen embracing in public. She took my arm tightly, turned me around and walked back up the street to the Metro station. Three kopecs were required again to get through the turnstile which once inside enabled you to travel anywhere on the Metro. Because Biblioteka Imeni Lenina station had four lines running through it, the number of choices of passages to take was enormous, all labelled in Russian obviously which I couldn't read. There were four routes going in different directions so that's 8 passageways plus four exits to different sides of the street connected by long tunnels. We needed the red line in the direction of University. I clung to Lena fearing that if we should get separated I would never find my way out. The escalator seemed to go down for ever but seeing as there are four lines here, some must go over or under each other. Even at 10 o'clock at night the place was throbbing with people and occupying every step on the escalator, both up and down. The scientist in me again thought 'I would love to see the machinery underneath to see what can move the weight of so many people such a distance.'

Standing on the platform, a rush of air indicated the oncoming train. Above the tunnel on the outbound side was a large digital timer which had just come to 2 minutes as the train stopped. There was very little time to get on until a pre-recorded voice said *"take care doors closing"* (obviously in Russian). As the train pulled out the digital timer reset to 0 as the system was so tightly controlled to allow one train every two minutes. The next stop was Krapotkinskaya followed by Park Kulturi and then Fruzenskaya. As the doors opened Lena pushed me forward through the crowded doorway as not everyone was getting off there. Up the never-ending escalator to a further choice of tunnels, one labelled **Вход** and the other **Выход**; one meaning exit and one meaning no exit but at a glance looked very similar in Cyrillic. Finally a sign saying **Выход на город** - exit to city.

That did it for me. If I am going to come here often I have got to be able to read some Russian and to know a few words of conversation otherwise I'm never going to be able to travel around on my own.

After the stuffy atmosphere in the crowded Metro, an icy blast of fresh air hit us as we pushed through the heavy swing doors. Above the doors we had come out of at street level was a big new building with mosaic frescoes around the top. This was a new library, which Lena had hoped to use for her studies but had not been opened yet. A short walk to her flat in *Nesvisky Pereoluk* took us first past a military academy followed by the apartment block with all the black Zils and Chaikas parked outside. At last we reached the relative safety of Lena's flat.

Lena introduced me briefly to her Mum, a small rotund lady with grey white hair.

'Doesn't your mum mind you bringing a strange foreign man home? '

'I don't make a habit of it and besides you are special.'

'Wow. Was she having the same feelings as I was?' I thought.

Her Mum indicated for me to sit down in the kitchen. It was a small room with a square table surrounded by an L-shaped bench seat around two of the sides and third side on the edge of the fridge. I squeezed my way in followed by Lena. The shelves on the opposite wall were crammed full of all sorts of jars of preserves pickles and dried mushrooms and there wasn't a space to be had anywhere. Mum had made a pot of tea which was now put on top of a samovar of boiling water. She pushed over a small plate of jam and a spoon.

'What do I do with the jam?' I asked Lena.

'You put a spoonful in your mouth and suck the tea through it.'

Mum bade us good night and disappeared down the corridor. Flats in

Moscow were allocated according to need so two people in one flat got a single bedroom large enough for a double bed. Lena had this bedroom whilst her mum slept on the converted sofa in the living room every night.

The next morning I woke with a start. 'What's that hammering noise,' I asked Lena. 'It's Mum cooking your breakfast,' she said. 'She's bashing a piece of chicken with a meat hammer.'

'For breakfast?'

'Yes. Russian men are sent to work with a big breakfast, as there are no places for them to eat during the day. They need lots of calories to keep the going until dinner time when they come home.'

After a quick shower, Lena escorted me to the tiny kitchen where Galina had put on quite a spread. Black bread and Beluga caviar, slices of osetrina and tea with jam from the samovar. This was followed by a well flattened chicken quarter fried in butter with lots of garlic. The samovar fascinated me. It was brightly decorated with an enamelled floral pattern, a tap towards the base and a lid, which neatly housed a small teapot. The procedure was to boil the water in the samovar, make a very strong tea infusion in the teapot and keep it warm, sitting on top of the boiling water. Guests took a small amount of the strong infusion into the cup and diluted it with boiling water from the tap to their preferred strength.

My stomach now full, Lena called for a taxi. I knew the procedure now and was soon speeding on my way back to the hotel. I saw Lena one more time during the stay and confirmed that I would be back next month, January. She was delighted and made me promise that I would ring her as soon as I was back in Moscow.

'Don't forget your warm clothes,' she reminded me. 'It can go down to minus 30°C in January.'

Chapter 10

Mr Pankratov

The next day I was to give a talk at the State Committee for Science and Technology on the use of Image Analysers in both Medicine and other sciences. My audience had been arranged for me and included doctors and professors from many different specialities. I loved giving these talks to mixed audiences especially when I was floored by a particular question that I could not answer but knew that there was somebody in the audience who could. It was a technique I had learnt on my first South African tour and always worked providing you had prior knowledge of the audience. It went something like this.

'Mr Hunter, how would you apply your image analyser to the study of *flibbety gibbets* (for example)?'

'Now that's an interesting question. (Thinking – what the hell is a *flibbety gibbet?*). Before I answer that I see that we are privileged to have Professor XYZ in the audience. Professor, would you like to comment on this first?'

Professor XYZ would then give his opinion and in the process help me understand what a *flibbety gibbet* was. Scientists love talking about their specialities and I could stand back and listen.

'Thank you Professor for that very enlightening answer. Next question please.'

This technique made it look like I was "all knowing" and everyone went away thinking that they had learnt something from me. I could now insert this topic in my next talk and increase my credibility as a speaker. After my talk had finished a man who I had never met before came up to me and said, 'Mr Hunter, I have enjoyed your talk very much and wondered if you might be able to come back next week to do it again. I have some visiting professors coming in from Vladivostok and I am sure they would like to hear it.'

'I would love to but my Visa expires tomorrow so I have to go home. One week is not enough time to get a new Visa and book flights.'

'If you are prepared to do it I will help you.'

'Then you will need my passport details in order to support my application.'

'Not necessary,' he said opening his briefcase in which was a photocopy of my passport. (n.b. photocopier).

At this point my legs turned to jelly. I had never seen this man before but he had all my details in his briefcase. Gulp.

'On Monday go to the Russian Embassy personally and apply for a Visa to come back next Saturday and book a flight ticket. If the Visa has not arrived in the post on Friday, just go to Heathrow on Saturday morning in time to catch your flight.'

'But they won't let me on the plane without a Visa when I check-in.'

'Just trust me.'

'Okay if you are sure. How many days would you like me to come for?' I asked but I knew there was no way they would let me travel without a Visa.

'Oh just two weekdays. You can have Sunday to yourself for some sightseeing.'

I was feeling even more unnerved now as he said this in such a way as if he knew exactly what I would be doing on Sunday. I would be going to see Lena.

The flight home was uneventful. The usual cheer as the Captain announced that we were leaving Russian airspace. I was sad that I was leaving but if all went well I would be back again next weekend.

I set off very early on Monday morning to get to the Russian Embassy by around 7:30am. I was second in the queue outside the high brick wall surrounding the Embassy. There was a turnstile gate and a loudspeaker next to it. Just after 9:00am a harsh voice crackled through the loudspeaker, 'Next,' and with a click on the ratchet, the turnstile was released. There was now quite a queue behind me and I was glad I had got there early. A few minutes later, 'next' followed by a click and I was in. The Visa section was in a high ceilinged room in what must have been some sort of Stately Home. There were several bank style cash desks with severe looking women behind glass screens. A large picture of Lenin hung on the wall behind them. I passed my application form and passport through the slit at the bottom of the glass window.

'My letter of invitation should already be here, supported by the State Committee for Science and Technology.'

'One moment...' I stood there nervously with my palms sweating. 'Ah yes, Mr Pankratov has been in contact with us.'

Another unnerving moment for me to think that over the weekend my man had telephoned the Russian Embassy, had a discussion about me and how he wanted me back on Saturday. Now I knew his name.

'It is quite urgent,' I said as politely as I could. 'I need to travel back to Moscow on Saturday.''

'I will see what I can do.'

Friday's post came and no Visa. I had booked a flight to Moscow on Saturday with British Airways and would have to leave in the morning before the post arrived. I was beginning to think that I had wasted the company's money and time but I must at least give my man the benefit of the doubt.

I got up early on Saturday morning, parked my car at Heathrow long-term car park and made my way to Terminal Two. There was the usual crowd of people milling around and I began to wonder whether I had done the right thing.

A tap on my shoulder startled me.

'Mr Hunter your Visa,' and a brown envelope was thrust into my hand. Before I could make out fully who this person was he had turned round and disappeared into the crowd. Well this gave me a real adrenaline rush. Whoever this person was knew what I looked like and where I was. How weird was that? I felt unnerved that someone had been watching me the whole time.

I checked my Visa and passport and it was all in order so off I went to check in. I didn't know yet where I would be staying but the INTOURIST desk at Sheremetyevo would let me know on arrival. To some travellers this would be a worry, not knowing what hotel you were booked in but I was now getting used to "the System" and knew that someone, somewhere would look after me. After all, they wanted me there.

It was the National Hotel I was booked into according to the INTOURIST lady who pointed to a man standing near me and said, 'and there is your taxi driver.'

For the sake of this chapter, which is dedicated to Mr Pankratov, I will not dwell on what I got up to at the weekend. I will allow you to wonder!

My lecture went well and Mr P introduced me to more potential customers. At the end of the day when we were just chatting he said to me,

'I would like to come and visit your production facility. Is that possible?'

'I don't see why not.'

'You would need to give me an official letter of invitation and deliver it to the Soviet Trade Delegation in Highgate.'

I did what was asked so back in the office I had to explain to my colleagues the importance of this visit and told them that I thought Mr Pankratov was my KGB minder. Most of them pooh-poohed this but agreed to put on a show for him. Dennis, the MD, was very keen on this visit and wanted to get involved.

Armed with Mr Pankratov's letter of invitation I set off for the Soviet Trade Delegation in Highgate, near to the cemetery where Karl Marx is buried. I drew up at the large metal gates wondering how on earth to get in. There was no bell or intercom visible but I did see a camera on top of the fence, which was now pointing at me. Eventually the metal gate slid sideways allowing me to drive in. 'What now?' I thought. I saw a sign for Visitors Parking and pulled up outside what I thought could be reception. In I went, to be greeted by, 'Mr Hunter, we were expecting you.' Just as I thought I was getting used to "the System" this completely freaked me out and made me feel uneasy. The knotted feeling in the pit of my stomach intensified. 'They really do know a lot about me!' I thought.

I was offered a cup of coffee which I sipped as we engaged in some small talk when it was suggested that I should come back and meet one of their Trade Delegates to look at some of the Russian made products that I might be interested in, especially their range of optical glass and filters which are known for their excellence.

I communicated with Mr Pankratov by telex and made arrangements for a specific day for him to visit me. The night before his arrival when I was just about to leave the office, I took a telephone call.

'*Good evening Mr Hunter. Special Branch here. We understand that you are entertaining a visiting Russian at your invitation and we would just like to know what your itinerary is for tomorrow.*'

'I – Ugh... No problem. I am picking him up from the station at 10:30am and driving back to our factory and office. I am taking him to lunch in a restaurant in Cambridge, back to the office for some final business discussions then returning him to station at about 4:30pm.'

'*That's fine Mr Hunter. Have a good day.*' The phone clicked off without another word.

I put the phone down thinking, 'what on earth have I got into. Special Branch is now questioning me.' I reassured myself with the knowledge that every trip to Moscow and every business deal I did was made known to the

Department for Trade and Industry and the British Embassy in Moscow so if I were doing anything wrong they would let me know.

I pulled in to the station the following morning at 10:15am to meet Mr Pankratov. Minutes after I parked, there was a tap on the driver's window and a warrant card thrust at me.

'Good morning Mr Hunter. We are from Special Branch. We understand that your are meeting a Russian visitor but we would like to have words with him first.'

'OK, shall I come to the platform with you and introduce you?'

'That wont be necessary sir. We know who he is. We will take him into the waiting room for a while and then you can have him.'

'Bloody hell,' I thought, 'he really must be KGB for Special Branch to be interested in him.'

The train pulled in and I saw the two men escort Mr Pankratov to the waiting room. They must have spent about 20 minutes with him before bringing him over to my car.

'Here you are sir. We have finished with him so you may take him now.'

'What was all that about?' I asked Mr Pankratov as we set off for the office.

'It was nothing. Just general questions about my visit,' he said, waiving his hand as if to bat the question away.

Back in the office the guys had set up several demonstrations for Mr Pankratov but mindful of the restrictions imposed on us as to the level of computer power we were able to sell to the USSR. Anything outside of our restrictions had been carefully removed so as to avoid any embarrassing questions. Dennis had seen my car comincg and was ready at the main entrance for an official welcome. All the staff were intrigued to see what a "real Russian" was like, particularly after the stories I had told about my trips to Moscow, and were keen to join in the demonstrations.

Time for lunch.

I had booked a table at the Garden House Hotel in Cambridge as it had beautiful gardens over looking the Cam with iconic views of punters poling their way under the bridges. Dennis joined us for lunch but as we drove towards Cambridge I was aware that a car had pulled out behind me as I left the office and had followed me all the way to the restaurant. I kept this in the back of my mind. Inside the hotel we were shown to our table but as we passed through the bar seating area I noticed someone sitting, reading a newspaper, held up high so I could not immediately see their face.

'I don't believe it,' I thought. The classic spy movie pose of someone trailing a spy but not wishing to be seen. This was just too obvious. And what a cliché! What better setting than Cambridge, where the famous group of three spies had been recruited namely Guy Burgess, Donald Maclean and Kim Philby.

'I wonder if they have bugged our table?' went through my mind. 'So what if they have. We are not doing anything wrong, just trying to do some honest business to improve our exports.'

Lunch was followed by a stroll around the gardens, which Mr Pankratov was enthralled over. Back to the office and again the same car that followed me to Cambridge was now tailing me on the way back. Just time for some final discussions on how we could develop our business relationship bilaterally and then back to the station.

There it was again. That same car was now following me back to the station. We bade our farewells in the car park and I made my way back to the office. The car had now disappeared.

He must be important if Special Branch put on this number of staff to tail him. And those were just the ones that I could see.

My next encounter with Mr Pankratov was even more bizarre. My relationship with Lena was progressing and as I hadn't got any business trips to Moscow arranged for some months I booked a weekend City Break with a travel company which meant that I travelled on a Tourist Visa, not business. The Mezhdunarodnaya Hotel was their chosen venue and I felt that I ought to let the tour guide know that I would not be doing any of the set excursions but going off on my own. She was a little concerned but after she knew my situation and my ability to speak and read some Russian now she relaxed.

I deposited my luggage in my room and went through the usual farce of ruffling my bed to make it look slept in and avoiding the Dezurnaya as I slipped out with my key in my pocket. When I returned the following morning to get a change of clothes and to check in with the tour guide to show I was OK, I found a slip of paper under my door. It was a square of graph paper folded in half with a business card enclosed. A shiver went down my spine as I read the English side of the card.

Dimitri A Pankratov

Deputy Head of Division

Department of Scientific and Technical

Cooperation with Foreign Countries

USSR State committee for Science

and Technology

This was the first time I had seen Mr Pankratov's title in full. No wonder Special Branch had an interest in him.

What was written on both sides of the small piece of graph paper was even more unnerving and I transliterate verbatim.

Mr. Hunter! Welcome to Moscow! I know you are here – operator gave me your room number. All my attempts to contact you by phone failed, you're always out. 10 o'clock. I reserved tomorrow morning (16.07.86) for a meeting with you at G.K.N.T. – State Committee for Science and Technology. I'll call you tonight after 10pm and tomorrow morning to confirm the meeting. Prof. Rubin will be present. Address of G.K.N.T. is Nezdanova street, 11. Russian spelling is ул. Нежданова 11. This is for taxi-driver. Best regards, Pankratov.

I mistakenly thought that as I was travelling with a tourist group, no one would know I was here. WRONG! Mr Pankratov knew and had gone to great lengths to contact me. He was obviously well educated in the English language by looking at his hand written note. Some very English word construction and attention to detail with punctuation marks.

Obviously I had to attend the meeting during which I had to explain why I was always out and my relationship with Lena. He already knew!

After the meeting I never saw Mr Pankratov again. I don't know what happened to him and probably never will.

Chapter 11

Yugoslavia and Zoritsa

I came to love visiting the reluctantly Communist Yugoslavia as it offered all the excitement of being in a Communist country but with less of the risks. I had appointed a distributor for our products in Yugoslavia and made regular trips to support him either by doing lecture tours or exhibitions.

On one of my first exhibition tours, my colleague Terry and I drove out to Zagreb in an estate car full of equipment and arriving at the Palace Hotel in Zagreb one Sunday afternoon, we started to unload the car and set the equipment up in our allocated exhibition room. While I was carrying boxes from the car to the hotel I missed my footing and slipped off the edge of the pavement. I heard a loud crack and a pulse of pain shot up my leg, taking my breath away. At first I didn't realise what I had done but after struggling for some half an hour or more trying to limp around I noticed that my foot was hanging loosely at the bottom of my leg and was excruciatingly painful. Terry, realising that something was seriously wrong rang round a few of his contacts and found a consultant radiologist who worked in the General Hospital. She told him to bring me in straight away and Terry obliged by driving me to the hospital.

I didn't have to wait very long as there was no one else there that Sunday afternoon - just me and the lady radiographer. She got me to lie down on a very cold x-ray table and out of kindness to me I suppose she decided to protect my private parts from any stray radiation by slapping a large lead shield across my crotch. This wasn't done with very much compassion and inflicted a second source of pain. After taking a set of x-rays of my ankle and examining the pictures she informed me that my ankle was broken and would have to be set and plastered.

I was then taken to the plaster room, sat in a very uncomfortable chair, and a male nurse knelt on the floor in front of me. He made me put the tip of my toe on the floor, cupped his hands across my knee and started to push my leg down in an attempt to straighten my ankle. I had got my hands on his shoulders and as he pressed, the pain got so intense I can truly say it was the first time in my life I saw stars. (I then realised the meaning of seeing stars). The more he pushed the more my grip increased on his shoulders until it got to the point where he was crying out in pain as well because my fingernails were digging into the flesh in his back. Eventually he managed to straighten my ankle at which point he slapped a wet plaster bandage on my leg up to my knee and I sat there waiting for it to set, still in extreme pain, not being offered any painkillers and sweating profusely.

After it had set he said, 'okay you can go now.' I was not even offered a crutch or any sort of walking aid so I had to hop out of the hospital with one hand on Terry's shoulder.

When we got back to the hotel we were met by Harry, the front hall porter. Harry was a real character, a guy who could fix anything for you. You just had to ask Harry for something and he could arrange it. Now Harry knew my penchant for attractive ladies and as soon as he saw my predicament he said 'Graham I know what will make you feel better. Go to your room and wait.'

I knew exactly what Harry meant so I hopped up the stairs to my room, stripped off and somehow managed to have a bath with my newly plastered, still very painful leg hanging over the side. I dried myself and just with a towel around my waist, I hopped over to the bed. I had I should mention at this point I had left the room door on the latch in anticipation and it was not long before the expected knock came. In walked a beautiful blonde.

'Harry tells me I have to make you feel better,' she said.

'Oh yes please,' I whimpered.

She proceeded to take her clothes off in front of the window and with the light streaming through her blonde hair was a real sight to behold. The back lighting made her glow and accentuated her perfect features. She removed all of her clothes and with each item that came off I could see that she was even more beautiful than I first thought. Now totally naked, she walked over to me. I could hardly contain myself underneath the towel draped across me. She very gently removed the towel and started to make me feel better. It was absolutely wonderful. She knew exactly what to do to make me feel good and for a short period of time, I managed to forget the severe throbbing pain in my ankle.

After we had finished I got dressed and went down to dinner. Harry said, 'did you enjoy that? Did it make you feel better?' unable to hide his smile.

'Oh yes! 'I said and winked at Harry. I couldn't wait to eat my dinner as I was starving now.

The following day I had to give a lecture and demonstration and was under a severe handicap in that I had no walking aid to assist with the heavy lump of plaster on my left leg. After I finished the lecture in the morning Terry said 'we need to find something to help you walk. Let's ring up the British Consul in Zagreb and see if they can help.' They were very obliging on the telephone. 'Yes we keep a stock of certain medical items so come in and we will see what we can find for you.'

Off we drove to the Consul and in a dusty old cupboard they managed to find a crutch. But what a crutch! It looked as if it had been a prop in a Long John Silver film and was quite simply a broom handle with a T piece nailed across the top. But beggars can't be choosers – it was a walking aid of sorts and I was very grateful to at least have something to help me hobble along.

Later that afternoon when we returned to the hotel we were greeted by Harry again who enquired about my ankle.

'Well it is still very painful today, 'I said.

'Would you like some more comfort tonight? 'Harry asked.

'Oh yes please,' I responded.

Harry said that he couldn't guarantee he could get me the same girl again but that he would get me someone else just as good. So I went back to my room and waited expectantly.

This time when the knock on the door came there was an equally attractive female outside but this one was tall and leggy with a huge curly shock of strawberry blonde hair and although she was a little over made up, she was an extremely attractive girl. "Sex on legs" described her accurately.

Her name was Zoritsa.

Zoritsa too managed to make me feel very happy and despite the huge plaster cast on my leg we managed to make love with a lot of energy and gusto.

Before Zoritsa went she asked me how often I came to Zagreb and at that time it was quite frequently. 'Here is my address and phone number,' she said. 'Perhaps you would like to visit me next time you come when the plaster cast is off. I thought that this was a great idea. I never expected all this female attention. It felt incredibly good after years of enforced celibacy.

The following day Terry and I had to pack up the exhibition and drive down to Belgrade. We stopped in the Metropole hotel and after unpacking our bags went to sit in the bar for a relaxing drink or two. Now, Terry was a bit of a ladies man as well but he liked to tease and while we were sitting in the bar as usual, a lady of the night came over and started chatting in perfect English. It was obvious that it was Terry she was after but he wasn't going to give her an easy time.

'Well,' he said, 'what have you got to offer? '

'I'll make you feel good and give you a good time,' she purred.

'No no, I want more detail,' he persisted. 'I am a tits man. Have you got good tits?'

On hearing this she accepted his challenge simply flopped the top of her dress down, whipped out her breasts and said to him, 'how about these? Are these good enough for you?'

'Hmm,' said Terry, examining her breasts carefully. 'Not bad but I also like a bit of thigh as well.'

At this she promptly hauled her already short skirt up to her bum and put Terry's hand on the inside of her thigh. 'Is that soft enough for you? '

I could see that Terry was getting a bit excited by now. 'Mmm. All right. Off we go.' With that they disappeared out of the bar and upstairs to his room.

Half an hour later he re-joined me in the bar for a beer.

'How was it then?' I asked him.

'Oh I wished I hadn't. It was like bonking a sack of potatoes. I didn't enjoy it at all.'

After finishing our work in Belgrade our next stop was Sofia in Bulgaria. Terry was happy to do all the driving as long as I was happy to continue with the tour.

I was booked on a Yugoslav Airlines flight to return to England and Terry was going to drive the car back home on his own. At the airport I got the full treatment as we had pre-warned them that I had a leg in plaster. I was met by a porter with a wheelchair who wheeled me onto the plane ahead of everyone else. The plane was flying to Zagreb first where we had to change. They allowed everyone else to get off first and then came to meet me with an ambulance. I was carefully escorted down the steps, into the ambulance, and then driven across the tarmac to the waiting plane, which I was allowed to board on my own. There I sat for an hour in a totally empty plane. I was beginning to wonder whether I was on the right one but eventually the crew arrived, people started to board and finally we set off back to Heathrow.

I a colleague met me in the arrival hall with a wheelchair. He had already heard that I had a crutch reminiscent of a prop from Treasure Island and being a bit of a joker he had brought with him and an inflatable parrot, which he proceeded to attach to my shoulder, much to everyone's amusement. With this I was unceremoniously wheeled across Terminal 2 to his waiting car.

After about four weeks of hobbling around clumsily, the plaster cast was taken off and lo and behold my ankle has healed, confirmed by x-rays taken at my local hospital. What a relief as I was expecting some problems due to the 'unusual' way my ankle had been reset in Zagreb.

It was some months later that I could fit in a return visit to Yugoslavia. Business had been good and I had no trouble in justifying a return visit. This time I was on my own and flew directly to Zagreb. Arriving at my favourite hotel I was greeted cheerily by Harry, the front porter.

'Ah Mr Hunter, can I do anything for you tonight?'

'No thanks,' I replied. 'I don't need any help tonight.'

After checking in I hurried up to my room and called Zoritsa.

'Hi, I'm back again. Are you free tonight?'

'Oo yes,' she said. 'Come round to my flat. You've got my address. It's not far from the hotel so you can walk.'

Off I set up the road to find her flat. Unfortunately I was not familiar with the way addresses were written. There were two numbers written in Roman numerals after the street name, one the number of the building and one the number of the flat. I was not sure which way round they were written and I knocked on several doors before I found someone who knew Zoritsa.

'Wrong flat. It's over there,' said a very surprised gentleman who answered the door.

Finally I found Zoritsa's flat and was greeted like a long lost friend.

'Come in. Come in,' she said with excitement. 'Meet my Butler, Alfred.'

What!!! A live-in butler! I was astonished that this lady could have a butler; after all, this was Yugoslavia, a Communist country.

The inside of her flat was beautifully appointed and well decorated. Crystal chandeliers hung sparkling from the ceiling and expensive carpets were arranged neatly on the floor between huge glass-doored, wooden display cabinets, which were full of fine cut glass.

She had prepared dinner for me, which I ate with relish. Then the phone rang and after a short conversation that I could not understand she said apologetically, 'sorry Graham but I have got to go out for a short while. Alfred will look after you. Do you play chess? – he is quite good at it.'

For the next forty-five minutes or so I sat engrossed in a chess game and not having played for years, Alfred easily beat me. It felt so surreal. Here I am sitting in a splendidly appointed flat in Zagreb playing chess with a working girl's butler.

A key rattled in the front door – Zoritsa was back. She strode into the living room wearing a pair of thigh high leather boots. Being long legged she looked very enticing in them.

'Come on,' she said, taking me by the hand. 'Bedtime.' She dismissed Alfred for the night, thanking him for entertaining me and led me to her bedroom. If I thought her living room was well appointed, the bedroom was palatial. The bed was at least a super king size, covered with colourful Oriental throws. The most prominent feature of the room was the headboard, which overlapped each side of the bed by at least two feet and contained the most amazing array of switches and controls. From this headboard she could control the lighting, the built-in music centre, the television and no doubt could also summon Alfred if required.

She seductively stripped off, leaving only her thigh high leather boots on. Boy was I excited. I returned to my hotel the following morning a very happy man.

Chapter 12

Miss Su 1

During my visit to Hong Kong, one of my objectives was to establish a distributor who could sell into both Hong Kong and China for me. I had interviewed a couple of companies but one in particular was keen to have the business and went out of their way to entertain me in style. This particular evening they arranged to pick me up from my hotel in a huge stretch limo and took me to a club. This looked as if it had come out of a Hollywood set - the canopy out to the street, the red carpet and the top-hatted concierge at the door. Inside the establishment was huge with a dance floor surrounded by hundreds of tables. The host took me over to the door at the edge, which led into some offices and introduced me to the Mama-San (the mother of the house). She led us through into another large room where lots of lovely young ladies were waiting to entertain. Mama-San selected one for me. She was very petite and although I know Chinese people look younger than they are I took some convincing to believe that she was over 16. Not a problem for the Chinese but it certainly would have been for me. After spending several hours in the club during which time we consumed innumerable bottles of champagne my hosts had to leave me alone so they could prepare for work the next day. They assured me my escort was mine for the evening and had been paid for. I caught a glance of the bill - at least £700 from my quick calculation from HK dollars. I didn't know whether to be horrified or not.

I don't recall any problems getting her into my room but when she took her clothes off she had so little pubic hair that I did wonder just how old she was. I also remember thinking that if we did appoint these distributors permanently it would cost a fortune to reciprocate in hospitality. I telephoned Dennis to tell him how I had been entertained and how much the bill had come to although I hadn't paid for this one.

We did sign them up as distributors and they proved very helpful the next time I was in Hong Kong as I will reveal.

I was very excited because I had been invited to take part in the first ever medical equipment exhibition to be held in one of the remotest parts of China in Xinjiang Province. It was the Forbidden City of Urumqi which was up in the far north-west corner of China with the borders of the USSR, Mongolia and Kazakhstan not far off. It used to be a major hub on the Silk Road during China's Tang dynasty and developed its reputation as a leading cultural and commercial centre during the Qing dynasty in the 19th century. Latterly it became a Forbidden City with no entry or exit from it unless Government authorised. It is regarded as the furthest city away from the coast anywhere in the world.

I had prepared well in advance and had a lot of demonstration equipment for the show sent out to our new distributors in Hong Kong. When I set off for Hong Kong it was with some trepidation because although I had travelled through China before I had never been to such a remote part.

After the usual exhilarating landing at Kai Tak airport in Hong Kong, I was met by our distributors who whisked me off to their offices to make preparation. The equipment had all arrived and was sitting in the foyer all neatly boxed up in the little wooden packing cases. I was told that we had to spend the next two days not only getting my Chinese Visa but also getting the licence to take the equipment into China and get it back out again. I was more than happy at the thought of spending two days and nights in Hong Kong as it meant I could spend two nights with Loli. I knew that I would certainly not be getting any female company while I was in China...casual sex was frowned upon.

After getting all the necessary paperwork together we set off-and what a memorable journey that turned out to be. We had to take all the equipment with us as cargo baggage, which meant that we had about 12 boxes all neatly nailed and screwed together by little Chinese carpenters and we loaded these in the back of two cars and drove off to the airport.

Kai Tak airport was very efficient and although busy it was not too much of a problem to get ourselves booked onto the flight to Beijing. However, things were very different once we arrived in Beijing. We had to stay overnight which meant that all 12 boxes of cargo we were carrying had to be offloaded and driven to the hotel. The following morning all had to be loaded back into two taxis and returned to Beijing airport.

I could not believe the melee of people at Beijing airport. It was just one throbbing mass of people who had no idea how to queue, all surging together trying to push themselves forward to book their places on various flights. It was chaos. We had identified which check-in desks were handling the flight to Urumqi and I was just plonked in the middle of the floor guarding a couple of suitcase trolleys with all our cases piled high on them while my distributors threw themselves into the fray and fought to get to the front of the queue. I was more than happy to stand guard over our goods and keep well clear of the heaving mass of bodies.

What I hadn't realised was just how much clout my distributors carried with various officials at the airport. Once they had identified themselves at the check-in desk it was absolutely amazing. It was as if a button had been pressed and doors were opened for them. We were booked on the flight with no problem. We were even given all the customs papers and stickers to fill in ourselves and apply to the boxes so that they were pre-cleared before being loaded onto the aircraft. Once we had put all the stickers on the boxes we were ushered through customs-or should I say ushered around, as we did not have to open any boxes and show the customs officers what was inside. We wheeled everything up to the boarding gate where eventually it was taken from us by another friendly official and loaded onto the plane.

Boarding the plane was yet another experience, as it was again apparent that Chinese travellers have no sense of queueing. That's one thing that the British do well at least. Once the flight was announced and people asked to board, there was another mad surge of people all shoving and pushing to get on even though they all had allocated seats. Once inside the plane there was a big battle for overhead luggage space. Unless you have travelled on Chinese airways before you will probably not believe some of the things that happen. People boarded the plane with small net bags carrying live chickens and one even had a small pig in a bag. To my absolute horror after we had taken off one family proceeded to get a Primus stove out from the hand luggage, pump it up in the middle of the aisle, and boil water for their own green tea.

The flight to Urumqi took us just over four hours, flying directly west from Beijing over the Gobi desert. Urumqi airport was something else. This city nestled between some mountains just at the side of the Gobi desert. The airport had one small terminal building and some custom sheds with probably only two or three flights per week. Our plane came in, unloaded, loaded up again and took off. The airport was now closed. A sudden chill came over me as I thought, 'there is no way I can get out of this place in a hurry.'

After we had located our baggage and all our packing cases we were again escorted around customs to meet some waiting dignitaries on the land side of the barriers. I was not expecting such a reception but when my distributors told me that I was the only European in this town, which in the past had been closed to visitors. I could understand why I was being given the red carpet treatment.

All the packing cases were bundled into a little open-backed truck while we were taken by Chinese limousine to one of the local hotels. The hotel apparently was a specialist hotel used mainly by overseas Chinese visitors i.e. businessmen from Hong Kong or other expatriate Chinese, but certainly not Europeans. The hotel appeared to have been built on a building site and rubbish tip. The drive up to reception was littered with building material, old packing cases and what appeared to be the contents of dustbins, with a few little wild pigs rummaging around for what morsels they could find to eat in the rubbish.

The interior of the hotel was rather dark and dingy with very few light bulbs working. Once checked in I was taken up to my room along a very dark corridor and as my eyes grow accustomed to the dark I could see that every 10 feet also there was a large chipped enamel spittoon. On closer examination, these spittoons appeared not to have been emptied for a considerable time as the contents were sloping over the top and seeping into the carpet below them.

My room was very sparsely appointed and on the glass-topped dressing table there were a few standard items of equipment. One was a very brightly coloured Chinese thermos flask full of hot water, which I was told would be replenished every day. There was a little bowl with green tea bags and a fly swat. I could understand the thermos and green tea bags but as there were no visible signs of flies about I was a little bemused as to why we had a fly swat. However, when my two distributors joined me later they showed me why I needed the fly swat. Before you go to bed they said you quickly whip back the covers of the bed with the fly swat in your hand and you bash all the little insects that are crawling around in your bed. It made my skin crawl at the thought of having to sleep in a bed infested with insects.

The bathroom was equally spartan with a tiny tablet of soap and something that resembled a face flannel as an apology for a towel. The plumbing was hanging off the walls and rusty screws were dangling in mid air leaving holes in the plaster through which cockroaches freely crawled in and out. We had had a long journey so I thought I might as well have a shower. I turned the water on to find that it was a bright orange colour. My attempts to get a lather with the soap failed miserably and after my shower, I ended up smelling of rust and feeling dirtier than I had before I got in. I had to use the small face cloth in the same way as a window cleaner would use a chamois leather, by drying small sections of my body and wringing out the cloth to remove surplus water.

That evening when I met my distributors for dinner I commented on the lack of facilities in the bathroom. 'Ah,' they said, 'don't worry because sometimes there is no water so there's no need for a towel. You'll get a clean towel every day providing it's not raining.'

Mystified I enquired, 'why don't I get one if it's raining?'

'Oh, because the laundry lady can't hang out the washing to dry if it is raining.'

That evening we were joined for dinner by several of the local dignitaries and once again, as the only European in town, I had to get used to the red carpet treatment.

One thing I always found about travelling in China was that regardless of how dingy or dirty or spartan the places were that you stayed in, the food was always exquisite. Bowl upon bowl of the most amazing dishes kept coming and I tucked into them with delight. Delicacies such as deep-fried whole baby birds, ducks tongues and something that resembled Dolmades except the filling, instead of being wrapped in a vine leaf, was wrapped in a webbed ducks foot.

Having filled myself up on all these lovely treats I was then told that the speciality of the house was about to arrive. I was absolutely gobsmacked when a whole barbecued sheep was wheeled in with all the ceremony you would expect on a Burns night when the haggis is piped in. The head chef proceeded to dissect the sheep in front of me. As the honoured guest I was given all the best bits, which included the sheep's head and other parts, which I did not attempt to identify. I was honour bound to eat everything I was given, as it would have been an insult to turn such delicacies away.

Over dinner people joked about how the British in general have difficulty in using chopsticks but complimented me on how well I handled mine. As an experienced traveller in China I had come to grips with chopsticks years ago and impressed my hosts by picking up single grains of rice, peas and quails eggs without any trouble at all. One of my hosts joked by saying that when you are really proficient at using chopsticks you can catch a fly in mid-air. Not one to miss rising to a challenge, I had noticed that a small fly had landed in my lap and I surreptitiously swatted it with the palm of my hand. While my hosts were engaged in other conversations I quickly put this fly between the ends of my chopsticks under the cover of the tablecloth then suddenly jumped up in the air and announced to everybody, 'look I've just caught a fly.'

This caused an uproar and was followed by copious toasting of my health with this evil concoction called Mai Tai. I can only describe this liquor as tasting like a cross between rocket fuel and petrol, not that I would know what they taste like.

When being honoured with a toast it was expected that you should down your glass in one go with the salutation of "gambey." You can imagine that after an evening of copious toasting with rocket fuel, the following morning I really did not feel like getting up and going to set up an exhibition stand. However, my distributors were up early, bright eyed and bushy tailed, and after a breakfast of steamed buns with red bean paste and liberal amounts of green tea we set off for the exhibition hall.

This exhibition was being staged in the military barracks and the exhibition hall was the soldiers' gymnasium. When we walked in I could not believe that this room was ever going to hold an exhibition as it looked like a rubbish tip. There was some semblance of trying to erect booth's and stands around the hall but the floor was littered with debris. While lots of people engaged in arguments as to where their equipment was and who was going to bring it into the hall, we were shown to our booth and my heart sank when I saw it.

There was a huge pile of rubbish in the middle of the booth and we had been given three tables to use, which looked to me as if they had come out of a Dickensian novel. They were old wooden school desks with wobbly legs. There was paint daubed all over them and carvings on the top. They looked disgusting.

95

Not being one to admit defeat easily I said, 'right, how can we smarten up these tables?' One of my colleagues volunteered to go into town and when he came back he had bought several metres of beautiful blue silk which we used to drape the tops of the tables. Once we had located our boxes we proceeded to get all the equipment out and set it up, and by the end of the day I was able to think, 'Hmmmm this doesn't look too bad.'

During the day I had constant visits from two Chinese customs officers who had been appointed to oversee our equipment, bearing in mind that the equipment was only allowed in on a temporary import licence and we had to ensure it was shipped out again after the exhibition. One of these customs officers was a very unlikely Chinese man who was about 6 feet tall, had blue eyes and very Mongolian features. The other was the lady who introduced herself as Miss Su. Miss Su could speak very good English but admitted that she had never met a European person before and had never had the chance to practice her English language skills with an English speaking person. So, unsurprisingly, she latched herself onto me at every opportunity.

That evening after we had to set up the exhibition stand and got rid of all the rubbish we began to feel that we might have a good week ahead of us so we happily went out for yet another banquet. Who should turn up at the banquet but Miss Su, still in her Chairman Mao customs uniform but minus the official badge on her lapel. She proceeded to seat herself next to me on the round table and continued to practice her English. Around the table were other dignitaries. There was the local General from the military barracks who annoyed me immensely by refusing to take his hat off during the whole meal. There was the Minister of Trade for the area plus the exhibition organiser. As I was the only European in town they all wanted to sit at my table and talk to me.

The banquet was absolutely fabulous again with lots of delicacies that I could not even begin to describe and of course lots more toasts with the evil Mai Tai. One of the two distributors bet that he could drink two glasses of the Mai Tai for every one that all the others around the table drunk. This was a challenge we simply could not refuse. Toasts were made for any and every reason to up the glass count. I don't recall how many glasses I drank that evening but certainly the following morning I felt dreadful. I remember lying in my bed thinking if I feel this bad I wonder how my colleague feels having drunk twice as much as I have. Much to my surprise, there was a knock on my bedroom door and there he was, bright as a button cheerfully saying, 'I'm ready for breakfast now. What about you?'

That morning the hotel chefs had put themselves out for me and conjured up some fried eggs, which are not normally an addition to the Chinese breakfast table. Several of my Chinese colleagues also wanted to try fried eggs for breakfast and I could hardly hide my amusement when I saw them trying to eat fried eggs with chopsticks. They just did not know how to handle them with the egg slipping all over the place. In the end they put the two chopsticks under the fried eggs, lowered their mouths to the plate, elevated the egg slightly and sucked. Eventually the whole egg was sucked inside their mouths and swallowed.

After breakfast, we were picked up again in the stretch limo and driven to the Exhibition Centre where to my amazement thousands of people were crowded outside trying to get in. We were shepherded through the crowds and in through doors and eventually got to our exhibition stand. Dust covers were taken off, final titillation and alignment of equipment, and we turned it on to make sure it was working. We were then ushered outside for the inaugural opening ceremony.

Outside in the grounds there was a table with various dignitaries sitting at it and a ceremonial red ribbon draped across the main door into the gymnasium. After a lot of speeches, not a word of which I understood, the Minister for Trade cut the ribbon and the crowd surged forward pushing to get inside. We also rushed back in, got to our stands and prepared ourselves for the throngs of people heading up the aisle towards us. My two Chinese colleagues from Hong Kong were doing a good job of demonstrating the equipment and interpreting the visitors' comments for me. As the crowd gradually died down Miss Su, the customs officer, came to me and said 'Graham can you show me how your equipment works?'

Not wishing to cause offence by a refusal I said, 'of course I can,' and took her through how it all worked. I showed her how to turn it on and off and to get results from it. She listened intently and after about half an hour she said 'thank you for that. I am just going to meet some of my friends and bring them back here. I won't be long.' Sure enough, after about 45 minutes she came back with a group of half a dozen very important people. They must have been important because they all had at least two ballpoint pens in their top pockets, which is normally a statement of importance in China. To my amazement, she proceeded to give a very plausible demonstration of the equipment to her visitors. Some questions were asked, which I answered, and then she turned to me and said, 'my friends want to buy this equipment.'

Very impressed by her abilities to demonstrate and sell I nevertheless had to shake my head. 'This is a problem. This equipment is only in on a temporary import licence and I have to take it back home with me.'

'No problem,' said Miss Su. 'I am a customs officer. Just leave it to me.'

'But what about payment?' I said. 'It costs $10,000.'

'No problem either,' she said, 'just leave it to me.'

After her friends had gone she explained that they were professors and doctors from one of the local scientific institutes and had some foreign currency that they wanted to use to buy my equipment. She explained that as a customs officer she would be able to prepare all the documents to enable the equipment to stay in China.

'But what about payment?' I insisted.

'Don't worry,' she said, 'trust me, you will be paid.'

After the exhibition closed that evening, Miss Su came to me and asked if I would like to go to dinner with her. I was quite flattered that she wanted to spend an evening with me and readily agreed. She arranged to come and pick me up from my hotel at 6:30pm. I went back to my room, showered in rusty water, dried myself on my pocket handkerchief towel and prepared myself for what I hoped would be an enjoyable evening. Miss Su appeared at reception promptly at 6:30pm. She hadn't changed and was still in the same Chairman Mayo style Custom's officer Jacket and trousers but had taken her badge off her lapel. We walked up the main street, round a few back roads and eventually she took me into a very dingy restaurant and said, 'this is where we are going to eat tonight.'

I was horrified. It was filthy. It was full of local Chinese, eating very noisily, spitting out all the bones onto the table and also, in true Chinese fashion, spitting great globules of sputum onto the floor whenever they felt the need.

Outside the restaurant, donkeys and carts clattered up the road as these were the locals' form of transport. Camels also wandered around freely and both animals' excrement was abundantly obvious, piled up in the road. The constant wind from the Gobi desert blew in clouds of dust and sand in swirls.

We had to wait a little while for a table to become free and eventually a group of men left, leaving a pile of detritus, chopsticks and crockery on the table. We were ushered to this table and while we sat, a waitress came over with a dirty rag, which I would have had trouble using as a floor cloth and proceeded to wipe all the bones and spittings out off the table and on to the floor. She then collected up all the dirty chopsticks, unravelled the dirty cloth, wrapped the chopsticks in it, and with a rolling motion on top of the table, wiped all the chopsticks. She then re-laid the table with these same chopsticks and at that point I thought, 'this is where I die.' I was at least comforted by the fact that I had had all my vaccinations before travelling, but I was convinced that I was going to catch something.

Miss Su ordered for me and the food began to arrive. I had to confess that it was delicious. The tastiness of the food dampened my worries about the dirtiness of the chopsticks and I tucked into this meal with relish. I kept finishing plate after plate as it was served up. It got to the point where I was absolutely bloated but more food kept arriving. I turned to Miss Su and groaned, 'when does this stop? '

She then explained that in Chinese custom, food is brought to a guest until he or she leaves some on their plate and it is only then that they are truly full. I have to confess that despite the dirty surroundings this was one of the best Chinese meals I had ever eaten. I staggered back to my hotel feeling very uncomfortable, accompanied by Miss Su.

The following day another thronging mass of people were queueing up to force their way inside the exhibition hall and I don't know where the time went because I was engaged in conversation with potential customers all day long. Miss Su was a frequent visitor, checking that I was okay and that I had adequate refreshments. At this exhibition there was no cafeteria and nowhere to get a drink but partway through the day, a tractor arrived in the military compound with a large trailer piled high with local melons. I had never seen melons shaped like this before. They must have been about 2 feet long, more like a marrow than a melon, and with very sweet yellow flesh. Each exhibitor was allocated about 25 melons, which were piled behind their stands. These melons were absolutely gorgeous and certainly better than glasses of bottled water or indeed the local brew, which was disgusting.

After a very busy day, Miss Su came along to me just before closing time to ask whether I would like to go to a Chinese dance with her. Again, not one to miss an opportunity to join in some local culture and custom, I quickly said, 'yes I would love to.'

She picked me up at 7:00pm having not changed from her business clothes again but merely removing her lapel badge again. We walked up a few streets and came upon another large building which obviously housed the dance hall. There was a queue of Chinese people waiting to get in and I was very conspicuous by the fact that a). I was head and shoulders above everyone else and b). Had a full head of blonde hair, not black.

Miss Su forced her way to the front of the queue and engaged herself in what appeared to be some very heated discussions with the doorman. She beckoned me to come over. There still seemed to be some problem and there was a lot of jostling and haggling going on. Eventually, she pulled out her customs officer badge from her top pocket, pinned it to her lapel and prodded at it quite violently. At this the doors opened, the heavies stepped aside and we were ushered in.

'What did you do?' I asked.

'I told them that I was a customs officer and if they didn't let us in I would bring some charges to bear on them.'

Once inside I could see that the dance floor was a throbbing mass of bodies, but it was obvious that the number of males outweighed the number of females by about 2 to 1. There was an old-fashioned brass band playing on the stage and Miss Su asked me if I would like to learn a Chinese style dance which of course I agreed to. The dance she taught me I can only describe as being like an English Quickstep, only in double time. After about half an hour of practising she thought I was getting proficient and said 'some of my friends would like to dance with you. Is that okay?'

'Of course, 'I replied, 'that would be wonderful.'

The first friend came over and to my horror it was a man. For those of you who haven't travelled to China, it is quite normal for men to dance with men but I have never experienced this. Having only had half an hour's tuition on how to dance the Chinese Quickstep, I was then given a male partner who insisted on leading so that I had to follow with the female steps. I remember thinking to myself, 'I am so glad that I am the only Brit here. I wouldn't want any of my friends to see me doing this and bring it up at a later date to haunt and embarrass me. As the evening went on more of Miss Su's friends were brought along to dance with me, most of them male, and at about 10:30pm I was taken back to my hotel feeling absolutely exhausted but not having had a single drop of Mai Tai.

The following day at the exhibition I recognised one of the people who came up to me as one of Miss Su's friends who wanted to buy the equipment from our stand. He was carrying a plastic bag, which he thrust into my hand and then rapidly disappeared. I opened the bag and to my amazement there were bundles of US dollars. Hurriedly I close the bag up not wishing the contents to be seen and put the bag in my briefcase under the table. The blue silk tablecloth hung down far enough to hide the briefcase. When Miss Su came along I showed her the bag.

'Oh good,' she said, 'now I can complete the paperwork.'

'But what about taking this money out of the country,' I said.

'Don't worry,' she said. 'I am a customs officer. Leave it to me.'

That evening the exhibition closed and we were invited to the celebratory banquet, which more local dignitaries would be attending. Again I was accompanied by Miss Su and the General, who still refused to take his hat off plus many others who I just did not understand as they didn't speak a word of English. The speciality of the house, the whole barbecued lamb, was again wheeled in and with great pomp and ceremony and dissected in the middle of the dining room floor. This time there was lots of posing for photographs and I was told that the exhibition had been very successful and was going to be publicised in the local and national press. People were jostling for position to have their photograph taken with me and the evening turned out to be yet another constant stream of toasting and swallowing that evil fluid which by now I had grown accustomed to.

The next day we had to go back to the hall to pack up all the equipment and were met by Miss Su's friends who took it all away. After we had cleared up and were getting ready to go back to the airport for a flight back to Beijing and Hong Kong, Miss Su gave me a small package.

'Just a little present for you to commemorate our friendship,' she said.

I opened it and inside was a beautifully handcrafted knife with brightly coloured stones embedded in the handle.

'This is lovely,' I said, 'but how on earth can I take this back home with me on the plane?'

'Don't worry, 'she said. 'I am a customs officer. Just do what I say and everything will be all right. Make sure you put the knife in your check in luggage and I will do the rest.'

That afternoon we were driven back to the airport in a cavalcade of Zils with of course Miss Su accompanying me. When we got to the airport there were lots of official handshaking and goodbyes and eventually we checked in our bags and went through to the departure lounge. As I was sitting in the lounge waiting for the plane to come in, which was the first and only plane on that day, I was very surprised to hear on the public address system and announcement in very Chinese English, 'Missa Hunta, pick up terephone for a terephone call.'

I found one of the house phones and picked it up. It was from Miss Su. 'Graham,' she said, 'don't worry about the knife. I have spoken to my friends at the airport and they will look after you and I'm just about to ring my friends in Beijing so you will have no problems.'

After I had put the phone down and the flight was announced I was met by an official who said, 'Missa Hunta prease come with me,' and guided me round through a side door, by-passing security checks and into the departure lounge.

I was beginning to feel quite smug now in the knowledge that perhaps I was going to get this knife home with me. During the flight from Beijing to Hong Kong I was reminiscing with my two Hong Kong agents and asking them how I could ever thank Miss Su for her hospitality and her present.

'Very easy', they said. 'Chinese people enjoy fairy stories and Miss Su reads English. Just send her some books; fairy stories from England.'

To cut a long story short, when I got back home and was sitting fondling the treasured knife, I tried to think of what books I could best send to Miss Su and in the end, came up with Grimm's fairy tales. I purchased the complete works and wrapped them up. I shall never forget the address I wrote on the envelope. There were just five words, which simply read Miss Su, Urumqi Customs, China.

'That's never going to get there,' I thought.

But it did and thereby starts another story.

Chapter 13

Miss Su 2

It was over a year since I had last seen Miss Su. I was sitting in my hotel room in Hong Kong after a really punishing schedule having just been from Zagreb to Belgrade to Moscow to Hong Kong to Manila to Seoul to Bangkok to Singapore and back to Hong Kong again.

The last part of this visit was to go to Urumqi to attend another exhibition. I had spent the day in Hong Kong getting my Visa for China and was looking forward to spending an evening with Loli before flying off the following day. This time it was going to be different. I wasn't going to be accompanied on the flight and I was a little nervous about attempting this on my own, as I had no knowledge of the Chinese language or written Chinese and I knew that I would again be the only European in Urumqi. However my Hong Kong agents had assured me that all the arrangements were in place and I would be met at Urumqi airport, taken to a hotel and looked after until they arrived the following day.

I had hoped as it was just me travelling with my luggage that I wouldn't have the same problems we had had last time when we had to carry all the packing cases and equipment with us on the plane. The first leg of my journey went fairly smoothly. It was a Cathay Pacific flight from Hong Kong to Beijing where the check-ins were perfectly normal, the boarding of the plane perfectly normal and everything seemed fairly civilised. However what I hadn't bargained for was that at Beijing airport I would have to join the thronging masses of bodies pushing and shoving to get to the check-in desk for the next flight.

'Oh well,' I thought. 'Here goes. I've got to do it.' Surprisingly I found it relatively easy to push and shove past a lot of the Chinese as I had the advantage of not only being head and shoulders above most of them but also considerably larger and stronger. Eventually I got to the check-in desk took my place allocated on the China airways flight and went off in search of the departure lounge. Beijing airport is huge and sprawling and it took ages to find out where the plane was leaving from and had to find a map to work out how to get to the appropriate gate. Boarding this time was not quite so civilised and certainly brought back memories of my last visit to Urumqi. People were getting on the plane with net carrier bags of piglets, chickens, ducks and all manner of disgusting food items which you couldn't possibly imagine eating. Most of them also carried screw top jam jars in their pocket in which they had brewed some green tea some time earlier. Every so often they would unscrew the dirty lid, sip some of the insipid liquid, and spit out the tea leaves all around the floor in front of them. Refreshments on board this China Airways plane on the four hour flight were pretty minimal. A stewardess came round with a huge teapot containing Green tea. This was supplied frequently during the flight and was about the only refreshment we got.

To this day I still cannot understand Chinese peoples' behaviour when travelling in an aeroplane. As soon as the plane touched down on the tarmac there was a mad scramble as everyone jumped out of their seats, grabbed their entire luggage from the overhead lockers and tried to be first in the queue to exit the plane. All this was happening while the plane was still doing 100 miles per hour along the runway with reverse thrusters on. As you can imagine when the pilot put the brakes on a little bit harder before turning off the runway all these people standing in the gangway fell over in a heap with all of their baggage on top of them, chickens, piglets, food and all. I just sat there and laughed in disbelief that an Airline would allow such dangerous antics.

Similarly once the doors were opened there was a huge dash down the stairs, across the tarmac and into the arrivals lounge where everyone pushed and shoved at the baggage carousel trying to find their luggage. Knowing full well my bags would arrive sooner or later I thought, 'I'm not joining in with this,' and stood back letting the seething mass dissipate. Sure enough as the crowd thinned out, I could see the carousel. There were my bags. I took them off quite calmly, went to a seating area and sat down to wait. I had every confidence in my Hong Kong agents' arrangements for me and indeed 10 minutes later a group of people came along to meet me.

'Mr Hunta preas come with us.' I hadn't met these people before but they were officials from the present exhibition organising committee and had been sent in a large limousine to pick me up and take me to my hotel.

Nothing had changed since my last stay in the Kunlun Hotel. The driveway was just as rough over potholed roads and the entrance to the hotel was strewn with piles of rubbish with little pigs rooting around trying to find something to eat. Once inside the hotel the sense of familiarity was almost comforting. There were the enamel spittoons placed along the passageway at 10 foot intervals, still full and slopping over onto the carpet. Once in my room, there was the comforting thermos of hot water and a bowl with two little green tea bags. There too was the fly swat. 'Fantastic!' I thought. 'I know how the system works this time.'

I walked into the bathroom and there before my eyes was - no towel! It was a no towel day as the day before it had been raining. I was hot and sweaty from travelling but I thought, 'I am not going to be beaten by this. I have a pocket handkerchief! If I can dry myself on a towel the size of a pocket handkerchief there is no reason why I can't use my real pocket handkerchief just as effectively.' So without more ado I jumped under the stream of comforting warm, rusty brown water, attempted to soap up a lather and finally patted myself dry with my handkerchief, ringing it out frequently. 'Oh that's better! Now I'm ready for the evening!'

The next morning after breakfasting heartily on red bean paste steamed buns and green tea. I eagerly awaited the arrival of my colleagues with all our equipment. They arrived on time, around midday, and decided we should all go out to lunch together which would enable me to meet some of the dignitaries and exhibition organisers. We all bundled into a big Zil and went off to a local restaurant, which actually looked quite smart for a change. It was in a hotel and I didn't realise there were such posh hotels around. The restaurant even had a carpet on the floor!

We were shown to a circular banqueting table, which held about 12 people. Gradually more people turned up and were introduced to me as the town dignitaries and exhibition organisers who had come to meet me and have lunch with me. I always looked forward to meals in China and as I have mentioned before, regardless of what restaurants may have looked like, without fail the food had always been good. Judging from what was being served up on the table this would be no exception.

Everyone was now seated and started to tuck in. A little way into the meal I noticed that one of our guests on the opposite side of the table was beginning to build up to a really huge spit. Chinese people are dreadful when it comes to clearing their throats and spitting. They make such a noise bringing up the phlegm and then evacuating it onto the floor. However this time the gentleman opposite me had gone through all the noisy performances of bringing up the phlegm from deep down in his bronchus and prepared to spit on the floor only to realise that the floor was carpeted. Without batting an eyelid he reached over to an empty soup bowl on the table, ejected this globulous lump of sputum into the empty bowl, put it back onto the table and continued eating quite nonchalantly. No one seemed to take any notice of this at all and we all carried on eating our meal.

After a fabulous lunch we drove to the local college where the exhibition was being held this time. This was totally different from my first experience in Urumqi and seemed to be a lot better organised. We were using the assembly hall of the college, which had been decked out in brightly coloured streamers and glittery baubles and looked more like Christmas than a scientific exhibition. We even had a proper booth erected for us this time with quite decent tables, which didn't need covering with tablecloths. We spent the afternoon unpacking and assembling the equipment and by the evening had a very presentable display. Feeling very pleased with ourselves we set off for dinner which in China is always taken early between 5:30pm and 6:00pm.

We went to another restaurant, which was also new to me and to my great delight, who was waiting for us there but Miss Su. She greeted me warmly but professionally with a handshake and sat down next to me at the banqueting table. We had so much to talk about as it had been over a year since I had seen her. She told me how pleased she had been to receive the present of books that I sent her and had read them all avidly. She confirmed that she would be looking after me again during the exhibition and would accompany me on many of the official banquets lined up for that week.

It was a very pleasant evening with much toasting with the usual evil Mai Tai and all of us hoping we were going to have another very successful exhibition. Miss Su said that unfortunately this time she didn't have any friends that wanted to buy our equipment but she would try hard to talk to any of the visitors that she thought would be interested when they came to our stand.

We got back to the hotel at about 9 o'clock and it was only then that I realised how much Mai Tai I had drunk as my legs refused to do what was asked of them. Apparently I was talking coherently but I had to reach out for one of my colleagues to support me as I walked out to the taxi. When we got back to the hotel and I said my good nights, I made my way to my room and it was only when I got to the end of the corridor that I realised how swaggering my gait was as I seemed to be bouncing off the walls. The hall was very dimly lit and at one point a couple of bulbs had gone. It was in this section while I was bouncing off the walls that I kicked something hard, heard a slopping sound and felt my feet getting wet. I realised I had kicked over one of the spittoons and was now standing in a pool of slimy, globulous sputum. I quickly let myself into my room and shut the door hoping that no one had witnessed my mishap.

I awoke the next morning with a headache, the likes of which I had never had before. I rang my colleagues room and said I was feeling a little under the weather. I insisted they had breakfast without me and told them I would meet them at the exhibition a little later on. When I eventually managed to go down to breakfast I noticed that the spittoon I had kicked over the night before had been picked up and cleaned, it's spilt contents cleared away and even the carpet miraculously cleaned so there was no sign of my little accident.

I had hoped that my usual ration of red bean paste steamed buns would settle my stomach and clear my head. Unfortunately they did not and during the taxi ride to the exhibition hall I had to ask the driver to stop at least six times so I could put my head out of the door and throw up! I felt dreadful! I vowed I would never touch that evil liquid again.

I arrived at the exhibition area to find the usual thronging crowd of people waiting to get in. How I managed to get through the day I don't know but I did, with Miss Su's support. She had seen my suffering and suggested that we took the afternoon off and she would take me around the city.

The main street was extremely wide and crowded with people across its width. There weren't many cars and those that wanted to get through honked noisily to part the crowds. Most of the men were dressed in military uniform and wore sunglasses, which still had the makers label attached to the lens. Little children would stare at me and come to my side to feel the blonde hairs on my arms. I was head and shoulders over everyone and with my full head of blonde hair was highly conspicuous. Little donkeys pulling carts also parted the crowds with the trip trapping of their hooves warning of their presence.

The buildings on either side were drab and grey with the crumbling pavements covered in sand and dust which had blown in from the Gobi desert. We took a side turning and entered a market area where vendors were selling silk fabrics, strung between poles with bits of string. A lady sat on a rickety stool with a piece of paper at her feet on which was a bowl of powdery granules, a dead rat and something written in Chinese. Miss Su translated for me. 'This lady is selling rat poison,' she said. The sign says 'Buy my Rat Poison. Look what it has done to this rat!'

Further on were traders selling spices and dried fruits from galvanised baths piled high with brightly coloured powders, berries, fruits and nuts. The method of weighing was a couple of brass dishes suspended by three metal rods in a pyramid shape. The apex of the pyramid had some string tied to it and both contraptions were attached to an old stick, which the vendor balanced on his finger. The produce was placed on one side and a variety of weights added to the other until a point of equilibrium was reached. 'Not very accurate,' I thought, the scientist in me coming out.

The next section was totally dedicated to barbecuing sheep in what could only be described as their version of a take away. There were at least ten areas in the middle of a small square sectioned off into three by three metre units using shoulder height, blue boards. Each compartment had a long oblong tin tray full of hot charcoal embers. To one side of each compartment was a dirty, formica covered table with rusty tubular legs on which a vendor sliced up pieces of lamb on a bit of tree trunk as a chopping board. These bits of meat were threaded onto metal skewers and balanced over the hot charcoal. Every so often an assistant would fan the glowing embers to get more heat, the ensuing clouds of smoke adding to the already murky atmosphere. All around the periphery of the square were small kiosks where butchers plied their trade. Sheep's carcasses hung up everywhere. Flies buzzed busily around making the most of all this meat on display. It was filthy, not helped by the sand covered floor, which was splattered with blood. I decided not to join the queues of people waiting for more skewers to be cooked.

My alcohol induced malaise had lessened by now and I was very thirsty. Miss Su found a café of sorts where I had a Coca Cola and she had an orange juice. We sat outside under a sheet stretched tightly over some bamboo poles. Men sat idly on their haunches, some whittling bits of stick, which they used as toothpicks. Others played 'Jacks' on the sandy pavements. Women carried heavy loads on their backs in woven wicker baskets. Everywhere was dirty due to the incessant winds coming of the Gobi Desert.

On the last day of the exhibition before we were due to leave, my colleagues confirmed that they had found a buyer for the equipment so we didn't have to take it back with us much to my relief. Just as we were about to pack up and go back to the hotel Miss Su appeared carrying a large brown parcel which she gave to me saying it was a leaving present for me. I thanked her very much but didn't have a chance to open it before we went back to the hotel but she said she would see me in the morning and would accompany me to the airport.

When I opened up the present I was gobsmacked to discover that it was a large hand embroidered silk tapestry of two pandas in bamboo. It must have been about 6 feet across and 3 feet high, embroidered with the most beautiful coloured silks. It must have taken someone a month of Sundays to complete. 'Wow,' I thought. 'How on earth can I compete with this?'

The following morning we made our way to the airport and there was Miss Su with her colleagues and all the local dignitaries, waiting on the tarmac to see us off. I said my goodbyes to all the gentleman and then turned to Miss Su and thanked her tremendously for the present she has given me. Without thinking, instead of shaking her hand, I took her hand and kissed the back of it. After all, this was what I had been used to in Eastern Europe a few weeks ago.

I did not immediately know what I had done.

There was an instant outcry from all the dignitaries, the mood visibly changed and my two agents started talking furiously to them in Mandarin. One of them turned to me and said, 'Graham, do you realise what you have done? You have raped her in public, in front of her bosses, by kissing her hand.'

I didn't know where to put myself. Miss Su herself did not seemed too bothered – it was her colleagues making all the fuss. There was an awful lot of heated conversation. At one point my two colleagues said to me, 'Quickly. Up the steps onto the plane.' I rushed into the plane and took my seat, watching their continued animated discussions through the window. Eventually they came on board and sat next to me.

'Don't ever do that again,' they said. 'You have raped her in public and they required you to stay behind in China and marry her.'

I gulped!

I felt that the whole plane was looking at me. A rapist on board and they had witnessed the evil deed. If it wasn't for the negotiating skills of my colleagues I might still be in China now, farming a paddy field.

Chapter 14

Moscow, third visit

I hate Christmas. Everything bad in my life to date had happened at Christmas and besides, being an atheist I didn't believe in it. I couldn't wait for January as I was returning to Moscow only a few weeks after my last visit. I wanted to follow up potential customers that we met at the exhibition in Sokolniki Park and to visit the major import export company Mashpriborintorg - Firma "Analit", who dealt with all imports of analytical equipment and raised the necessary letters of credit for payment. Letters of credit were a safe way of getting paid but often included punitive clauses if the terms were not exactly adhered to, so it had to be right first time. The letter of credit would describe the equipment being purchased, the agreed price, acceptable delivery times and method of delivery. If all this was carried out correctly and the required documents presented to the nominated bank on time, payment would normally follow. However if there were any mistakes, the bank could legitimately withhold payment until corrective measures were taken. One example of how frustrating this could be was attention to spelling in the documents. If there was a typing error in the order, and frequently there was, all subsequent documents raised had to use this typing error otherwise they would be rejected. Often customers would state their preferred freight forwarder or cargo airline and this also had to be adhered to.

One thing I had learnt pretty quickly was the use of the correct INCOTERMS on quotations. This is an internationally recognised set of abbreviations that describe the sellers and buyers duty in the contract and the point at which risk and ownership of the goods moves from seller to buyer. The easiest and cheapest term is EXW or Ex Works. This means that as soon as the seller notifies the buyer that the goods are ready for collection, this is where his responsibility ends. All risk passes to the buyer who has to organise collection and delivery plus insure the goods whilst still in the company's warehouse. The best term for the buyer is DDP or Delivered Duty Paid. This means that the seller pays all costs until the goods are delivered to the customer's premises, insured for 110% of the stated value and all customs duties paid. This is extremely difficult to carry out and involves a lot of upfront costs to the seller and delayed payment until all actions are completed and the documents are presented to the bank correctly.

At risk of boring you with these details, dear reader, I wanted to make the point of how important the negotiations with Mashpriborintorg were and how this meeting alone justified my current trip to Moscow.

For my flight on this visit I had chosen Japan Airlines as they did a stopover in Moscow on their London to Tokyo route. As a lover of Japanese food I found the meal service very tasty and they even offered Sake, warmed to the correct temperature. The approach into Sheremetyevo airport was a bit wobbly to say the least as it was snowing quite hard. The reverse thrusters on the 747 were put on immediately on touchdown and I felt as if I was being pulled out of my seat. I presumed that this was done because of the snow on the runway and to prevent skidding.

My hotel was to be the Mezhdunarodnaya again which, while it was a very comfortable, modern hotel to stay in, it meant that I had to go through my performance of getting past the Dezurnaya and the door security guards if I wanted to visit Lena. The roads from the airport to the hotel were piled high with snow at the sides but traffic was moving quite easily. The "snow gobblers" as I called them were out in force removing the snow off the roads effortlessly. If you haven't seen one it is quite difficult to describe. Imagine a fire engine with a large escape ladder mounted on the back, with the ladder overhanging the front of the cab by a long way. Now replace this ladder with a continuous conveyor belt with transverse slats across it. Add a large shovel at the road end with two oscillating arms that reached out and pulled the snow onto the conveyor belt. This is the snow gobbler. It drives along scooping the snow up with the large shovel and onto the conveyor belt, which then tips out at the top into an open-backed tip-up lorry which keeps up with the gobbler. Once full, the lorry moves off to the Moscow River where it is tipped in. A fleet of lorries supporting each gobbler effectively keep the roads free of snow and the traffic moving freely.

As soon as I had checked into the hotel and had been escorted to my room by the Floor Lady, I immediately telephoned Lena. Her mother answered.

'Can I speak to Lena please?' I said as clearly as possible in the hope she might understand.

'Lena nyet, nye doma, zavtra,' she replied.

Lena wasn't home, call back tomorrow is what I understood. I was so disappointed but there was no way I could have contacted her in advance to let her know I was coming. Telephone calls from the UK to Moscow were difficult to organise and had to be booked 24 hours in advance. They were almost certainly listened to and a call to a private number would have raised the authorities' interest. For business use the telex was the main means of communication, albeit slow and difficult to use.

I consoled myself with a vodka and orange juice in the hard-currency bar and spent a happy hour people watching. Now I knew what went on here I could work out who was who and see whether the "official ladies" got any takers.

After eating my fill of the unusual combination of breakfast items at the Mezhdunarodnaya, I set off in the falling snow to meet Mashpriborintorg. The meeting went very well and they were obviously keen to buy from me. They did ask if I could do something else for them. They needed to buy a special film emulsion that was sensitive to radiation and required shipment on dry ice under very strictly controlled timings and asked if I would be prepared to obtain it for them. Apparently other people had shied away from this because of the difficulty involved and it required a special export licence. I agreed on the condition that the manufacturer would sell it to me. I would let them know definitely when I returned to my office. They were delighted with this and out came the secret bottle of Vodka to toast the successful meeting.

My next call was at the business section of the British Embassy in Moscow. It was always good practice to keep them informed of what I was doing in Moscow and who I was seeing. It was really cold that day and although I had a sheepskin coat on and my fur hat, I was wearing a business suit underneath and what I hadn't bargained for was the effect of the cold on my legs which only had regular thickness trousers covering them.

After my visit to the Embassy I had trouble finding a taxi and as I could see the Mezhdunarodnaya hotel around the bend in the river I decided to walk. It was probably less than a mile in total along one side of the Moscow river on Krasnopresnenskaya Naberezhnaya, a wide eight-laned road. Within minutes my moustache had frozen and was covered in white frost. It was so cold that for the first time I experienced "fairy breath." This is a phenomenon where when you breathe out, the water vapour in your breath freezes instantly into very small ice crystals which flutter to the floor and sparkle in the sunlight. It was -25°C and at this temperature it was dangerous to breathe through your mouth as you could cause frost damage to the lining of your respiratory system. It was best to breathe through your nose covered with a scarf and keep pinching it to break up any ice crystals as they formed. After 10 minutes of walking my legs started to go numb with cold and I felt my pace slowing down dramatically. I was beginning to worry and realised the stupid mistake I had made in trying to walk any distance in this extreme cold and with thin trousers on my legs.

I kept looking back to see if any taxis were coming but there were very few cars at all on the road. It was pointless trying to flag a taxi going in the opposite direction as it was illegal (and impossible) to do a U-turn across eight lanes of traffic. Eventually I managed to flag one down and with great relief climbed into the back seat. It only took a matter of minutes to get to the hotel but heaven knows what damage I would've done to myself if I had continued my walk.

I decided to run a bath to warm myself up but had forgotten to bring my bath plug and there wasn't one in the bathroom. The only way was to sit in the empty bath with your heel firmly pressed in the plughole and carefully run the taps without burning or freezing your foot. Feeling very miserable with the cold and now no bath plug I let out a loud cry saying, 'I hate this place. I come over here to do business and can't even get a bath plug in my room.' I didn't know why I did it but it made me feel better to let off steam.

Once I had warmed up I tried telephoning Lena again and to my great joy she answered the phone.

'Hi Lena. I'm here in Moscow again for a few days. Can I see you?'

'Of course you can. I'll come and get you in a taxi so wait outside for me in about half an hour. Make sure you wrap up warm as it's very cold today.'

'I know,' I replied relating the story of my walk today.

I hurriedly dressed but this time I put my thermal long johns on plus a long sleeved thermal vest.

'Real passion killers,' I thought as I looked in the mirror.

'What do you think?' I said addressing the mirror personally in case someone was watching at that moment. I had put two pullovers on followed by my sheepskin coat, hat, scarf and gloves but now the problem was reversed. I was getting very hot in this overheated room. I quickly ruffled up my bed and had a quick peek outside my door to see if the Dezurnaya was at her post. She wasn't. I turned to the mirror and said, 'don't forget my bloody bath plug,' and quickly made my way up to the lifts.

As I crossed the foyer I could see that the thugs on the door had come inside for a warm-up so I was able to slip outside unseen. This time it was a great relief to get back outside in the cold as with all the layers I was wearing I was sweating profusely. The taxi rank outside was fortunately under a large canopy so I was relatively sheltered for my short wait until Lena's taxi pulled up. I knew it was her straight away despite not being able to see much of her face as it was nearly all covered by her silver arctic fox hat and fur collared coat. She rolled down the window and said, 'Get in quickly.'

We went back to her flat where her Mum had cooked some food for me. It took me awhile to take all my warm clothes off in the hall but I still felt too hot with my long johns and thermal vest on, as Russian flats are always too hot in the winters.

'I'd like to take you to meet some friends this evening. We will use the Metro as it won't be as cold as the streets and I can teach you how to use it.' Off we went again having put all the warm clothes back on. A short walk along Nesvizhski Street to Fruzenskaya Metro Station where we pushed our way through the very heavy swing doors. The station foyer was awash with dirty, melting slush from peoples' boots. Lena gave me three kopeks and asked me to follow her through the turnstiles after inserting the coins in the slot. Down, down, down we went on the seemingly endless escalator where it was now getting quite warm again, but I couldn't strip off.

We had to go three stops to Biblioteka Imeni Lenina then change lines. It couldn't have be a worse station to learn about the Metro as this one had four lines to choose from. There were so many choices of passageways with a multitude of signs in Cyrillic, all of which I could not read. The other problem for me was that the Metro was so well used all day long that there were thousands of people who all knew their way, walking along briskly and carrying me with them. Lena pulled me over to the side and explained the signage.

выход в город means Exit to City so don't go along that passage until you have reached your destination. The first problem for me here was unless you are very observant, выход is Exit whilst вход is entrance and to the uninitiated looks very similar, especially when being swept along with the crowd. It is very easy to be going completely in the wrong direction if you muddle these two.

Next comes the choice of line. Biblioteka Imeni Lenina is on the Red line and there are three other stations meeting at this point, Borovitskaya on the Grey line and Arbatskaya on the Dark Blue and Light Blue lines. We want to travel to Chekhovskaya, which is on the Grey line so we need to look for "переход на станцию Боровитскауа" which means "Crossing to Station Borovitskaya" and is conveniently written in a Grey flash. Part way along that passageway we need to decide which direction to go in and it will be signed with the name of the Terminal station on each end of the line.

My brain was reeling from trying to take in too much information in one go. I hung on tightly to Lena's arm and let her guide me. 'If we get separated down here I will be totally lost,' I thought as a sense of fear came over me and I clung to her even tighter. 'I really must make more effort to learn some Russian.'

The problems didn't end there. Once on the crowded train you needed to know when your station was coming up as you had to start pushing and shoving your way to the doors before it got there. If you were not near the door at your stop the chances are that you wouldn't be able to get off as the train only had about 30 seconds before it set off again. There was a train every 2 minutes so they didn't hang around.

The sweat was pouring off me by now, partly due to nervous tension and partly due to being clad in layers of winter clothes in a very hot, crowded train. It was a welcome relief to get to Chekhovskaya and out through the heavy swing doors into the cold of the night. Just a short walk up the road and we were at Genya and Elena's flat. This couple had been good friends of Lena's for a long time and she valued their opinions on a lot of things. I learnt afterwards that she had taken me to meet them so she could get their opinion of me.

Genya was a tall man with dark hair showing signs of premature male pattern baldness. He wore large framed black-rimmed glasses, which gave him something of a professorial look. He worked in one of Moscow's museums and looked after a large collection of Russian historical artefacts. His wife Elena was round faced with beautiful chestnut brown hair, dark brown eyes and also wore large framed glasses. They both spoke English, Genya more than Elena, and we had a lovely evening discussing a lot of topics. Little did I know at this stage the part I would come to play in their future lives.

The following evening Lena took me to meet another girlfriend, Marsha. Marsha was a very talented artist but unfortunately was deaf and dumb. A very pretty girl with an amazing talent. Her flat was full of oil paintings but she explained that she had problems getting hold of artists' materials. Looking round the room at her pictures I could see that a lot of them were spoilt by having very shoddy frames made out of what looked like recycled wooden pallets held together with nails. No nice mouldings and no neatly mitred corner joints. She could paint anything - life-like portraits, Russian Winter landscapes and more. She was currently working on an almost life-sized painting of Lena for which she sat once a week.

'Your work is amazing,' I said. 'I am sure I could sell some for you back in the UK.'

'That would be fantastic if you could but you know it is illegal to take works of art out of the Soviet Union,' she conveyed to me in sign language and writing.

I didn't know that but it made the paintings even more desirable if I could get them out.

I knew my luggage would be X-rayed on the way out but I was sure that wooden stretchers on some unframed canvases would not show up. The nails would show but if I packed them in my suitcase with my toiletries randomly scattered around them they may go through undetected. It was worth the risk as what could be the worst-case scenario. If discovered, they would be confiscated and I would be taken off to a side office somewhere in the airport, given a good talking to, enough to scare me, and eventually allowed onto my flight. It was certainly not a crime that I could be sent to Siberia for.

I knew that I was going to be a regular visitor to Moscow but couldn't tell Marsha at this point when I would be coming back.

'No problem,' she signed again whilst miming the words. 'I am not going anywhere. 'Instead of bringing me any money from the sales of my pictures, would you buy artist materials for me as they are so hard to get here and would be of more value to me. Oil paints and brushes would be very useful.'

I selected two beautiful Russian winter landscapes where Marsha had really captured the texture of the snow on the silver birch trees, glinting in the winter sunshine. Bubble wrap was unheard of in the USSR and any packaging material hard to come by. We ended up wrapping the paintings in old newspapers and tying with string in order to protect them on the way back to Lena's flat.

My third and last evening with Lena before my return flight I spent with her in her flat enjoying her company and her body. She played the piano for me and we spoke about our families. I told her that I was separated from my wife and waiting for a divorce to be settled. She too had been married at a very early age but it only lasted a year. She never knew her father as he had left her mother when she was only one year old. Her cousin Olga, who she regarded as a sister, had a one year old daughter and asked me if it was possible to buy some shoes for her and bring them over on my next visit.

'How will I know the correct size?' I asked.

'I will get Olga to draw around her feet tomorrow morning and if I come to the airport with you I'll give it to you then.'

This comment took me by surprise but pleased me immensely. She wanted to come to the airport with me to see me off and spend more time with me. This was getting serious and in such a short time but I was thoroughly enjoying it.

My return flight was again with Japan Airlines which left Moscow at 5:10pm. This meant I needed to be there three hours ahead at around 2:00pm so I had arranged a taxi for 1:30pm. I spent some time in my room carefully packing my bag to give some protection to the two paintings. I had to wrap them in my dirty shirts and put a shoe around two of the corners plus my razor and aftershave can to try to disguise the nails. My toilet bag went round another corner and I hoped this would now do the trick.

I had asked Lena if she would join me for lunch in the hotel but she was somewhat reluctant to start with.

'What's the problem?' I asked.

'The security guards won't let me in.'

'I'll tell them you are my guest.'

'You can try but you might have to bribe them.'

I was waiting outside when Lena's taxi arrived at 12:00 midday. I helped her out and walked over to the hotel door arm in arm. The thugs immediately jumped in front of her and with some very brusque exchanges in Russian blocked her way.

'They won't let me in,' she said sadly. 'I told you so.'

Feeling very annoyed I started to talk to them in English in a very firm voice.

'What is the matter? She is my guest for lunch and I am a resident in this hotel as you know.'

'Problyema,' said one thug in a tone I recognised from the waiter outside the restaurant who would not let us in. He wanted a bribe.

'Passpart pazhalsta,' he said holding his hand out.

I quickly took the twenty rouble note out of my pocket that I had put there for this very occasion, and slipped it into my passport as I handed it to him. He took some time scrutinising while surreptitiously removing the money and pocketing it.

'Okay,' he grunted as he stepped aside and gave me my passport back. This to me was the final proof that Lena was a normal girl and not KGB.

Lena looked very nervous as she came into the hotel.

'Don't worry. You are with me,' I said, trying to reassure her.

We got a table in the restaurant and I let her order as she could read what was written on the menu. I noticed that the waiter treated her very brusquely as well, not the sort of behaviour I would expect from restaurant staff to a customer. I was feeling very annoyed but resisted saying anything as it would only have made things more uncomfortable for Lena. She only nibbled at her food and kept looking round very nervously.

'What's the worst thing that could happen to you if someone saw you with me?'

'You don't know what it's like living here. Someone could make my life very difficult if they wanted to. You never know who works for the KGB so the best thing is not to trust anyone until they have proved they are worthy of your trust. There will be people who are jealous of my friendship with you and might want to spoil it.' I couldn't understand this as I was naturally a very trusting person and couldn't envisage someone wanting to backstab me.

We finished our lunch quickly and went over to reception to retrieve my bags. I had already checked out with the Floor Lady and had given her a couple of ballpoint pens, which were well received. I didn't know when I might see her again and need her assistance.

Lena was only too relieved when our taxi arrived. I felt sad climbing in next to her as I was going home and I didn't know when, or indeed whether, I would see her again. She gave me the traced footprint from her cousin's baby girl's foot and also asked me if I could get her some lipsticks, preferably light pink. We travelled for most of the journey in silence. She had asked if the driver was going back to the city, which he was and agreed to take her back home.

At the airport I got my bags out from the back of the taxi, gave Lena a big hug and off she went. I couldn't have felt more saddened to see her driving off. Inside, the queue for my flight was already starting to build up but with no sign of anyone staffing the customs desk. I was feeling somewhat nervous as I had the two paintings from Marsha in my suitcase and hoped that I would not get caught. Eventually a stern looking man in official uniform started to process the queue. Every bag was going through the X-ray machine and every customs declaration form scrutinised to check for any black market money dealings. I had left all but three rouble notes of my currency with Lena and that was allowed in case you needed to hire a baggage trolley on any return visit. As I approached the checkpoint I could see a notice showing what items were banned from being taken out of the USSR. Up near the top of the list was "works of art," which sent a shiver down my spine. My nervousness was momentarily lifted as I got to the bottom of the list where "men's underpants" and "umbrella spare parts" were listed. Who on earth was going to take out umbrella spare parts? I didn't think that they were repairable. As for Russian-made mens' underpants, well I had to chuckle.

My turn came and I loaded my bags into the X-ray machine as the officer took my form.

'Any roubles?' he asked.

'Only these three rouble notes,' I said opening my wallet and offering him a view of the contents, hoping it would distract him.

He stamped my customs form and Visa, keeping both and now turned to view the X ray screen. I held my breath. He had not seen anything suspicious and allowed me to take my bags out. I breathed a sigh of relief as I walked across the large open space, a sort of no-man's-land, to the airline check-in desk. Phew.

My Japan Airlines flight home was via Frankfurt where I changed to Lufthansa. I was looking forward to the flight based on my outbound experience of the in-flight service. The snow was now falling heavily and snowploughs were kept busy running up and down the runway and sending great clouds of snow outwards and creating large piles on the side. Planes on the stand were being sprayed with de-icing fluid at regular intervals to stop too much snow from building up on the wings of the aircraft. Our Jumbo was there, having just come in from Tokyo and I could see crates labelled "live fish" being offloaded, obviously destined for the Japanese restaurant in the Mezhdunarodnaya hotel where I had just come from.

We were all seated and the final de-icing spray had been carried out. The snow was settling fast as the tug pulled us out of the stand and pointed the huge aeroplane in the direction of the runway. We had to wait at the end of the runway for the last couple of snowploughs to clear off the remaining snow. Apparently the procedure in a take off during snowy conditions like this, when the snow might have built up after the last de-icing, was to engage full thrust with the brakes firmly on, letting the aircraft shudder under the strain for a few seconds thereby shaking off any residual snow. At last the brakes were released and the mighty beast began to accelerate. Suddenly to everyone's horror the plane hit a patch of ice and slid sideways off the runway, coming to an abrupt stop in a pile of snow. The kinetic energy released was such that several of the overhead lockers sprang open and a whole section of food trolleys in the galley emptied their contents all over the floor. I sat there not knowing what was going to happen next. The cabin crew were now rushing up and down the aisles reassuring nervous passengers and replacing items in the overhead lockers that had fallen out. Eventually the captain came on the intercom and apologised for the incident. He told us that a tug would come out to pull us from the snowdrift. After a bit of pushing and pulling the tug eventually got us back onto the runway but now we were one third of the way up. The captain then announced, '*cabin crew take your seats for take-off.*'

'Bloody hell, he's going to try taking off again but with only two thirds of the runway left,' I thought.

The cabin went deathly quiet. We all sat in nervous anticipation of what might happen next. The plane accelerated again and with little left of the runway we were airborne. He could certainly not have aborted that take-off so it was all or nothing. I shudder to think what could have happened. We might have been on the 6 o'clock news that evening!

Once the seatbelt signs went off, the cabin crew started to clear up the mess that had spilled from the food trolleys. It was amazing but there was no sound of seat belts being unfastened. We all sat there with them firmly buckled up. The captain came on again with more apologies and letting us know that the meal service might be a bit restricted as a lot of it had ended up on the floor.

Okay, we had safely got airborne but we still had to land in Frankfurt. My worry was that the abrupt stop in the snow might have damaged the wheel mechanism and prevent it from coming down again. A nervous silence reigned again as we descended into Frankfurt, which fortunately had no snow. I heard the familiar sounds of the wheels being lowered but a lot further out from the airport than normal. I presumed that the pilot was giving himself some safety margin in case a problem occurred. Bang and we were down, full reverse thrust on, which slowed us down in time to turn off the runway when a loud cheer and applause erupted from the cabin. We were all so relieved to have landed safely. I have had some scary experiences flying in my years of international travel but this one sticks firmly in my memory.

Chapter 15

Moscow, May 1986

May's itinerary was looking very busy. I had been invited to visit the Russian Trade delegation in Highgate again to discuss further business. Apparently my efforts to get the special heat sensitive film emulsions were well appreciated and I was being rewarded with more contracts. Mr Kolosov who I met, knew I was going to Moscow again later in the month for seven days and had arranged for me to see Mashpriborintorg again. But before this I had a week in Rome with my new Italian distributors.

After the Far East and behind the Iron Curtain, European countries were easy and nothing much of special interest to this book happened so I will skip this week.

I flew out to Moscow on the last Sunday of the month on good old British Airways. I had been put in the Intourist Hotel this time, a large tower block just round the corner from the National Hotel and convenient for the Metro at the Biblioteka Imeni Lenina station.

Moscow in May is green and verdant as it the start of their spring. The temperature goes up rapidly after all the slush has disappeared and is a comfortable 19°C. As each winter draws to a close, the female balsam poplar, by far Moscow's most abundant tree, produces hundreds of sticky, sweet-smelling brown buds. Warmed by Russia's brief spring sun, the buds grow into catkins. Upon maturity, the catkins split into two parts and the ripened seeds, shrouded in white, nearly weightless tufts, are released into the air. Freed, they drift by the millions before accumulating in rain puddles and sticking to car windscreens. This season in Moscow is a period when windows remain shut, when yawning outdoors is an act of foolishness, when Muscovites shrug good-humouredly at their "summer snow," but when they also carry handkerchiefs, wear sunglasses and diligently wash down the streets. Why this happens here, and in no other major city, is the subject of much speculation and myth. The main reason, of course, is obvious: there are 300,000 to 400,000 poplar trees in Moscow, and a good number of them are female.

It goes without saying that I spent the nights with Lena but my first appointment on Monday morning was at 10:00am at the Institute of Bio-organic

Chemistry so I had to get back to the hotel fairly early to change. The Metro was very busy that morning and it took me longer than expected to get back to the Intourist hotel. I was in a bit of a rush and showered and changed quickly, gathered up my papers and rushed out to find my taxi. As usual, there were at least a dozen taxis waiting outside the hotel but one taxi driver caught my eye as I walked out and I assumed that it was my driver. I jumped in the back of the taxi and continued to check my paperwork in my briefcase. Satisfied that I had got everything I sat back and relaxed to enjoy the drive. Within 20 minutes we had pulled up outside the Institute of Bio-organic Chemistry and a chill went down my spine. I had not told the driver where I was going but he obviously knew. I thought I was getting used to "the system" in Moscow but occasionally something happened to remind you that you are constantly being watched.

Dr Dolganov at the Institute was very impressed with the specifications of our new equipment and expressed a wish to buy. I told him I was seeing Mashpriborintorg the following morning and would talk to them about his requirements.

Mr Bacharev at Mashpriborintorg greeted me affectionately and offered me Russian tea, which I readily accepted.

'Good news Mr Hunter. I have just authorised the purchase of another one of your analysers and here are the documents for you to sign if you agree.'

'But shouldn't we discuss what specifications you require this time?'

'No just the same as the last one and of course – the emulsions. You did a very good job of getting them shipped to us last time so we would like some more please.'

I was gobsmacked. This was amazing. All the paperwork for the next order was on his desk so all I had to do was to read them and sign them if correct. I could take an order back home with me, which would really give me some brownie points back in the office. We spoke also about Dr Dolganov's requirements and it was agreed that his would be the next order but it might take a few weeks to get the paperwork organised. Yet another feather in my cap.

On Wednesday I had a lunch appointment with an English lady who had met me at an exhibition and who had an office in Moscow. She wanted to see if there was any room for some sort of cooperation. I can't say too much about this meeting but nothing transpired afterwards.

On Thursday I went back to see Dr Dolganov to report on my meeting with Mashpriborintorg then off to the Russian Institute for Non-Ferrous Metals in the afternoon.

Friday morning was spent at the Commercial Section of the British Embassy where I had organised for some typing to be done. After lunch another meeting with Mr Pankratov and lastly a meeting with Mr Bakharev who was one of the organisers of the next exhibition in Sokolniki and was trying to persuade me to take my own stand instead of sharing Terry's.

My last night with Lena was very emotional for me. Despite having spent some time with Loli, I had seriously fallen in love with Lena. I had brought her the lipsticks she wanted plus the shoes for her cousin's little girl. I gave her my schedule for the next three months, which included five weeks away in the Far East and Australia before coming but nothing planned for Moscow until October which was nearly five months away..

'I hear they do good copies of designer handbags in Singapore. Please could you get a Louis Vuitton handbag for me.'

'Of course I can. Is there anything else you would like?'

'Maybe some baby clothes for little Ksenya.'

After making love we snuggled up together and Lena went off into a deep sleep. I laid awake for some time, thinking about all the things that had happened to me over the last year. I had a girlfriend in Hong Kong who thought the world of me, another in Korea who moved in with me whilst working out there, Pauline in Cape Town and this lovely lady lying next to me, who I adored. The problem was that the other three were free to travel anywhere but Lena was behind the Iron Curtain and the chances of me getting her out were slim to non-existent. We were lucky to have gotten this far without any interference from the KGB.

I had to get back to the Intourist Hotel in the morning to pack my bags and order a taxi to the airport. Lena wanted to come with me to the airport again which pleased me no end but always saddened me as I said goodbye to her. I could never be sure that I would see her again if the KGB objected to our relationship.

On the way to the airport Lena said to me, 'why don't you try telephoning me while you are at home and see if we get connected.'

'But won't that give you some problems?'

'Maybe, but it is worth a try to see what happens. After all, you are doing well in business here and the people in high places seem to like you.'

I agreed to try and we continued the journey to the airport in silence, cuddled up to each other.

Chapter 16

Far East, second visit

My next big trip was to Hong Kong and China again but first I had a couple visit to Holland and Belgium. These were easy as I could drive there and nothing remarkable happened. I only mention it to show my readers how intense my travel program was.

My flight to Hong Kong was with Cathay Pacific, a lovely airline to travel on. Direct flights were still not popular so a stopover in the Middle East somewhere was always required. I was sitting next to a man who was only travelling to Abu Dhabi but during our conversation it transpired that he had paid more for his single ticket to Abu Dhabi then I had paid for my return to Hong Kong. I couldn't understand the pricing policy but happy that my travel agent could get a good deal for me.

I was to be met by my agents in Hong Kong and this time I knew what to expect during the landing. I could now pick out the regular travellers from the first timers. The regulars sat calmly, continuing to read, whilst the first timers clutched the arm rests with white knuckled hands and looked out of the window with a fearful look. It didn't matter which side of the plane you sat on as there were high rise flats on both sides. However if you were on the right side you would experience the wingtip nearly touching the ground whilst on the left side, the land would suddenly disappear and only sky would be visible.

The jumbo touched down exactly on time at 9:15am. Kai Tak airport operated so efficiently that within 30 minutes I had collected my bags, cleared customs, met my agents and was sitting in their car making my way to their office. I spent the whole day with them in the office going over the plans for the next couple of weeks. I was grateful for not having to do much on my first day as an eighteen hour flight and an eight hour time difference was quite disorientating. They asked me if I wouldn't mind looking after myself in the evening as they still had a lot of preparation to do for our two weeks in China.

'Great,' I thought. I would have woken up by then and could go and see Loli, after all she had some of my equipment in her flat that I needed.

Back at my hotel I gave Loli a call. She was working tonight but I could go to the club and take her out. If so she would bring my stuff in a carrier bag. I readily agreed.

I treated myself to a leisurely bath with a cold beer. I was wide-awake now as it was 12 midday body time. I needed something to eat so just had a quick supper before going out. I now knew what taxi to get to take me to Kowloon and was soon outside the Playboy club. The doorman gave me a knowing nod as he stepped aside to let me down the red carpeted staircase. I also knew the procedure at the bar. An Executive drink and specifically asked for Lolita. It wasn't long before she appeared, resplendent in her bunny outfit with the little bobtail perched on her perky bum. She gave me such a hug and kiss and took me over to a secluded table. We had so much to catch up on.

'What have you been up to since I saw you, back in August? That must have been at least eight months ago!'

'Well I've been to India, Yugoslavia, Moscow twice and a few trips inside Europe.'

'And how many other girls have you met?'

'I have to admit there was one in Yugoslavia who was very nice and a lovely girl in Moscow. I do like her very much but she lives behind the Iron Curtain and I don't know if I will ever see her again. The Communist State doesn't allow relationships with foreigners. I am going back in May and hope to see her again.'

'Don't forget me,' Loli said. 'Looks like I've got some strong competition.' When we finished the bottle of sparkly Loli whispered, 'why don't you take me out and I can get to work on you.'

No sooner said than done. I tipped the doorman HK$20 on the way out as I needed to keep on good terms with him I thought. Loli had brought my demonstration equipment with her and although I had to pay to get her out of the club, I owed her a meal as per my agreement with Dennis.

We managed to sneak back into my hotel unseen by the security guard and quickly locked my room door.

'Aren't you embarrassed to be seen with me?' asked Loli.

'Why on earth should I be?'

'Well I am obviously Hong Kong Chinese and you are British.'

'So what? You are lovely and what does race matter?'

'If I were to come to England would you still want to see me?'

'What! Are you coming over?'

'My cousin lives in London and I have always wanted to visit her.'

'Well if you were to come I would be happy to see you.'

I think my answer satisfied Loli and we settled down to a night of passion.

The following morning, after seeing Loli off in a taxi, I was picked up by my agents. We had to go to the Chinese consulate to apply for my Visa. After a lot of form-filling and questions, everything seemed okay and my Visa would be ready for collection in two days. The afternoon was booked for me to give a lecture in the Queen Mary Hospital Medical School – Hong Kong University. It seemed to go down well. So much so I was asked if I could come back on the following morning and deliver it again to a new audience. It really does something for one's ego when you have held a captive audience for 45 minutes and then asked for an encore the next day. 'I must be good,' I thought.

My Chinese Visa was ready for collection as promised and after collecting it I was given the rest of the afternoon off. Guess what I did? You're right. I called Loli.

'I'm free for the rest of the afternoon. Can we meet?'

'Of course. Have you been up Victoria Peak by the funicular railway?'

'No I haven't.'

'Okay I'll meet you at the lower station at 3:00pm.'

I was so excited about doing some sightseeing in Hong Kong and especially in the company of Loli.

The Peak Tram, as it is affectionately called, carries both residents and tourists to the upper levels of Hong Kong Island. It starts from Garden Road in Victoria District and runs up to Victoria Peak via the mid levels on a system of cables and pulleys. There are four stops on the way up and an area of double track in the middle, which acts as a passing place for the up and down trams, which run simultaneously.

Victoria Peak is 1,312 feet above sea level and gives an amazing view of Central Hong Kong, Victoria Harbour and Lammas Island. It has to be one of the most iconic views in the world and there I was, with a lovely Chinese lady, experiencing something that many people would never see in their lives. It was really breath taking. There were so many skyscrapers packed together in Central District but it made you wonder how there was room for people to walk the streets between them. A sense of humidity hung in the air, which intensified the heat and smells. Star Ferries, another Hong Kong icon, busily crossed to and fro across Victoria Harbour from Hong Kong Island to Kowloon. I know I have said it before but I had to keep pinching myself to check that it was real.

I don't know how long I stood on the peak, tightly holding onto Loli, but she eventually gave me a nudge and said, 'are you okay?'

'Yes I couldn't be better. I am just in awe of where I am and who I'm with. I need to maximise on my experience.'

'When you are ready why don't we go back down and take the Star Ferry across to Kowloon, have a drink, then come back on the ferry to your hotel. We could have dinner in your room and make love as many times as you are able.'

The Star Ferry is another unique experience. It has been described as one of the 50 things that you have to do in your lifetime. This fleet of double-decker ferries, painted green on the bottom half and white on the top, take workers and tourists from Hong Kong Island to Kowloon mainland and back. They ply their trade from the Tsim Sha Tsui Pier on Hong Kong to Wan Chai. The smell as you bob across the harbour is also memorable as is the view of Victoria Peak from sea level.

We got back to my hotel room at about 7:30pm just as it was getting dark. Victoria Harbour took on another appearance at night with lights everywhere including on the sampans that were bobbing round the harbour. Apparently as Kai Tak airport was right in the middle of the city, no flashing lights were allowed which might distract the pilots. All neons were constantly illuminated and competed with each other in their brilliance and colour to attract to the punters. We ordered a modest dinner from room service and sat together on the sofa in front of the open curtains with a glass of wine just enjoying the moment. Dinner came and went. Loli took my hand and lead me over to the enormous bed.

'Now let's go and get down to business,' she said as she started to undress me.

I don't know what the time was when she left but we had agreed that we would meet up again in two weeks time when I returned from China. She had promised me another unique experience but wouldn't tell me what it was. If this was a competition for my affection, she was really trying very hard.

The next two weeks were going to be a challenge. We were going to base ourselves in Zhenzhou, a large city of some 10 million people and based in the University, do a series of lectures and meet a lot of scientists, some of whom were travelling large distances to come and see me. Zhenzhou is in central China and as such is a good location for people to come to.

To get to Zhenzhou we first had to go to Canton (now called Guanzhou) by train from Kowloon station. The train went through the new territories and it did not take long until we got to the Chinese border, a distance of some 142 km. Here we came to a halt to allow Chinese customs officers on the train and examine passports and visas. This was quite a lengthy procedure as you can imagine as the train was packed. It was very noticeable how the scenery changed once inside China. From the opulent houses built for the rich to the poor peasant cottages where extended families lived under one roof. Old ladies were outside the houses with what looked like home-made brooms, sweeping the dust off tarmac roads. Others were doing their morning exercises practising the art of Tai Chi. To me it looked like a lot of arm waving and balancing on one leg but I suppose it did them some good. We had to spend the night in a hotel as our flight left at 7:15am in the morning. We took a taxi to Canton airport where we purchased our tickets to Zhenzhou. No booking ahead. It was just like a shuttle service. The planes for the internal flights in China were old Russian Tupolevs which had seen better days. The seats were simple metal tubes with canvas stretched over them and were very uncomfortable. Health and safety was non-existent. People moved around the plane as they pleased and when coming into land they all jumped up to get their luggage out before the plane had even taxied off the runway.

Chinese people do not know the concept of queueing. It is more like a free for all scrum as people push and shove to get up to check-in desks.

It was now 10:00am as we checked into the International Hotel, the flight from Canton having taken two and three quarter hours. I was already feeling dirty and sweaty so went to the bathroom for a shower. Oh no - a no towel day. It must have rained yesterday. UGH! We spent the day in the hotel making phone calls and checking on who was coming to see me so I resigned myself to being dirty for the day. I supposed that everyone else would be in the same situation so we would all smell together!

The group for lunch has now increased to 10 and by dinner (at 5:30 in the evening) it had gone up to 12. Everyone wanted to talk to me but couldn't speak English so I was totally dependent on my two guys to interpret for me.

The day dragged by for me, not fully understanding what was going on. Monday was just as bad. I spent the morning with the same five professors but by now we had run out of conversation topics. I was told that we would be going back to Hong Kong probably next Wednesday, which was eight days away. I hoped that I would have more to do than just stay in the hotel talking.

Tuesday came all too slowly but the good news was there were towels and hot water. The water was a bit discoloured and smelt of rust but at least I had a wash. After breakfast we went to the University where a visiting Professor gave a talk on Image Analysis and stereology – in Chinese – so I didn't understand a word. I was to give my talk in the afternoon using an interpreter. The meeting room we were in was dirty and dark. There were metal bars covering the high windows and two light bulbs dangled from the ceiling on bare wires. They were not on. We were having one of their regular power cuts. This made my talk very difficult as I could not use my slides.

They asked me if I would come back tomorrow and try again which I did. Nothing else to do. This time they had set up a generator outside the room so at least I could use my slides. The problem now was that I was competing with the noise from the generator but as they couldn't understand me at all it didn't really matter.

The next few days were more of the same. At last I was told that we were going back to Hong Kong on Monday for a flight that left at 7:00am so it would be a very early start. Eventually we got back to Kowloon station at 2:00pm on Tuesday, totally drained. I had two more nights in Hong Kong before returning to the UK. I pampered myself with a shower in a proper shower cubicle with oodles of hot water and fluffy white towels to dry myself on. What a luxury after the last two weeks. I rang Loli to tell her I was back and could we meet up again. She couldn't make that night but said she would organise my surprise for tomorrow.

We arranged to meet outside my hotel the following evening, just as it was getting dark. We took a short taxi ride to one of the piers on the harbour where we boarded a small sampan, the iconic little boats that typified the scenery in Victoria Harbour. Loli explained that we were going on a short trip by boat to experience the Hong Kong scenery by night and then on to an area where other sampans were sailing around. From each sampan came a delicious smell of food cooking. This was going to be our dinner. One by one the sampans and sailed up to us and offered us portions of what they were cooking on board. It was an amazing experience as Loli had promised. We could leisurely eat each course before the next boat arrived whilst gently bobbing up and down in the harbour. Yet another moment when I contemplated how lucky I was to be able to do this as part of my job.

Needless to say we went back to my hotel to finish off this trip with a night of passion. Loli left with a carrier bag with my demo equipment as I was coming back the following month to do an exhibition in Shanghai. This guaranteed that I would see her again in three weeks time.

I saw Loli twice more in April and took her to dinner as a thank you for looking after my stuff again. We went to a Japanese restaurant in Food Street, a street in Hong Kong which is totally dedicated to restaurants. There were over 3000 restaurants in Hong Kong which meant you could eat in a different one every night and take nearly 10 years to try them all.

Loli recommended starting with a lobster dish. These were kept alive in an aquarium at the front of the restaurant. The waiter selected one and brought it up to us on a silver platter.

'Is this one okay sir?'

'Yes,' I replied not knowing any difference. With that he wrenched the head of the poor beast and very skilfully removed the shell from the tail chopped it into small portions. These were put into a small dish and offered to us with Wasabi sauce. The bits of lobster meat were still wriggling. I put one in my mouth and I could feel the meat moving on my tongue as I chewed it. I couldn't see the point of serving the meat in such a condition but I presume it showed that it couldn't be fresher. The head and shell were taken to the kitchen where they were transformed into a wonderful soup served with Udon noodles.

Loli was becoming quite a habit and I enjoyed her company in the heady atmosphere that is Hong Kong. She had not travelled out of Hong Kong and I often wondered what our relationship would be like in a different country or whether it was just the magic of Hong Kong that made it special.

Chapter 17

Far East and Australia

After returning from Moscow at the end of May I only had 21 days to prepare for my longest trip away yet, 34 days. During this preparation time I also had to support our Dutch distributor with a two day visit to Amsterdam.

I had a very good travel agent who arranged all my flights and hotels for me. He used to get what was called a round-the-world ticket, which although I did not circumnavigate the globe, as long as I kept travelling in an easterly direction and came back directly, I qualified for a cheaper ticket. Apparently this is how my seat on a recent flight to Abu Dhabi was cheaper than my co-passenger. My schedule was to be Hong Kong, Taiwan, Korea, Singapore, Jakarta, Denpasar and Sydney.

My first two days in Hong Kong was spent helping my agents with follow-up visits plus a bit of training on some new products. Naturally my two nights were spent with Loli who told me that she was travelling to London with her sister, to visit a cousin of theirs and was leaving Hong Kong on 4th of July. She asked if we could meet up in London, which of course I was more than happy to do. I gave her my contact phone numbers and arranged that she would call me between 11:00am and 12:00md on Monday the 28th which would be my first day back in the office from this long trip.

Our last night together was very emotional and it felt strange as she left me that the next time I would see her would be in London. I recalled my feelings during my last stay in Hong Kong when I wondered what our relationship would be like in another country. Now I would get a chance to find out.

The next morning I was off into the unknown, well for me that is. A Cathay Pacific flight to Taipei, Taiwan. I had done a bit of research before I left to learn about the political situation in Taiwan. Taiwan used to be known as Formosa but after World War II when the Japanese surrendered their occupation of the island it was renamed. It is also referred to as ROC, Republic of China, as opposed to PRC, People's Republic of China (mainland China) and the two should never be mixed up.

I was met by my distributor, Alex, a very personable Taiwanese national who would be my guide for the next couple of days. He had organised a packed day on Friday as this was the only working day and on Saturday he would be my tourist guide.

We had four visits to do, all in different departments of the University, namely Zoology, Botany, Microbial Chemistry and Horticulture. All had very different potential applications, which we discussed at length. Alex was delighted with what we had achieved and was sure that he could turn this interest into orders after my visit.

Saturday was my "day off." Alex was very knowledgeable about his city and after a drive around we visited the Palace Museum. The next stop was a short drive up a mountain to a swimming pool and bar. I was a bit surprised at this but it proved to be a beautiful experience. The pool was an infinity pool which looked out over the mountain range. Alex had timed this visit to perfection as the sun set behind the mountains, which were perfectly aligned with the end of the infinity pool. We sat in the warm water with a glass of Taiwanese beer and watched the ever-growing golden orange globe disappear behind the mountains, shimmering as it went.

Next was dinner. The Chinese always eat their evening meal early compared with us but I was ready for it. I let Alex do the ordering, giving him free rein to get anything that was representative of local cuisine. It was delicious but I had to remember the Chinese custom of leaving something in the bowl to signify that you had eaten enough.

The last treat caught me completely by surprise. The Taiwanese have a long-standing tradition of the barber shop culture. Not only could you get a haircut and shave but you could also get your ears de-waxed! This was followed by a shoulder massage by a pretty little girl followed by other bits of you being massaged underneath the draped cloth. I honestly didn't see that coming, so to speak, and all for the modest sum of NT$180 per half hour. Alex grinned as I walked out of my cubicle.

'I think you might need another beer after that.'

I was driven back to my hotel just before midnight, totally relaxed and very happy. I slept soundly that night.

The next stop was Seoul in Korea. I was booked in the Manhattan hotel in downtown Seoul and made my own way there by taxi. The receptionist greeted me politely and informed me that Miss Ko was already checked in and was waiting for me. What a lucky guy I was. Three countries in less than a week and a different girl in each country. Ko He-Rang was waiting expectantly for me in my room....

Mr Im had arranged a punishing schedule over the next five days to maximise on my time there. Day one was a visit to the Ministry of Construction where I was taken to two departments, each with a very different measuring problem. Day two we went to Han Dok Pharmaceuticals in the morning after which Mr Im took me to lunch for a new experience. I have already mentioned the Korean mix up of the Ls and Rs plus their Fs and Ps which I was beginning to get used to.

'In this restaurant they make a special soof out of lips!

'A soup made of lips,' I repeated in a questioning tone.

'Yes lips,' he repeated pointing to his chest.

I still didn't get it so Mr Im tried again.

'Lips, lips,' he said again, frantically drawing his outspread fingers across his chest.

'Ah ribs is it?' I said emphasising the R and B.

'Yes lips,' still not being able to copy my pronunciation.

It was indeed a very unusual soup and was like a beef bouillon with large pieces of meat-covered ribs, some noodles and of course loads of garlic. A portion of kimchi accompanied the soup, which again was loaded with fermented garlic. I was so dosed-up with garlic that I now began to secrete garlic-smelling sweat in the humid, high temperatures. Ordinarily I would not have met business customers stinking the way I did but everybody did it here and my smell went unnoticed.

In the afternoon a visit to the Gold-mining Research Centre and Chong Kun Dang Pharmaceuticals.

On Thursday I had a change of accompanying personnel. Mr Im had some urgent business to attend to so I was taken around by Miss Lee from the sales office. As she did not drive we had to use a combination of taxi and train to get to the Korean Institute of Metallurgy where I spent all day with them in two different departments, looking at various measuring techniques in a variety of metals.

Mr Im was back on duty on Friday and explained that we were visiting KAERI, the Korean Atomic Energy Research Institute which was a long way out of town in Daejeon. We took a taxi there, which took us about two hours 10 minutes and an express bus back which took two hours 30 minutes. It was a pleasant drive and gave me the chance to see some of the country from a higher point of view in the bus.

By the time I got back to He-Rang's flat I was exhausted but she knew how to make me feel better and we spent what, unknown to me, was to be our last night together in her huge bed enjoying some new positions that I have not experienced before. Saturday was going to be a complete day of travelling, flying from Seoul to Taipei and then Taipei to Singapore. I had left He-Rang at 8:00am and eventually arrived at the Orchard Hotel in Singapore at 8:30pm that night. This was my first time in Singapore and I was really excited at being able to spend the next week here.

Orchard Road was alive. It was one of the main shopping streets and was lined with camera shops, watch shops and tailors plus quite a few doorways advertising "Massage" over them. Bright lights illuminated the whole street into daytime. I decided to walk up and down and take in the atmosphere. No sooner had I stepped out of the hotel then I was accosted by salesmen inviting me to come and see their shops or have a suit made. The watches in the window of the shops were obviously real judging by the price but when I told one persistent salesman that the Rolexes were too expensive for me he invited me to come into the back of the shop saying, 'cheaper ones in back. Come see.'

I went through a small door at the back of the shop into another room with several glass display cases.

'Look – Rolex, much cheaper. $100.'

He persuaded me to hold one in my hand and at once I could tell by the weight that it was a fake. However it was a very good imitation and if it kept time would be an interesting purchase.

'$100?' I repeated.

'Yes very cheap.'

'What about $50?'

'No can do. $100 very cheap.'

'What about $75?'

'$80'

'OK,' and shook his hand.

The watch was placed in a replica box and I walked out a satisfied customer.

Now I needed to find a handbag shop as Lena had asked me for a Louis Vuitton version. It wasn't long before I found one and the moment I stopped to look in the window the salesman pounced on me inviting me in to the shop. He had a whole range of designer bags so I asked him for a Louis Vuitton. There were several choices offered, all at silly prices compared with the real thing. It was fairly obvious that they too were fakes as the material was definitely not leather, more of a plasticky feel to it. However they did look authentic with the Louis Vuitton logos plastered all over them. I chose one and after a bit of bartering got what I thought was an acceptable price.

Shopping over I started to walk back to the hotel up the other side of the road. I fended off more eager salesman but was stopped in my tracks by someone offering, 'Massage sir. Pretty girl.'

'Why not,' I thought so followed the man up two flights of stairs to a reception desk where an attractive lady of mature years greeted me warmly. She asked me where I was from and when I had arrived and quickly ascertained that I must be weary from travelling all day.

'I get you very pretty girl for soothing massage? S$100?'

She showed me up to a private room and invited me to take a shower and wait on the couch for my lady to arrive. I was not sure of the etiquette, this being my first time in Singapore, so I opted to wrap the fluffy white towel tightly around my waist and laid on the couch facedown. It wasn't long before a lovely little Singaporean Chinese girl came in and introduced herself. She was wearing a very skimpy top and a pair of hot-pants. We engaged in some small talk before she climbed on top of me, legs astride my hips and starting work on my shoulders. Her fingers were very agile and found every knot in my back as she worked her way down. She got to the top of the towel and loosened, it exposing my bum which she worked on with her elbows. Next she got to my thighs and very seductively massaged them, gradually working round to the inner muscles at the top. As she rubbed up and down she would just touch my balls, which started to arouse a passion in me!

'Okay back done. Turnover.'

Feeling a bit apprehensive I thought, 'let's see what happens now,' so turned over exposing my now erect penis. She moved up the couch again, now straddling my hips from the front and sitting on my now throbbing gland. She worked her way down my intercostal muscles between my ribs and finally arrived at my proud organ.

'You want happy ending. Only S$50 extra, cash.'

How could I resist? She placed the towel over my abdomen, squirted some more oil on my bits and gently started to caress them. This was sheer heaven. Her strokes got stronger and more frequent until my back arched and I finished all over the carefully placed towel. She certainly knew her stuff.

She cleaned me up and told me to rest for 10 minutes before getting dressed and she would be back to collect her money. The lady at reception said goodbye and asked if she would see me again.

'Quite possibly,' I replied. 'I'm here for a week.'

I was much more relaxed now as I walked back to the hotel and feeling rather peckish. I quickly took my purchases to my room and came back down to the large atrium where the bar and restaurant were still in full swing. The atrium was well known for its huge chandelier, the size of which I have never seen before. The lifts were in one corner directly opposite the entrance and reception close by. Seating for the bar and restaurant occupied half of the floor space in the atrium and gave you a good view of who was coming and going. I ordered a beer and a noodle dish and sat "people watching," one of my favourite activities when time allows.

A well-dressed man in a smart suit was wandering around apparently aimlessly and I reckoned he must be the hotel security guard. A European man walked into the hotel with a girl in arm, who was very obviously Chinese.

'Ahah. I know what's going on here,' and watched intently. The couple headed for the lifts and the smart suited man casually walked over behind them. The couple got into the lift followed by the man and I could envisage what was going to happen. Two minutes later he was back down and walked over to reception to speak to the receptionist.

I was right. He was hotel security and he was reporting to reception which room the man was in with an unregistered guest.

I finished my meal plus another beer and as I was about to leave, the Chinese girl came out of the lift and hurriedly exited from the front door. The smart suited man went over to reception obviously to report that the unregistered guest had now left and all was well. What a memorable first night in Singapore, I thought, as I drifted off to sleep in my king-sized bed.

Sunday morning came quicker than expected but I knew that I was not meeting Tan, my new Singapore agent until after lunch. I decided to have a leisurely breakfast and spent the morning lazing by the rooftop pool. As I lay on my sun lounger, quaffing my second pre-lunch beer, my mind wandered and I considered how my life had changed. I was now spending time in environments that were so different that acceptable behaviour in one was regarded as a sin in another. Having made a couple of faux pas already I would have to be careful not to muddle up where I was. I also had several girlfriends in similarly diametrically opposed environments and lived a luxurious lifestyle in hotels around the world but slummed it in China.

My mind was jolted back to the present as the pool barman approached me with a cordless phone saying, 'Mr Hunter, a telephone call for you.' It was Tan who wanted to confirm this afternoon's arrangements. He would pick me up after lunch and spend the afternoon showing me some of the attractions of Singapore.

My first impression of Singapore was that it was so clean, free from litter and everything neat and orderly. The vegetation along the road was neatly trimmed and hedges cut. It was a punishable offence to chew gum in the street and worse still to spit it out onto the pavement. There were two distinct regions, old and new. The new was where I was staying in Orchard Road the old was round the harbour.

The entrance to the harbour was guarded by two large Merlions, half mermaid and half lion. Lots of little fishing boats gently bobbed up and down in the sheltered waters. Around the edge of the harbour were all the old buildings, mostly 2 to 4 stories high, which are now listed. Behind them in contrast are lots of skyscrapers in the very modern Business Centre of the island. On the other side of the harbour, standing in a defiant position with arms crossed in front of him, is a white marble statue of Sir Stamford Raffles, the founder of Singapore and after whom the famous Raffles Hotel is named.

One thing that has to be done is to go to the Long Bar in Raffles Hotel and drink a Singapore Sling. This famous cocktail was developed by Ngiam Tong Boon sometime before 1915 whilst working as a bartender in the hotel.

Singapore's Central Business District had been suffering from traffic congestion for a long time and the Government had recently introduced a car-sharing scheme to try to overcome the problem. They made it illegal for a car to enter the CBD with only one person travelling in it and installed cameras on the main roads entering the area. Anyone photographed with only a driver was fined $100. Some enterprising schoolboys had come up with a money making scheme. They would wait at the roadside just before the cameras and for a modest tip would travel with the driver past the check point and get out the other side, walking back for the next one thus saving the occupant $100 and making a tidy sum for themselves!

Tan had organised a full week for me, both lecturing in the Singapore Institute for Scientific Research plus visiting potential customers and took it in turns with other sales people from his office to accompany me. I was taken to a different restaurant every night but two stick in my memory.

One was known as the Banana Leaf restaurant in which all meals were served up on a banana leaf. The leaves were pre-cut into rectangles and were the only thing at your place setting. No cutlery, no chopsticks - nothing else. Everything had to be eaten by hand. The restaurant was famous for its fish head curry, which of course I had to try. One waiter came round and put a dollop of rice on the leaf. Another followed with a large bucket and ladle and put a large fish head on top of the rice, looking straight at me. He also ladled some of the curry sauce onto the rice. A third came round giving out poppadums from a large rusty tin, in a manner resembling a croupier dealing out cards in a casino. Observing social etiquette I had to eat with my right hand only, the left hand being reserved for certain body functions and was regarded as dirty. I pulled the fish head apart to find the best bits, which were the cheeks and the eyes plus the sauce soaked up in the rice. When finished the waiter simply wrapped the remaining bones in the leaf and threw it away. Very simple and no washing up. The only problem I had now was that the turmeric in the curry had stained my hands and I had bright yellow fingers, which took days two days before it eventually washed off.

The second memorable meal was in a Vietnamese restaurant which Tan and his wife, Irene, took me to. Irene was Vietnamese and I asked her to order for me. A plate of pickled red chillies was served with the beers as nibbles. I went to take one but Irene immediately took my arm to prevent me from putting it in my mouth.

'They are very hot and not many Europeans are able to eat them.'

Well that was a challenge to me. I loved hot curries and regularly had vindaloos so I eased my arm out of Irene's grip and put the chilli in my mouth. Irene looked amazed and put one in her mouth while observing me closely. My goodness, they were hot but very flavoursome. After swallowing my chilli I reached out and took another. Irene also took up the challenge. Then another, then another. Irene couldn't believe it. At number five she said, 'okay stop. So you can eat hot chillies. Most unusual for a European and you have my respect.'

By now I couldn't feel my lips and my tongue was painfully on fire, so hot that even another beer couldn't extinguish it. After about 30 minutes it gradually died down and I was able to enjoy the rest of the meal.

I had another surprise experience coming that I was not quite prepared for. 'It is Durian season,' said Tan. 'We will go to the Hawker Food Centre and you can try some.' Durian is a fruit much loved in parts of Asia and can only be described in appearance as the size of a watermelon but with evil spikes on it. They can weigh up to 10kg each. During harvest time there are normally a couple of fatalities per year if one of these fruits unexpectedly falls from the tree onto the head of the person underneath.

'Here we are,' said Tan.

I was aware of a very unpleasant smell in the area but thought it was just the open drains. Tan bought three large slices of durian and bought them over to our table. The flesh looked like that of an avocado pear and similar in colour.

'Now be warned. The fruit has an awful smell which you will get first but don't be put off, bite into it.'

I picked up my slice and raised it to my lips but before I could take a bite I smelt this disgusting smell and immediately put it down.

'My God what's that awful stink?' I said.

'Try again,' Tan said, 'it's worth it.'

I tried to hold my breath as I raised it to my mouth for a second time. I was there, past my lips and into my mouth. I bit off a chunk and started to chew. It was delicious. I could see Tan's point but such a smell. I can only liken it to eating a bowl of strawberries and cream inside a public toilet after an outbreak of dysentery!

'Well done,' said Irene, 'you are the first one of our European visitors to eat durian.' I felt that Irene was beginning to regard me as some demigod and totally non-European.

Now I could understand the funny signs in the hotel. It was a symbol representing a durian fruit with a big red cross through it. Hotels do not allow guests to bring durian into their rooms as the shitty smell pervades the whole corridor.

The next morning I was beginning to wish that I had not showed off with the chillies. The human body never ceases to amaze me but I still cannot understand how chillies can wreak so much havoc in the mouth and then disappear into the gastro-intestinal tract without any signs of discomfort. Then suddenly the following morning it feels like Mount Vesuvius is erupting out of your bottom. I couldn't walk properly for quite awhile as my sphincter was stinging.

I had a lecture to give and customers to meet in the morning and managed to get through that without exhibiting too much discomfort. In the afternoon the Managing Director of the company took me to his tennis club for a few afternoon beers, which were most welcome as the humidity was beginning to get to me.

Singapore is a funny place to get used to. Being on the equator there are no seasons, no changing daylight hours and no changing weather. The sun rises at 6:00am and sets at 6:00pm every day. The temperature was always around 30° or slightly more and the humidity is up in the 90%. It always rains heavily every afternoon around 2:00pm for half an hour and within minutes of it stopping, the pavements were steaming and soon dry out. I was in Tan's car for the first time when we had a deluge and I commented that he did not have to put the windscreen wipers on as the rainwater was easily running off the screen and not obscuring his vision. They used a product on their windscreens that was originally developed for helicopter screens and acts as a surfactant. The rain cannot stick to it, as there is no surface tension. I've got to try this at home I thought and asked Tan where to buy it.

'Most garage accessory shops sell it. I'll get you some when I fill up with petrol.'

In my last day in Singapore Tan managed to get in a visit for me. A soft drinks manufacturer that has a specific measuring problem in their quality control laboratories. I managed to solve the problem and left on a high. After lunch and a few beers Tan took me to Changi airport where I was taking an overnight flight to Australia.

Singapore to Jakarta to Denpasar to Sydney. Although it was overnight we had two changes of aircraft so I had a little sleep. I have trouble sleeping on a plane at the best of times but to have to get out twice in the middle of the night made sleeping nigh on impossible. My body was already on local time in Singapore at eight hours ahead so the two hour difference when I landed in Sydney was not too bad. The Managing Director of the company selling our products in Australia, Tony McD, met me at the airport even though the plane had landed at 7:10am. He had booked me into a lovely hotel on the seafront called the Shore Inn. Even though it was a Sunday he was going to show me around as it was my first time in Australia.

We did the usual things like the Opera House and Sydney Harbour Bridge and for lunch, under the shadow of the bridge, we had prawns and beer, a favourite combination for Aussies. The prawns were not prawns as we know them, they were enormous and would put a small lobster to shame.

The beer however was a different matter. Fosters draft, and very cold. For a real ale lover like me, fizzy Fosters didn't do it for me. Number one it was so gassy you ended up with the burps. Number two it was very low in alcohol but number three it was so bloody cold that you would die of hypothermia before getting pissed. I remember buying a postcard to send home to my parents with a picture of prawns and beer and a rhyme which was a bit of a piss take on our 'wish you were here' postcards and read:

If you were here we'd have prawns and beer.

Seeing as you're not I'll eat the lot.

My first week in Australia was to train staff in the use of Image Analysis in readiness for the following week's exhibition plus a lot of customers to visit to sort out specific problems. On the weekend they had organised a trip to a favourite diving site and took me out to sea looking for sharks. I didn't dive, although I had qualified as a diver with the British Sub Aqua many years ago but hadn't done it for a long time. We stayed in a motel out of town and feasted on barbecues with freshly caught fish both nights.

We had to get back fairly early on Monday as we were setting up a major laboratory equipment exhibition which would last until Thursday. It was three days of constant customer visits to our stand and come Friday morning I was shattered. My flight home was leaving later in the afternoon and I had to admit that I had had enough and wanted to get back home. I eventually arrived back at Heathrow at 7:00am on Saturday morning.

After 34 days of living in hotels I got what I nicknamed the "Baked Bean Syndrome." Eating out for every meal of the day may seem idyllic, especially for a foodie like me, but after this length of time I just longed for some baked beans on toast or a boiled egg with dippy soldiers.

Chapter 18

Loli in London

My first day back in the office after 34 days away was manic. Everyone wanted to catch up with me. I was now spending more working time overseas than in the UK and I had a lot of catch ups to do as well.

During my time away the company had installed a clocking in system to make pay and holiday entitlement easier to work out. However they hadn't accounted for me. Out of the 253 working days in the year, for the last 12 month period I had been out of the country for 221 days and this included a lot of weekends for which UK based employees would normally be entitled to a day off in lieu for each weekend day worked. If I worked out how many weekend days I had worked plus my normal holiday entitlement I didn't have enough working days left to be able to take days off in lieu. With only 30 or so office days I needed these to do all my follow-up work and preparations for the next overseas visits. It also meant that I had minimal contact with other members of staff, some of whom didn't even know that I worked for the company. I did share a very capable secretary who did as much as she could for me but if something needed my signature like a Visa application, I had to be there to do it personally. I wasn't too worried about all this as my trips overseas were very enjoyable and some of the things I had done, "normal" people would never be able to do in their holiday periods. I left it to the personnel department to sort out my entitlement.

As arranged, Loli telephoned me just before lunch. She was staying in Paddington with her cousin and sister and was looking forward to seeing me again. I was staying with my parents as I had left my house to my estranged wife and hadn't found a place of my own yet. No wonder - I wasn't in the UK for long enough to go flat hunting. Loli was going back to Hong Kong the following week so I decided I would take Friday off to make a long weekend.

When I got to where Loli was staying, I was greeted by her sister first who took me aside.

'I wanted to speak to you alone just to let you know that Loli thinks a lot of you and I don't want her to get hurt emotionally. Please don't do anything to upset her.'

Before I could digest what her sister had just said Loli walked into the room and gave me a big hug and kiss. It felt weird, as all of our meetings up until now had been in Hong Kong. She was ready for a day out in London with me so off we went.

The first difference I noticed was that Loli was feeling the cold all the time. Although today was the 1st of August it was our summer but was nowhere near the 30°C and high humidity that she was used to back home. We did some of the usual touristy stuff and my next problem was finding somewhere to eat. Since being in the UK she was struggling with our food and found our Chinese restaurants disgusting. I must say I agreed with her on this one as I reckoned that if you hadn't eaten Chinese food in China you hadn't eaten Chinese food at all! We ended up in Chinatown where the food was something like that she was used to at home.

After a tiring day I took her back to her cousin's flat but there was the next problem.

'I'm sorry but I can't ask you to stay and we won't be able to have sex tonight.'

What a disappointment for me. I couldn't take her back with me either as I was staying with my parents. We arranged to meet again the next day and Loli asked if I would go shopping with her. Not my favourite pastime but I agreed. We spent the day going round to the Department stores and especially the cosmetic departments. Loli spent a lot of time with the shop assistants, leaving me sitting on a stool twiddling my thumbs.

After she had filled several carrier bags she asked if she could meet my parents and see where I was temporarily living. No mobile phones in those days so I was not able to warn my parents that I was bringing her back. During the 45 minute car ride she again asked me if I felt comfortable walking with her round the streets holding hands. I told her I had no problem but she obviously felt something as this was the second time she had asked me this question. I wanted to know what she was thinking but didn't want to push her.

My father was a little taken aback to see me on the doorstep with an attractive Chinese girl but greeted her warmly and invited her in. Tea and cakes were offered which Loli found quaint. She had heard of the English passion for afternoon tea but couldn't drink it with milk in. There was no problem with conversation as my mother and father wanted to hear all about life in Hong Kong.

After a couple of hours I had to take her back to her cousins flat as she needed to start packing for her return journey back to Hong Kong. No sex again! As we parted with an affectionate hug we arranged to meet up in Hong Kong in a few weeks time as she still had my stuff in her flat, which I would need.

The whole two days had been surreal for me. I still felt a lot of affection for her but how different it had been in a new environment. I knew it was only her first visit to the UK but how she struggled with our different ways of life unlike me who loved going to Hong Kong.

Chapter 19

The Proposal, August 1986

After my weekend in London with Loli my thoughts went back to Lena. I had no work planned in Moscow until October and I could not wait that long to see her again. I had an idea. Why not go on a City Break holiday to Moscow with a tourist company. I checked with Thompsons and yes, they had a 4 day mini break in Moscow in August and there was just enough time to get me a visa if I booked it straight away.

I had also promised Lena that I would try to telephone her so that evening I called the International operator and asked how to arrange a call to Moscow. She told me that it needed 24 hours to set it up, heaven only knows why, and would I like to book one for tomorrow evening. Bearing in mind that there is a three our time difference between the UK and Moscow I opted for a 6:00pm call. The operator accepted this and said I would be called back tomorrow evening to be connected.

I was very nervous as 6:00pm approached the next day. I didn't know what to expect and was taking a chance that Lena was home. Two minutes before six the phone rang. 'Good evening sir, International operator here. I am just connecting you to Moscow. Hold the line please it might take a few minutes.' My heart was pounding and my hands trembling. I could barely hold the phone still against my ear. I could hear the switchgear whirring and clicking and then followed the ringtone on a single "burr" not the familiar "burr burr" that we are used to. Then a female voice answered in English with a very strong Russian accent. Good evening Moscow, London calling. Please could you connect me to, and she gave the number. My heart rate must have doubled at this point and I could feel my pulse pounding in my ear against the telephone. My palms were now sweating profusely. I felt like a spy. I wondered just how many people in the UK made personal phone calls to Moscow and what the repercussions might be for Lena and myself. Another ringtone was audible which seemed to go on for ages.

'Hello,' I heard a familiar female voice say and then the Russian operator spoke over the top in Russian first and then in English.

'Hello London. You are connected now. Go ahead please.' Some more whirring and clicking in the background and I started to speak.

'Hello Lena, it's Graham here,' my voice uncontrollably trembling.

'Hello Graham, it's so nice to hear your voice. What is your news? When are you coming back to Moscow?'

'I can get a tourist trip to Moscow for three nights later in August (and I gave her the dates). Is that okay for me to come and see you?'

'Oh yes please,' she responded enthusiastically.

We continued chatting for a while and agreed that I would call back next week to confirm that I have booked the trip. There were a few more whirrs and clicks and then the line went dead. I hung on for a while and the London operator came on the line again.

'Sorry. The line from Moscow has been disconnected. Would you like me to try again?'

'No thank you. I'm going to call again next week.'

I flopped into an armchair, exhilarated but totally drained. What have I just done? I have managed to make a private call to Moscow, which had obviously been listened to, probably at both ends, and have now officially made it known that I was having a relationship with a Soviet citizen.

The next day I confirmed the city break to Moscow and sent my passport off to get a Visa. This would be a tourist Visa and would be dealt with by the travel company. Much easier than the business visas which I usually travelled on, but more restrictive so I would have to be careful.

I was back in the UK for a few weeks and busied myself with lots of follow-ups from my previous visits and planning the next trip. Lena was constantly on my mind, so much so that I confided in a colleague as to what I was doing.

'Don't do it Graham,' said Simon. 'You'll never be able to get her out of the Soviet Union and you will only get hurt.'

I was taking a bit aback by his response but I knew he was only considering my best interests. I continued with my plan undaunted.

At last the day came when I was leaving for Moscow with a small tourist group. After some small talk with the Tour Director who was accompanying us, I explained that I was visiting a girlfriend in Moscow and would not be coming on the organised tours. She was a little concerned at first but when I showed her that I could now speak and read some Russian (I had been practising with a self learning tape) and was confident enough to travel around Moscow on my own, she relaxed. I agreed that I would check in with her every day to prove I was okay and to receive any instructions on the leaving arrangements.

Lena and I spent a wonderful couple of days in the warm summer sunshine, just enjoying each other's company. She took me to places where your average Russian spends time relaxing like Park Kulturi and Alexander Park. On my last afternoon we were walking hand-in-hand along the embankment of the Moscow River, in front of the Kremlin wall. Lena was dressed in a pure white skirt and jacket, which emphasised her size 8 figure. She wore a string of artificial pearls around her neck with matching earrings. She looked gorgeous.

'Lena, you know that I am still waiting for my divorce to be finalised but when it is, and if it's possible, would you wait for me and marry me?'

She went quiet for a while, obviously trying to take in the consequences of what I had just said.

'And what would you do if we were married? Live in Moscow?'

'No. I will try to get you out and you could come to the UK and live with me.'

She went quiet again for some time as we strolled along the embankment. Eventually we started talking again as if I had never asked the question.

'What have I done now?' I thought to myself. 'Have I just upset her or even scared her off.'

My group was leaving the next morning and Lena came with me in the taxi back to the hotel. She could not come to the airport with me this time as she was not part of the group. We said our goodbyes after which she embraced me quickly and jumped back into the taxi. As she did so she turned to me and said, 'yes I will,' and the taxi sped off before I could say anything. I stood transfixed to the spot. It was my turn now to take in what those three words meant to me. Simon's words were ringing in my ears. Had I started something that I could not finish? Would I be able to get her out? I put these negative thoughts out of my mind and renewed my determination to follow my plans.

Back in my room I quickly packed and made my way down to reception to meet up with my group for the return journey home. My fellow travellers were intrigued to know where I had been so I had to tell them something. They had all enjoyed the few days in Moscow seeing the regular sites and I could imagine how they felt as I recalled my emotions when I first came to Moscow. What a long way I had come since then I thought as I boarded the coach back to the airport.

At the time of the events I am writing about there were no mobile phones, no Internet and information on the Soviet Union was restricted to what the Authorities wanted you to know. I thought that I would give my readers some information that I have recently obtained from various sources, which will help you understand the enormity of the task I had taken on and perhaps appreciate my reasons for wanting to write this book.

After the end of World War II a lot of personnel who had been stationed in Eastern European countries had taken foreign wives, especially Polish and Russian and had settled in those countries.

On 15th of February 1947 the Supreme Council Presidium passed a Decree on "Banning Marriages Between Soviet Citizens and Foreigners." The lawmakers explained that this was to benefit women as they would feel uncomfortable in these new countries and would be discriminated against. This was propaganda as many USSR citizens dreamed of going abroad. The Soviet Union put itself forward as the best country in the world where all the needs of citizens were met and life was good. The mass exodus of its citizens didn't quite match the propaganda and hence something had to be done.

Up until the passing of this Decree, participants in mixed marriages were merely intimidated or disciplined at Party Assemblies but from that point on any marriages to foreign citizens were prohibited by law. In addition abortions were banned and divorce procedures made unduly complicated. Even worse International marriages that had taken place before the Decree were annulled and were regarded as acts of High Treason. However it has to be said that it was now very difficult to violate this law as the Iron Curtain did not let many foreigners into the USSR.

After Stalin's death in 1953 Nikita Krushchev came to power and annulled the prohibition but the persecution of Soviet citizens marrying foreigners was not over. Those who had affairs with foreigners were accused of immorality and fired from their jobs. When they tried to find other jobs they found many obstacles and ended up being unemployed. It was dangerous to be unemployed in the USSR without good reason such as a disability and was known as "Social Parasitism." This was a crime and "parasites" were expelled to the far reaches of the country such as Siberia or the Russian Far East, to work as labourers.

After Leonid Brezhnev replaced Krushchev, the persecutions stopped but new problems emerged. It was said that all registry offices received secret "for official use only" letters with the new rules for marriage to foreigners in them. Those rules were not published anywhere so your average citizen was not aware of them. This meant that the registry office could always refuse a marriage registration for whatever reason they wanted to give. It is hard to tell if these rules really existed but most probably it was the red tape that caused the problems, as you will see as you continue with my story.

Chapter 20

The next steps

When I got home I still couldn't believe that I had heard those words – "yes I will," and the significance of them. Lena had agreed that she would wait for me to get my divorce completed and then to look at what was necessary to get married. Working on the premise that she had agreed to both parts of my question my next task was to find out if it was possible for me to marry her as a British citizen. I quickly penned off a letter to the Nationality and Treaty Department of the Foreign and Commonwealth Office to which I had a very quick response.

The letter started off with a disclaimer saying that the Foreign and Commonwealth Office was not competent to give authoritative advice on the marriage laws of the Soviet Union and that I could find out from the Registry of Acts of Civil Status in Moscow via a letter to the Consular section of the Soviet Embassy in London.

It went on to say that they understood that the Soviet authorities required a certificate of no impediment and a certified translation of all the pages in my British passport including all stamps and visas. These documents needed to be presented by both parties in person and simultaneously to the Soviet Registry Office in Moscow when giving notice of marriage. Only then could an appointment to be made for the marriage to take place, usually between 1 to 3 months later.

They then gave a list of all documents required to be sent to the British Embassy in Moscow via the diplomatic service from the Foreign and Commonwealth Office in London for translation and legalisation.

a). Certificate of no impediment

b). Photocopies of all the pages in my passport

c). Full names and addresses of myself and my fiancé in English and Cyrillic   script.
d). My fiancé's father's full name in English and Cyrillic script.

e).Evidence of any termination of any previous marriage i.e. a decree absolute

Once these documents had been translated and legalised I could collect them from the British Embassy in Moscow.

I would also need a special Visa issued by the Soviet Embassy in London in order to travel to Moscow for both giving notice to the Registry Office and again for the actual wedding ceremony. I could not travel on a business Visa for these activities for reasons I would learn about later.

The last paragraph was the killer. A Soviet emigrant's passport and exit Visa would be required for my spouse before she would be allowed to leave the Soviet Union and an application may only be made after the wedding had taken place. There was no guarantee that this would be granted.

So having gone through all this bureaucracy and officially getting married there was the possibility that I would never get her out. Simon's words started to ring in my ears again.

I quickly put these words out of my head and concentrated on the first thing I had to do before any of this list could be tackled. That was to get a Decree Absolute granted on my divorce. I do not want to enter into any mudslinging but the divorce was taking longer than I anticipated due to my ex being in no hurry. As I was paying all the bills it made no difference to her how long it took and she was not inclined to help me.

Chapter 21

Zagreb, Belgrade and Far East

My time back at home and in the office flew by. I had to travel to Yugoslavia again and five days later after this visit I was off to the Far East and China for another long trip of 33 days.

I was booked into the Palace hotel in Zagreb again and of course I went to see Zoritsa in her flat. Now that I knew where it was I had no problem finding it. Alfred greeted me as a long lost friend and sat chatting with him for some while before my attention turned to Zoritsa. We stayed in on the first night but on the second she took me to an Argentinian restaurant, which I would not have believed existed in Yugoslavia at that time. I believed that the Yugoslavs were the most reluctant communists and the furthest away from interference by Russia and hence were not so impoverished as the other Soviet bloc countries.

I can hear you all saying,

'What is he doing going to see Zoritsa? He has just proposed to his girlfriend in Moscow and here he is being unfaithful already.'

Well yes, it was a proposal of sorts, which I intended to follow through but we had no exchange of a ring and no discussions as to how we would do it and no guarantee that we could. The other relevant point is that I was still not officially divorced yet so technically I could not get engaged to her until the divorce was complete. Besides I am a man who had been deprived of a loving relationship for years and yearned for female attention

When I left the Palace Hotel en route for Belgrade, Harry caught me by the arm.

'Mr Hunter, could I ask you a favour? The next time you come back to Zagreb could you bring me a credit card sized calculator?'

'Of course I can Harry. You have always looked after me so I am only too happy to be able to do something for you.'

My flight from Zagreb to Belgrade was only fifty minutes and soon I was checked in to the Metropole Hotel. Nothing special to report here so let's go straight back home.

I only had five days in the office before setting off again. I needed to get a cholera booster vaccination so spent Monday morning going to the

Medical Centre. I also had to pick up some anti-malaria pills as I was going to visit a malarial infested area. My flight on Saturday was on my beloved Cathay Pacific from Gatwick to Hong Kong, arriving in Hong Kong at 9:00am. My connecting flight to Manila left at 10:00am but the flight crew knew of my tight connection time and radioed ahead to keep the on-going flight informed of our pending arrival.

No problem, just a hurried sprint across Kai Tak airport to get to my next departure gate. I eventually arrived in Manila after one and a half days travelling plus an eight hour time difference.

This visit to Manila was another first for me, one that I had been looking forward to for some while. Just this year the Marcos administration had been toppled by a peaceful People's Revolution and the family forced to flee to Hawaii. Imelda Marcos was rumoured to have left over 3000 pairs of shoes behind.

As I got off the plane, the heat hit me. 33°C and high relative humidity, which brought me out into an instant sweat after the cool air-conditioning during the flight.

The ride to the hotel was interesting to say the least. Mr Tee, the owner of the company now representing us, picked me up from the airport. Up until World War II they had driven on the left as we do but when the Americans liberated the Philippines from the Japanese, they insisted that they changed to driving on the right. This was partly a political statement by the Americans to show that they had conquered the Japanese but also an economic measure as it made importing cars from the USA easier and cheaper. The most remarkable feature on the roads was the hundreds of brightly coloured Jeepneys that were used for public transport. These were large American Jeeps, which had seating for 12 people allegedly. Each one was uniquely decorated in brightly coloured patterns, and flowers and with chrome plated ornaments. These Jeeps were left over from World War II and had been stripped down and rebuilt with a roof for protection from the sun plus two long parallel benches to give more room for passengers. These gaudy vehicles would stop without warning to pick passengers up or drop them off. Health and Safety didn't seem to be an issue with many passengers clambering up to the roof if the inside was full. The term Jeep had been evolved from the use of the abbreviation GP for a general-purpose vehicle and when coupled with the suffix from another word Jitney, an American taxi, became Jeepney. The whole place was chaotic with no sense of organisation. Thankfully Mr Tee skilfully wove in and out of the traffic but with no regard to lane control and got me safely to my hotel.

I had appointed Mr Tee's company as our new distributor in the Philippines and my job was to give their sales team some training and accompany them on some customer visits. He explained that he had a sales force of twenty, all of them girls, who he thought made better sales people when dealing with male customers!

My first two days were taken up with training the girls on all the company's products. For a hot blooded man like me it was such a distraction having twenty very pretty girls standing around you and giving you their undivided attention. They were all shorter than me, with jet black hair, so I stood out like a sore thumb being blonde and a good six inches taller than all of them. On the second evening we all went to a Chinese restaurant followed by a disco. By the end of the evening I was exhausted as all the girls wanted to dance with me and I had little opportunity to sit down.

The third day was taken up with my lecture at IRRI and I was looking forward to a quiet evening. No such luck. We all went to Josephine's restaurant where there was a cultural show and dancing.

'Please no more dancing,' I thought.

Being the only European in the establishment I was continually invited up onto the dance floor to make an exhibition of myself, but the girls loved it.

At last, on the Thursday morning, I had some time off to relax before setting off to the airport for my flight to Hong Kong. I was looking forward to three nights in my favourite place in the company of my little bunny girl, plus doing a bit of work in between to justify my visit. I won't spend any more time on the details, as I am sure you now know what I got up to!

Next stop Seoul. I had three days and nights there, but this time He-Rang was not there as Mr Im had organised some other activities for me. It had struck me some while ago that being entertained in some Far Eastern countries always involved the supply of pretty, nubile girls for my pleasure. This visit was no exception.

I had barely had time to freshen up after my late afternoon arrival in Seoul before I was whisked out by Mr Im. First dinner, with lots of soju and to top up my garlic levels and then on to the Manhattan nightclub. It wasn't long before a couple of lovely girls were brought over to our table by the Mama San for our approval. I have to say that in my opinion Korean girls are among the prettiest in the world. Mr Im agreed with the Mama San's choice and the girls joined us at our table. My companion could speak a little English and we managed to make some small talk for a while. She pointed to the door over in a dark corner of the club where the Mama San was seated.

'You can take me in the special room if you would like,' she whispered in broken English.

How could I turn down this opportunity? Mr Im was also going to use the room but suggested I went first. The Mama San unlocked the door and we entered a darkened room with dim red lighting that reminded me of a photographer's developing studio. In the centre there was a piece of furniture, which looked like an adjustable dentist's chair. The door lock clicked as the Mama San locked us in and my companion stripped off.

'How would you like me?' she said, pointing to the adjustable chair.

'I don't know, you choose,' I replied.

'I get on top of you, okay?'

'That's fine.'

I stripped off and got onto the chair, which was plastic covered and my now perspiring back slipped and squeaked on the padding.

'Put your feet here,' she said, pointing to the stirrups at the foot end.

With that she pressed a button and the chair adjusted its position until it was at 45° to the ground. At the level of my thighs there were two steps protruding from the sides of the chair onto which my naked companion jumped. There were also two handles at the head end, which she gripped and gradually slipped herself onto me. Slowly at first she started up and down on me, gradually increasing the tempo. It didn't take long until it was all over as much as I tried to make it last longer.

She passed me a towel and said, 'go clean yourself over there at the sink.'

When we had both dressed she tapped on the door so we could be let out. I paused by the Mama San expecting to have to pay but no, Mr Im had already settled the bill.

'You enjoyed?' she asked.

'Oh yes, thank you,' I replied and walked back over to our table with somewhat wobbly legs.

'Thank you Mr Im. Now it's your turn.'

Back to work the next day. I was on my best behaviour as I was being taken around by the MD of the company to visit Yonsei University's anatomy department. I was in my element on this visit - in the dissection room were at least twelve dead bodies lying around in various stages of dissection by the students. I hadn't smelt this smell since my pathology days and once smelt never forgotten. This was followed by a quiet dinner with more garlic and soju and an early night – unaccompanied!

I awoke refreshed and raring to go again. Mr Im was accompanying me again to visit both the EWHA Women's University Anatomy Laboratory and the National Institute of Health's Department of Animal Management. I was very impressed with the quality of sales leads that we were following up and equally pleased with my ability to solve their individual measuring problems. That was another two guaranteed sales from the days work so that warranted some celebration.

Mr Im explained that he was going to take me to a special place that was not advertised and you had to know where it was. It was a little one-street village, way out of the city, called Me Ar Ree. Not all the taxi drivers knew where it was so Mr Im had to direct him. All the traditionally built houses on either side of the street has large glass fronts, brightly lit, in which were gathered lots of pretty girls just lounging around. We walked up and down both sides and Mr Im asked me to choose where I would like to visit. It was so difficult as all the girls were gorgeous but I eventually made my choice. Once inside we were greeted by the Mama San and asked to choose our two girls. We were taken to the back of the house and shown into a dimly lit private room with a central, low glass table and cushions spread around on the floor. Once seated with our companions, plates of "food" were brought in including such delicacies as dried squid and fried locusts followed by large bowls of fruit. Soju was served with the compulsory single glass, which we all had to share in turn around the table. After the dishes were cleared the Mama San came in carrying a tray of miscellaneous items and announced that the girls would now put on a private show for us.

They both stripped off and began to dance around us erotically. Their show was to perform a variety of tricks using just their vaginas. The first trick was to insert a long candle until just the wick was showing. She gave a little grunt and a look on her face that showed she was straining. I was then invited to take hold of the wick and slowly withdrew said candle. The candle came out like a string of sausages hanging in a butchers shop. She had snapped the candle in at least four places just using the muscles in her vagina, the sections only connected by the central wick.

The second girl then sidled up to me with an unopened bottle of beer plus a bottle opener with a large plastic handle. I was invited to insert the bottle opener between her legs, which I did with trembling hands. I then had to hold the bottle of beer firmly whilst she positioned herself over it and skilfully engaged the opener with the crown cap. With a little twist there was a pssst as the cap came off and the beer started to froth out of the bottle. She quickly took the bottle back and poured the beer into a glass for me.

The next trick was a little more dangerous and I was glad that my companion had no pubic hair. She took a long match and inserted it into herself, asking me to sit between her legs, holding the matchbox with the striking side upwards. With a single stroke she ignited the match and after the initial sparkly flare, asked me to blow it out.

There were four more items left on the tray, a raw egg, a stainless steel kidney bowl, a felt tip pen and a large piece of paper. My companion picked up the raw egg and very carefully inserted it, without breaking it. She gave me the stainless steel kidney bowl and asked me to hold it between her legs. With a little squirm she squeeze the egg back out into the kidney bowl, still unbroken. She then picked up the egg, cracked it on the side of the bowl and tipped out the raw contents. Quick as a flash she scooped up the yolk in half of the broken shell, asked me to open wide and popped the complete raw egg yolk into my mouth. I managed to swallow it without too much trouble but needed a swig from the "specially opened" beer bottle to wash it down.

The last trick involved to the felt tip pen and paper. I am sure you can guess by now as to where the felt tip pen went. She placed the piece of paper on the corner of the table and asked me to hold it down.

'What is your name?' she asked and I told her.

With her legs straddling the corner of the low glass table and with gyrating hip movements, she wrote "to Graham with love'" after which I was invited to remove the pen.

After a bit of tidying up my naked companion took me by the hand, led me out of the room and up the corridor to a ladder which went through a hatch in the ceiling. She went up first and I followed. The ladder led into an attic room which appeared to have a low thatched roof. It was simply furnished with a blow up mattress, a bucket and several bottles of beer. She helped me undress and to my surprise got me to kneel in front of the bucket. Using a standard bottle opening technique this time she then poured the beer over my privates to wash them, then gently drying them on a towel. Then we got down to business on the mattress although I was a little reluctant at first, having seen what she could do with a candle! Needless to say it was amazing sex with her totally in control. Another quick wash over the bucket with beer and on went my clothes before descending the ladder and back to our room where Mr Im was waiting. It was quite obvious from his dishevelled looks that he too had been "entertained" in my absence. He had already paid the bill and after another couple of sojus we said goodbye to the girls and left.

Getting a taxi back into the city proved to be a bit of a problem. I can't remember what the exact time was but it was well past midnight. There were no taxi ranks in Me Ar Ree and the only thing to do was to wait until some more male visitors were brought in and quickly grab the taxi before he shot off.

'What an evening,' I thought to myself in the back of the cab. 'How on earth could anyone beat that experience?' I was soon to find out as I was leaving for Bangkok in the morning!

The Thai airlines flight from Seoul to Bangkok took about five hours and was extremely comfortable. The lady flight attendants were beautifully dressed in Thai national costume and looked like they had all had to pass through a template at interview, as they were all of an identical size. The meal and drinks service was impeccable and no request was too much trouble for them.

Thai people are very gentle, family orientated people who couldn't do enough to be helpful. I was met at the airport by Theera, the Managing Director of the company, who was accompanied by his wife. We spent a very enjoyable first evening in a restaurant, sampling some fantastic food that I had never heard of before but the best bit for me were the huge oysters that had to be cut into four with a knife and fork before eating.

Bangkok was also very hot and humid and after a day of being driven round to visit potential customers, I was soaking wet with sweat and feeling quite tired in the oppressive heat. Theera took me back to my hotel and informed me that he had booked something special for the evening and he would be back in an hour with his wife and two children. After a quick shower and change into some dry clothes plus some rehydration therapy with a large beer, I got my second wind and was ready for more action.

Theera had booked a table on a cruising restaurant boat that sailed up river for a couple of hours then turned round and made the return journey in one hour in the strong river current. We ate and drank fabulous food, just watching the world go by on the riverbanks. There are patches of river that were completely covered with lilies, which grow like weeds and were a huge problem choking the river up. It took regular dredging to keep control of these weeds and to maintain a navigable passage for the many ships using the river. Theera's son and daughter, aged eight and six, were delightfully behaved and his wife a good conversationalist in English. Towards the end of the meal she said to Theera, 'this is Graham's first time in Thailand. Why don't you take him for a Thai body massage? I will take the children home in a taxi?' My ears pricked up at this as I had heard about Thai body massages. After docking, I said goodbye to Theera's family and jumped into his car wondering what was coming next.

We drew up outside a building, which looked like a block of flats. Inside it was totally different. In the reception area there was a large glass partition with rows of tiered bench seats behind. Perched on these benches were numerous beautiful girls, each with a number pinned on their skirts. Some looked totally bored and indifferent while others were actively signalling to me to choose them. Theera asked me to take my pick, which was very hard as they were all lovely. I eventually chose number 69, as I thought this might be a good omen. She was let out of the glass cage and led me to the lift. I discovered that all the girls had their own rooms and each corridor was serviced by a lady selling drinks from a trolley.

69 unlocked her door and let me in. The room was furnished

seductively, with purple velvet drapes and low lighting. On one side of the room was a large, round bath in a tiled area and a blown up plastic mattress next to it. Above the tub on a pivoting attachment was a TV screen, constantly streaming porn movies. In the middle of the room was a large heart shaped bed supported on a central pillar. The mattress was covered in what looked like red felt but had no sheets on it.

I downed my Coca-Cola and stripped off. 69 was already in the frothy, bubbling bath tub and beckoned me in. The water was comfortably warm and the bubbles tickled as they rose up my body. The porn movie on the TV had already had an effect on me and the tickly bubbles heightened my sensitivity. 69 set to work, washing every square inch of me, paying particular attention to a certain organ, now almost reaching bursting point. After the best bath I had ever had, she asked me to step out, still covered in froth, and lie face down on the inflatable mattress. This proved to be a little difficult as "something" was getting in the way.

Now I understood why it was called a Thai body massage. It is not just a Thai person massaging your body, it's a Thai person using her whole body to massage you. 69 slipped and slithered all over me, replenishing the froth as required. I turned over and she slithered up and down on her bum over my chest and abdomen, occasionally and very seductively slipping me inside her for a brief moment. Eventually I could take no more and had to release what she had built up very skilfully. What an explosion. 69 looked pleased with her result. She gave me a nice white fluffy bath towel to dry off with and indicated that I should get up on the heart shaped red mattress in the middle of the room. Sitting there naked with my arms drawn around my knees, I felt like the classic picture of a fairy sitting on top of a fly agaric, the red toadstool with white spots.

After about ten minutes rest 69 joined me on the top of the giant toadstool and set to work on me again. It was quite surreal but very enjoyable. Little did I know then that some of the girls' rooms had peep holes in the wall where for a cheaper price, men could watch the activities going on. She brought me to a climax again and by now I was completely exhausted.

Back down in the foyer, Theera was waiting for me, drinking a beer.

'Did you enjoy that?'

'Yes thank you but tell me, how does your wife accept you visiting a place like this?'

'No problem,' explained Theera. 'If a man pays for sex and tells his wife it's okay. It is when he has a secret affair that it becomes a problem.'

I was beginning to understand now how Mr Im back in Seoul could justify having extramarital sex with no worries about what his wife thought.

After another full day's work we had dinner in a department store, which I found strange. It was my last evening in Bangkok and Theera wanted to take me to a typical Thai cocktail bar. We went to the Valencia Cocktail Bar where the first thing that greeted me was a naked girl on a raised platform behind the bar, gyrating evocatively around the shiny chrome pole. Waitresses were also walking around totally naked and as I sat down on a stool by the bar, one came along and sat on my lap, asking me what I wanted to drink. She leant over the bar and called to the bartender to get me a beer and settled back down on the ever increasing lump in my trousers. Her name was Rapee and was extremely attractive, with a bit of black African blood I thought. Theera explained that it was illegal to have naked girls in the bar so there was always a look out on the door who, on sighting the police, would warn the girls to go and put their bras and panties back on. That was acceptable. Rapee's function was to encourage me to stay in the bar and to keep buying drinks, not for sex, although I am sure that could have been arranged somehow.

Tomorrow was Saturday when I had a 10:25am flight to Singapore but then had the rest of the weekend to myself. I needed a bit of time to relax after the frenetic activities of the past two weeks. I had an idea of something that I wanted to try - to telephone Lena in Moscow from another country. From the comfort of my plush hotel room I telephoned the International Operator and asked if I could make a call to Moscow.

'No problem sir would you like me to connect you now?'

'Why not,' I thought, 'it is Saturday so let's give it a try to see if she was at home.'

'Yes please,' I responded to the operator

The line went dead for a while then followed by the familiar whirrs and clicks.

'Hello Moscow. Singapore here. Please could you connect me to....'

After a few more noises the operator said, 'you are connected now sir. Please go ahead.'

Lena was at home and very pleased to hear from me. Winter was approaching in Moscow and there I was languishing in the tropical heat and humidity of Singapore. We chatted for a while and then Lena made a suggestion.

'Why don't you try sending me some picture postcards from all your destinations. I would love to see where you are. They may not get here but it is worth a try. It indicates that we are in a relationship as the cards will be read.'

I agreed and after putting the phone down went straight to reception to buy some postcards. I selected ones that portrayed an experience that I had had, like eating Durian fruit and drinking a Singapore sling in Raffles hotel. Lena would love these, if she actually got to see them.

(I know that I am jumping forward in my stories here but I would like to let readers know that I must have sent over 100 postcards in total over a short time but she only ever received six. Where the others ended up I do not know and never will).

During my week in Singapore I had more culinary delights including a meal in the outdoor Hawker Food Centre. One stall caught my eye but I was horrified to see what was being cooked. Terrapins! The poor creatures were kept alive in tanks but when taken out, retracted their head and limbs back into their shells. In order to kill them, a chopstick was forced up their back passage to which they reacted by sticking their heads out. A swift blow from a meat cleaver on a blood stained wooden block remove their heads in one shop and into the pot they went. Drunken prawns were also on offer that were prepared by throwing live prawns into some hot alcoholic liquor in a pot and watching them jump around in the death throes.

I opted for chicken satay skewers first which were being fanned with a banana leaf over some hot coals. This was followed by barbecued prawns which were so big I could only manage two. The aromas in the centre were intoxicating. Waiters rushed around noisily taking the freshly prepared food to the diners who was seated in the central eating area. Drinks were ordered from a separate waiter and everything payable in cash as soon it was delivered to the table. The atmosphere was electric and very warm and humid, well into the late evening.

The following day I got a phone call from my office back home. Some equipment in Manila had gone wrong and seeing as I was in the Far East already, could I go and fix it! They obviously had no concept of distances here but I agreed I would try. I still had over a week to go back to Hong Kong and then on to Urumqi in China for seven days before my flight back home from Hong Kong. This could not be changed as it was part of my cheap, round the world flight. After looking at the available flights to Manila from Hong Kong the only way I could do it was a return flight on the same day as my journey home. I booked the 10:05am flight from Hong Kong to Manila, arriving at 11:45am and Manila back to Hong Kong at 7:15pm and hoped that there would be no delays as my homeward journey left Hong Kong at 11:00pm. No stress there then.

My working week in Singapore was busy as usual but I wouldn't have it any other way. After all I was there to help them make sales and to teach them new techniques. Patrick took me to lunch at his tennis club one day while Affendi – a Muslim had to go to prayers during the working day and asked me in to see his mosque. I am not a religious person but I can admire the architecture of a beautiful building. Singapore is a multicultural society with many different religions. They have the best of all worlds when it comes to holidays as they all celebrate each other's religious festivals and have lots more days holiday then we do.

My last night was spent in the Banana Leaf Restaurant again with my favourite dish, fish head curry. I didn't have any customers to meet the following day so my yellow, turmeric stained fingers were not embarrassment. Back in my hotel room I decided to call Moscow again. No problem. Straight through. It must only be calls from the UK that are regarded as sensitive and need special attention.

Saturday morning was an early start. An 8:30am flight to Hong Kong arriving at midday and 3:00pm flight to Beijing with an overnight stopover. Sunday morning was another early start with a flight to Urumqi again, travelling for some four and a half hours across the Gobi desert.

After an exhausting week in Urumqi I was desperate for a rest but there was no let up. On Sunday morning an 8:00am flight Guanzhou arriving at midday and then a connecting flight to Hong Kong. I was booked into the Hyatt hotel for two nights and had an important meeting with the British Trade Commission on the Monday. Tuesday was manic. I left my bags in the left luggage department at Kai Tak airport and caught my flight back to Manila. This was followed by a speedy car ride to the customer whose equipment had developed the fault. It took me a couple of hours to fix it and test it but the customer was very impressed with my service. A late lunch with Mr Tee then back to Manila airport for the 7:15pm flight to Hong Kong, only just managing to collect my bags in time to check into the night flight on Cathay Pacific back to Gatwick.

I only had two days in the office for the remainder of that week with some speedy debriefings and getting ready for my next trip to Moscow, Warsaw, Kracow, Budapest, Zagreb & Prague on Sunday.

I really was burning the candle at both ends but I have to say I enjoyed it and the fringe benefits were fantastic. Not the life for a family man but it suited me down to the ground during this period of my life.

Chapter 22

Moscow, October 1986

I only had two days in the office after my long Far East visit, to prepare for my next trip behind the Iron Curtain, which was to be very difficult and demanding. Fortunately I was working with Terry who had done most of the preparation for me. I was to fly to Moscow on Sunday for a week whilst Terry loaded a hired estate car and drove to Warsaw. From Moscow I had to fly to Poland and meet up with Terry to do a lecture and demonstration tour taking in Warsaw, Kracow, Budapest, Szeged, Prague and Zagreb. That made five Soviet bloc countries to visit in 17 days. Fortunately I had two passports, one "dirty" and one clean. This meant that while I was away in the Far East on one passport, my very efficient secretary could get my visas in the other, so long as I had left all the appropriate forms signed beforehand. Time wise it was pushing it, as it would only have taken one application to go wrong to ruin the whole visit.

I had not seen Lena for just over two months although I had spoken to her on the telephone a couple of times. The joy of meeting her again was almost overwhelming when I arrived at her flat on Sunday evening. Remember that her last words to me when I left Moscow in August were, 'yes I will,' and we hadn't had an opportunity to talk about this since. I must confess that my eyes 'watered' a bit as I hugged her close to me. I didn't know where to start with our discussions but I had prepared a list of everything I needed to do back in the UK. There was nothing we could do in Moscow until my divorce was finalised and got all the required documents translated into Russian.

'I am so happy that you said yes but I hope that it does not give you too many problems. You are very brave to take me on and I will do everything in my power to marry you and get you out of the Soviet Union.'

'Life in Moscow is very hard and I have always dreamt of living abroad. I love you so much and trust you to do what you say,' she confessed.

'What about your mother and the rest of the family? How do they feel?'

'I haven't told them much yet but I know they would be happy for me if I had a better life in the West.'

I showed Lena my list of documents required from my side and she too had been doing some homework. She gave me her list which read:

1). Translation of your passport into Russian.

2). Permission from your Embassy for marriage and translation into Russian.

3). Legalisation in the Ministry of Foreign Relations in the USSR.

4). Copy of the verdict of the Court about the dissolution of your marriage with translation into Russian.

5). If no document 2 your Embassy must state that "decision of the court comes into effect legally from..... (date)."

6). Visa with stamp of the hotel to prove you have travelled on the correct type of Visa.

'For safety it would be better if you had both documents 2 and 5. The biggest problem we have to overcome is that the issue of a license to marry a foreigner takes six days and must be done on a private Visa, not business, but they only validate it for five days in order to make a problem for you.'

'There is one more problem for me that I had not bargained for,' she said with a tear in her eye. 'They need a letter from my father giving me permission to marry you and I have no idea where he is or whether he is still alive.'

I mentioned a few chapters back that Lena's father had left her mother when she was only one year old and he had not kept in contact with her. She had no memory of him and did not know what he looked like, either then or now. There were no family pictures to go by and she had no idea of where to start looking for him.

'Mum has agreed to help me on condition that she doesn't have to see him if we do find him. She remembers some of his friends that he used to go around with and where they used to hang out and she will try to find them. She had a feeling that he had moved out of Moscow but didn't know where to.'

This was a real blow to both of us and added what seemed to be an impossible obstacle to an already long list of difficulties.

'What about Public Records Offices? Can you search any databases that might give you an idea of where he is?' I said, trying to keep her positive.

'Yes we had thought of that and will give it a try.'

I held her tightly to me and gave her words of encouragement.

'We both love each other very much and have a very special relationship which has developed even with geographical and political barriers between us. We can do it but it will take a great deal of effort from both sides.'

She seemed comforted by my determined words and agreed that she would start the search for her father.

'Apart from this new problem, we can't do anything else until my divorce papers come through and my estranged wife is in no mind to hurry it along to help me. I left her with everything, including the family house but she still can't bear to see me happy again. My solicitor tells me it could be another couple of months yet.'

My schedule for the week in Moscow was not too hectic so Lena and I had some time together during the forthcoming days that she could take me to visit more friends and relatives.

My first appointment on Monday was in the Institute of Bio-organic Chemistry where one of their analysers has broken down. I soon found the faults and identified the spare part needed to fix it so called Dr Dolganov over to explain the problem.

'It is the XYZ circuit board that has a fault. I can get one sent to you as soon as I get back to the office but I won't be back in Moscow for another month to replace it.'

'Why don't you telephone your office and ask them to send it while you are here?'

'I could try but it takes 24 hours to book a telephone call to the UK and then a couple of days to organise a delivery with all the correct paperwork.'

'I can help you. Come with me to my office and call your company now. They are three hours behind us so their working day is just about starting. This is what you need to tell them to do....'

He gave me some instructions, which made the hairs on the back of my neck stand up as we walked up the corridor. At the end of the corridor was a normal looking office door but when he opened it, it revealed a second padded door with sunken buttons in leather, looking like a mattress on the bed. Once inside he closed both doors and invited me to sit at his rather plush desk, not the sort of furniture I was expecting for a Director of a Scientific Institute.

'Please call your office now. Just pick up the phone and dial.'

'What? Don't we have to book a call?'

'No just dial.'

I picked up the phone with trembling hands and it was it good job I was sitting down as my legs had gone to jelly.

After a few of the usual noises I was now used to, I heard the UK ringing tone and a familiar voice answered. It was my secretary.

'Good morning Sharon, Graham here in Moscow. I need to speak to the Service Manager urgently and get him to do something for me, which he will need your help with. Please do not question what I'm going to ask you to do but do it today without fail. Can you get him on a conference call so you can both talk to me at the same time?'

She sensed the urgency in my voice and quickly got Brian on the line.

'Brian - I am sitting with Dr Dolganov in the Institute of Bio-Organic Chemistry in Moscow. I need an XYZ printed circuit board to repair his analyser while I am still here in Moscow. Please would you put it in a jiffy bag and simply address it for the attention of "Graham Hunter – Moscow". Then get a motorcycle courier to take it to the Aeroflot office in London so it can be put on tomorrow morning's flight from Heathrow.'

'Don't I need a proper address for you?'

'No. Just do as I say please and trust me. Aeroflot will be expecting the package. It will be arranged from here!'

I could sense that Sharon had been scribbling notes as we spoke and I knew that I could trust her to support me.

'Thanks guys. I will tell you all about it when I get home,' and put the phone down.

'Relax,' said Dr Dolganov, sensing my nervousness. 'Let's have some Russian tea.'

'That sounds like a good idea,' I said. My mouth had gone completely dry and I was still in a state of shock from what I had just done. I thought to myself, 'this man has got some clout if he can organise all that for me. I wonder what will happen tomorrow?'

The Russian tea arrived in tall glasses on an ornate silver tray. There was a pot of sugar lumps but no jam. I knew how to drink tea with jam but do I put the sugar lump in the tea? Dr Dolganov showed me how to do it.

'Just put a lump of sugar in your mouth and suck the tea over it.'

The sweet warm liquid was just what I needed and I crunched up the remaining sugar in my mouth and swallowed it. That felt better.

Dr Dolganov walked me back up the corridor and said that he would pick me up at my hotel tomorrow afternoon and take me to Sheremetyevo airport to pick up the package.

'You can have the rest of today off and tomorrow morning as well,' he said with what I was sure was a knowing smile.

I quickly got a taxi and asked the driver to take me to Lena's flat. I was getting quite good with my basic Russian now and was confident in getting around Moscow on my own. As I sat in the back of the taxi I thought came over me.

'I didn't tell Dr Dolganov what hotel I was staying in.. He knew!'

It was wonderful having some time to spend with Lena and not to have to get up early in the morning to get back to my hotel. We visited some more of her friends and Lena taught me how to flag down a private car and ask for a lift for a small reward, like a packet of Marlboro cigarettes.

I returned to my hotel after lunch and did the usual untidying of the bed. I still did this even though I knew that they knew that I had not been in it overnight. At the appointed time I went downstairs to wait for Dr Dolganov outside. A black Chaika (Russian for seagull) pulled up and one of the tinted windows came down. It was Dr Dolganov.

'Jump in next to me,' he said pointing to the passenger seat.

The journey to the airport took about 40 minutes. He could speak very good English and we chatted a lot about life in the UK. He had visited London once and was quite knowledgeable about life in the West, something that the authorities normally tried to keep hidden from the general public.

We approached Sheremetyevo airport, past the huge iron tank trap, which was a memorial to show how far the Germans had advanced towards Moscow in World War II before the weather closed in and stopped them. Instead of taking the now familiar road to the main terminal, Dr Dolganov took a back road, round the barbed wire perimeter fence. He pulled up at a checkpoint and the barrier rose almost immediately, allowing him to drive onto the tarmac runway. I was aghast at this. A director of a Scientific Institute allowed direct access onto the tarmac of an International Airport. We drove over to where the Aeroflot flight from London just parked after landing. He pulled up at the bottom of the steps and after a few minutes a man came down from the aircraft carrying a jiffy bag. He came up to my open passenger window and said,

'Mr Hunter, your package,' and handed me the brown packet.

We turned round and went back to the barrier in the barbed wire fence that again opened quickly on his approach and we were on our way back to the

Institute. At this point I didn't have words to describe my feelings over what had just happened. I sat quietly for a while, trying to take in what I had just achieved. It felt surreal. That was the only way I could describe it. This was the stuff of James Bond films!

Back at the Institute it didn't take me long to replace the printed circuit board and to get the analyser working again much to Dr Dolganov's delight and thanks.

'They like me here,' I thought as I made my way back to Lena's flat.

Chapter 23

Poland, Hungary, Czechoslovakia and Yugoslavia

I was always saddened to leave Lena but we had made some plans as to what we needed to do plus I was coming back in four weeks time to do an exhibition. It seemed strange leaving Moscow on an Aeroflot flight to Warsaw. The plane had that characteristic smell of Russian soap coming from the toilets that regular travellers had nicknamed "Breath of Lenin" due to the formaldehyde-like "fragrance." The cabin crew were miserable and were reluctant to answer any call on the call button. The meal service was terrible – always chicken on Aeroflot but at least they did have Russian champagne.

Looking out of the window during the flight, the scenery below seemed grey and drab whichever way you looked. Warsaw airport was equally unwelcoming but the queues and waiting time for passport control not quite as long as in Moscow. I managed to get a taxi but realised that I had not got any Zlotys. No problem. The driver was more than happy for a few US$ and a packet of Marlboro.

I was booked in the Forum hotel where hopefully Terry would be waiting for me with the car and all my equipment. He had arrived earlier that day and as arranged we met in the bar. It had taken him two and a half days to drive from the UK to Warsaw and he was feeling a bit tired. We agreed that as it was Sunday the following day, we could take our time setting up the equipment for our seminar on the Monday morning.

My talk went down well as everybody in the audience could speak English. Several people had brought samples to challenge my ability to solve their problems, which I did. The afternoon was taken up with meetings with the Government purchasing agencies, which went on a bit longer than we expected, resulting in a late departure to Krakow. We eventually arrived at thirty minutes past midnight, but at least I was able to share the driving with Terry now.

I won't go into too much detail about our travels around Poland, Hungary, Czechoslovakia and Yugoslavia but would like to relate some specific stories of events that happened during the trip.

As you can imagine, we had to cross several country borders and having expensive equipment in the car, had a lot of hassle with customs at each checkpoint. At every one we had to unload the car on exiting a country to allow the customs officers to scrutinise the contents and compare it with what was declared on our paperwork. Then, after reloading it into the car and driving the short distance across no man's land, had to unpack it again for inspection before we were allowed to bring it in to the next country. At one particular crossing into Czechoslovakia I was driving and was beckoned by an armed official into a shed for what was going to be a thorough search of the car as well as the equipment we were carrying. Not being used to the controls on the hired car, as I got out I inadvertently pressed something that set off the burglar alarm with a high pitched wailing. Before I could work out how to turn it off, four soldiers surrounded me, all pointing loaded automatic rifles at me and forcing me against the car. Terry somehow managed to explain to one of the soldiers that it was a hired car and eventually they released me. I was shaking for some while after this incident as never before had I been faced with four loaded weapons aimed directly at me and treated like a criminal.

After this little incident, our inspection was even more thorough with one guy crawling under the car with a mirror, presumably looking for hidden contraband. We eventually had our papers stamped and allowed to go. I should mention at this point that driving round Eastern Bloc countries was made more difficult by the lack of garages and often the lack of petrol in them when you found one.

Our hotel for the night had an underground car park and as we drew up, we were met by a man who appeared to know Terry. He asked if we needed any petrol, which we did, and after an exchange of US$, said he would help us. Once out of earshot of him I asked Terry, 'what was all that about?'

'In this car park you have to pay for your car to be guarded overnight. If you don't you will more than likely get petrol siphoned out of your tank. This guy is going to do just that and come tomorrow morning we will have a full tank of petrol.'

The drive across Czechoslovakia was amazing with lots of "fairy tale castles" on top of hills and beautiful countryside. After a week of seminars in each country my final destination was Zagreb in Yugoslavia where Terry dropped me off and continued the drive home on his own. I had one day's work to do before catching a flight home.

As usual, my itinerary was very intensive and I only had Friday and Monday in the office before leaving for Moscow again on Tuesday.

Chapter 24

Moscow, December 1986

Decomber was the month for the big scientific exhibition in Sokolniki Park again. I had managed to pack all the demonstration equipment for the truck delivery to Moscow after my drive around Eastern Europe and Terry had done the stand organisation. I had also managed to fit in a one-day flight out to Zagreb and back to install a newly delivered analyser.

I had stocked up with duty frees at Heathrow with all the usual bottles of whisky and Marlboro cigarettes, some lipsticks for Lena plus I had already purchased six pairs of ladies tights in Marks and Spencers as these were always in demand in Moscow. At Sheremetyevo airport I put my bags through the X-ray machine and the officer asked me to open them.

'Strange,' I thought. 'I've got nothing in them that was either banned or over my limit.'

The stern faced officer found the six pairs of tights and asked me,

'You are a man aren't you?'

'Yes,' I replied.

'Then why have you got ladies' tights in your luggage? Maybe you have a girlfriend in Moscow?'

'Might have…' I replied cautiously, not wishing to upset him.

'Import duty payable on ladies' tights.'

'Okay. How much?'

'Two ballpoint pens for me,' he said with a grin.

This was the first time I had met a Russian customs officer with a sense of humour and happily handed over a couple of pens. I quickly re-packed my case and wished him a nice day - American style, and went off to find my taxi.

I was very pleased to find that I had been put in the National Hotel, right opposite the Kremlin and Red Square and very convenient for the Metro. It was a beautiful, old style hotel with a grand winding staircase and banister rail and had recently been used as a location shoot for the film "Russia House" with

Sean Connery. It somehow gave you the feeling that you weren't actually in Moscow until you got to your floor and there was the Dezhurnaya. This Hotel was obviously a showpiece being right in the centre of the city and opposite the Kremlin. It often held small exhibitions in the foyer.

I did my usual and made my bed untidy for the benefit of the camera and packed a couple of carrier bags with the stuff that I was taking to Lena. I don't know why but I looked up to the ceiling to see what I thought was a ventilator duct and over the air outlet hole was a piece of material that looked as if it had been torn off in the corner.

'Someone has done something with that recently and replaced it very untidily,' I thought. I pulled a chair over and stood on it to inspect the material. The corner had originally been glued and now peeled back but without any glue to replace it so it was hanging loosely. I gingerly peeled it back again to reveal a microphone. At last I had actual evidence that my room was bugged. I carefully put the material back again and replaced the chair. Now I had a conundrum to solve. Had that been placed there recently because I was to be in this room? Have they seen me in the camera behind the mirror and now knew that I knew that there was a bug in my room? Would this influence how I would be treated on this visit?

Lena was naturally delighted to see me again but was anxious to see what I had brought in the carrier bags. The lipsticks were a perfect choice of colour for her and the tights would be a source of income. She could sell them to her friends or use them as rewards for favours asked. The whisky and cigarettes would be saved for a special bribe if required. I had also managed to keep the newspaper I had bought at Heathrow, which had not been confiscated by the customs officer. This was a real treasure for her. An English newspaper with actual news about what was really happening in the world plus adverts for products that would never be available in Moscow.

Although I was going to be busy during the coming days at the exhibition, Lena had arranged a few social events in the evenings. It got dark early now and was very cold so indoor events it was to be. Genya and Elena plus two other friends were coming round one evening and Lena asked me if I could get some meats from the deli section of a Beriozka shop. She was also going to take me to a cinema to see a film she wanted to see. It would be in Russian but I might be able to follow a bit with my limited knowledge of the language.

There was not a lot we could do as far as our marriage was concerned. Lena had been trawling through some documents in the library to see if she could find her Dad whilst her mother and two aunts had been making enquiries of people who might know where he was. One of Lena's aunts was a tailor and dressmaker and had a small shop on the outskirts of the city. She had regular customers who had been coming back to her for years and hoped that one of them might come into the shop one day and be able to answer her questions. The other aunt was a retired schoolteacher and now lived quite a long way out of Moscow and could not help much, other than asking her long-standing friends whether they knew of anyone who still kept in contact with Lena's Dad.

Every time I had been in Red Square I had always been amazed at the length of the queue waiting to get in to Lenin's Mausoleum and wondered just what the attraction was. As I was staying in the National Hotel which was immediately opposite Red Square, I thought that I could go and join the queue one morning before going to the exhibition, as long as Terry was in agreement. Of course he didn't mind so we agreed that I would do this the following morning.

At breakfast I could see from the first floor restaurant window that the queue was already starting to form. I gobbled down my hard-boiled eggs and black bread, quickly finished off my lukewarm coffee and made my way over to the Kremlin. I had never been in such a long queue before and questioned the decision I had made to join it, but I was here now so I might as well stick it out. At the stroke of 11 o'clock the doors were opened and the queue started to shuffle forwards. It took about 45 minutes before I got up to the steps in front of the Mausoleum and with some trepidation, walked through the huge bronze doors into the gloom. As my eyes grew accustomed to the low light, I could just make out a long descending marble staircase with an armed soldier standing in every corner. We had been told not to talk, keep our hands out of our pockets and not to make any sudden moves. I could see the soldiers twitching nervously if any of the descending queue stepped slightly out of line. The staircase led into a square chamber, dimly lit with a red light and in the middle was a glass sarcophagus with Lenin lying under black drapes in an open coffin with his head slightly elevated on a black pillow. People made their way slowly around three sides of the glass case, incurring grunts and pushes from the soldiers should anyone dare to pause for a longer look. It was very spooky, cold and quite threatening. The queue then made its way up a second staircase, emerging into the light behind the Mausoleum and in front of the Kremlin Wall Necropolis with the rows of commemorative plaques. The whole experience only lasted a matter of minutes but the queueing was certainly worth it.

I decided that while I was here I would pay my respects to one of my heroes, Yuri Gagarin, who was buried there. In my best Russian I asked one of the guards where his plaque was and with a disinterested grunt, he pointed a little further along the wall. I was only standing in front of the plaque for 30 seconds before another guard moved me along.

Work wise, the exhibition went well but this time we had a different lady translator. The KGB did not like their interpreters getting too pally and familiar with their British exhibitors so they changed them around every so often. Tanya was a young mother and very "mumsy" in her character, but her language skills were equally as good as Vladimir's. She always needed to be home after the day's work as her mother was looking after her child and needed to be relieved in the evenings. This meant that there would be no outings like Vladimir organised but this suited me as I would be going round to Lena's flat every night.

I had one appointment outside the exhibition during the week and that was to visit Dr Dolganov at the Institute of Bio-organic Chemistry to check on the instrument I had fixed during my last visit and to see if I could sell some more. He was very happy with everything and said he would come and visit our exhibition stand later in the following week. (Russian exhibitions used to last for 10 days which was a hard slog). Terry had suggested that I needn't go back to Sokolniki Park after my meeting and could have the afternoon off. I decided to go back to the National Hotel and treat myself to a lunch in the beautiful restaurant on the first floor with the magnificent view of the Kremlin and Red Square and then to change out of my suit into something more comfortable before making my way round to Lena's flat.

When I arrived she was practising on the piano and continued to play for my entertainment after I made myself comfortable. She played beautifully. She could play a lot of the classic well-known pieces without referring to sheet music, which, as a non-musical person, I found amazing. After she had had enough of the piano, she changed into her ballet point shoes and proceeded to give me a showing of the recent ballet she had learnt. I had to double as her partner, offering my hand as a balancing support whilst she did some pirouettes on tiptoe. She truly was a very talented girl. How lucky was I?

On Saturday evening Genya and Elena plus two more friends, Sasha and Lisa came round for eats and drinks. I got on very well with all of them and found myself the centre of attention, answering lots of questions on what life was like back in the UK. Genya expressed a specific wish to travel to Sweden as he had heard a lot of things about their lifestyle, which interested him. Working in a museum, he had access to a lot of information that of the average person could not get hold of.

The following evening we went to the cinema but I have to confess I can't remember much about the film. It was in Russian and I struggled to understand any of it as it was spoken so quickly. However I did enjoy "people watching" and spent more time looking around at the audience then watching the film.

Genya and Elena had invited us to their flat, which we went to on my last evening in Moscow. Elena was an expert mushroom gatherer and had lots of jars of preserved mushrooms of different kinds in her kitchen, plus home-made Kvass. Kvass was a mildly alcoholic beer-like drink made by fermenting Russian black bread. It was palatable enough and I did manage a few glasses.

My visit came to an end all too quickly and soon it was time to leave for the airport. I had now got a long list of things to bring back on my next visit which would be in two months time, after another trip to South Africa in between. Tanya, our interpreter, had asked for a babygro and shoes for her little daughter and had given me a drawing of her foot. Genya asked for a pair of black shoes-size 11, as he was a very tall man. The two ladies wanted tights and cosmetics. Before leaving Lena, I had asked her for her ring size as I wanted to get an engagement ring for her when my divorce was finalised. I had already purchased a sapphire in Bangkok and I wanted to take it with me to South Africa to get a ring made there, as diamonds were a bit cheaper. She guessed what I wanted to do and gave me a ring that she didn't often wear, which was her exact size - a K. I just hoped that I could manage to get this out as I had not got it declared on my incoming customs declaration document.

It was becoming the norm for Lena to accompany me to the airport so as to be with me for as long as possible but I hated saying goodbye. Each time I wondered whether I would see her again. If the KGB had a mind to, they could have taken her away for having a relationship with a foreigner. I arranged to telephone her regularly, at least weekly, so we could report on how we were each getting on with our individual tasks.

Fortunately I got through the security checks without the extra ring being discovered so at least I could get on with having an engagement ring made for her.

Sitting on the plane my thoughts went over the events of the last 12 days. Nothing had happened to give me a fright; the only event was finding the microphone in my hotel room. Maybe it was because they wanted the goods that I was selling and liked my efforts to support them, that my relationship was tolerated without any interference.

Chapter 25

South Africa and Moscow

1987 started with a 10 day trip to South Africa based entirely in Johannesburg. My company had launched a new product and our distributor in South Africa had purchased a complete demonstration package, which required a lot of training. My first three working days there concentrated entirely on training their staff with the exception of Kieren, their Cape Town based salesman. He was unable to get up to Johannesburg for family reasons but Bob had agreed to send him to the UK for some training in the next few months.

The following two working days had been set aside for a couple of in-house seminars and letters of invitation has gone out to all the customers in the region. Bob had been staggered by the response and we anticipated at least 20 people on each day. As before, customers had brought a selection of samples with them to see if this new piece of kit could help them. It was a great success and they anticipated that a lot of sales would be forthcoming.

To celebrate a good week, Bob took me and a few of the sales team to Gold Reef City for the evening.

What a place!

It was a cross between an amusement park and a museum. It was built on an old goldmine, which had closed in 1971 and was themed around the Gold Rush that started in 1886. The buildings had been constructed to copy those of the period and had many exhibits and demonstrations covering extraction of the gold from the mine to making pure ingots.

Lots of beers were consumed that evening followed by an enormous pile of steaks and ribs. During the evening I had the chance to speak to Bob about my sapphire and what I wanted to do with it. He agreed that if I left it with him, he would get a jeweller friend of his to design and make a ring around the sapphire using South African diamonds. Then when Kieren came over to the UK he would bring it with him and I would pick up the cost of his accommodation for a few nights. This was a win-win situation for both of us as there were restrictions on Rand to Pound conversions and this way no money exchanged hands and we both benefited from the deal. Perfect.

For a change I had flown on Air France to Johannesburg and my return flight was via Paris with a stopover in Abidjan, on the Gold Coast of West

Africa. It was a pleasant enough flight that took 19 hours in total, which was a bit of a killer. I was exhausted.

Back in the UK I had the luxury of 10 days without any travel so I started a property search for a flat to buy in the town where my office was based. I found one which took my fancy on paper, but as I was travelling to Moscow again shortly, I made an appointment to view it on my return.

Off to Moscow again for seven days as Dr Dolganov had purchased some more analysers which had been delivered but needed installing and commissioning. While I was there I asked if he wanted me to check over his other equipment.

'That won't be necessary,' he said. 'They have been moved to another site.'

I didn't think anything of this at the time but subsequently learnt that his Institute was regarded as "safe" by the export licensing authorities back in London but I had no idea where the equipment ended up. It was not my problem as everything I did in Moscow was with the full knowledge of the Trade Section of the British Embassy there and the Department of Trade and Industry's Russia desk in London plus Special Branch, as I was to discover later, and probably MI6 as well, but who knows.

Work aside, I was able to spend all my evenings with Lena. I had managed to fulfil my shopping list and arrived at her flat with loaded carrier bags. As usual she was delighted to see me again and attacked the carrier bags like a child opening Christmas presents. I could sense that there was something else on her mind as she was even more cheerful than usual.

At last it came out over supper.

'Graham, I have some good news to tell you. I didn't want to talk about it on the phone but we have found someone who knows where my father is. The only downside is that he is now living in Yalta in Crimea, which is nearly 800 miles away. I have written to him explaining what I want to do and I am hoping for his reply soon.'

I jumped up from the table and went round to give her a big hug. We didn't yet know how he would react but that was one big hurdle overcome.

'If he agrees to see me, Uncle Slava has said he will come with me as he was his brother-in-law once.' I was beginning to feel a little more optimistic about what we were trying to achieve but realised that there were many more hurdles to jump yet.

I shared my news about my flat hunting and had brought a copy of the Estate Agent's details with me. This was something alien to Lena as in Moscow, flats were allocated according to need, free of charge and all services supplied as well. The thought of having to spend tens of thousands of pounds on the flat, which had to be borrowed and paid back over many years, freaked her out.

'And you have to pay for electricity, gas and water as well?'

'Yes that's right. So although you thought I was earning a good salary, a lot of it goes on these expenses first.'

I had noticed that both Lena and her Mum did the washing up under a running hot water tap and often, if the phone rang, they would go and answer it, leaving the hot tap running. This would be a steep learning curve for Lena when (not if – let's be positive) she came to the UK.

My week came to an end all too quickly for me with some more sad goodbyes at the airport. I had another big trip to do to the Far East and China but would be back in Moscow the following month. Naturally I left with a shopping list of goods to bring back next time.

Chapter 26

Far East and China

It was going to be another of those hectic weeks between trips. I had got back from Moscow late on Tuesday evening and spent Wednesday having a debriefing session in the office. Thursday morning was with my solicitor trying to hurry the divorce proceedings along. He said that it shouldn't be too much longer now before the Decree Nisi would be issued and then twenty eight days after that comes the Decree Absolute.

London was my next stop to pick up my Visa from the Chinese Embassy followed by a visit to the Department of Trade and Industry in Victoria Street to apply for another export licence.

It was now Friday the 13th, not that I am superstitious, and it was the day for me to view the flat I was interested in. It was on the top floor of a block of five flats, two on each floor below, and was grandly called "the Penthouse". It was currently owned by a retired Doctor of Philosophy who smoked cigars, as I immediately found out as soon as I entered the flat. It stank of stale cigar smoke and had not been decorated for years. All the ceilings were brown from years of cumulative smoking and in the kitchen there were streaks down the walls where the condensation from the cooking had left dribbles of nicotine, as the drips ran down the wall.

The doctor made a half-hearted apology for the state of the place and explained that his wife had bad arthritis in her hips and could no longer do the cleaning. Neither could she manage the three flights of stairs, which was the reason why he was selling and moving to a bungalow.

Once I had got over my initial shock at the grime and smell, I could see the potential of the property. The sitting room and master bedroom were very big and both had a balcony on which you could have a table and chairs. The bedroom side had a commanding view over the rooftops into fields of wheat and barley, which were the main crops grown in this area. The sitting room side was not so picturesque as there was a builders' supply merchant next door and the view was blocked by the brick wall of a large warehouse. There was a small second bedroom, an adequate bathroom and a kitchen, which needed a total refit.

As I could see the potential of this flat I was very interested in buying it, but knowing that there was a lot of work needed to get rid of the nicotine stains and smell, plus putting in a new kitchen. I had already got a mortgage agreed in principle so went straight round to the Estate Agent and put in an offer, pointing out all the negative points that needed attention and why my offer was a lot lower than the asking price. I pushed the point that I had no property to sell so no chain and could complete as soon as everything was in place. Apparently the doctor hadn't started looking for a bungalow so it would be his side that would be slow.

It was now approaching closing time on a Friday afternoon and the agent told me that he probably couldn't give me an answer until Monday. I pushed him hard, telling him that I was leaving on Tuesday morning for a long business trip and I needed an answer before I left.

I had a weekend free - an unusual event - so I went to stay with some friends who I hadn't seen for a while. We had a lot of catching up to do and they were especially interested to hear about Lena.

Monday morning came and I had a call from the Estate Agent. The doctor had accepted my offer and would now start looking for his new bungalow. I supposed they could see that I was the ideal purchaser for him, as I had no chain behind me and no urgency to move in as I was hardly in the UK. I contacted my mortgage provider and gave them all the details but had to explain that I was leaving the country in less than 24 hours time and wouldn't be back for three weeks.

I was off to the Philippines early on Tuesday morning and had to be at Heathrow by 7:30am. I had booked a Thai Airlines flight via Bangkok and I was looking forward to a new experience. The flight landed in Manila at 3:30pm the following day where I was met by Mr T (I could now call him Richard) who took me to my hotel, waited for a while for me to change and freshen up and then took me for drinks and dinner.

Looking back on my life I couldn't keep up this exhausting schedule now but in my mid 30s I was lapping it up and enjoying every minute.

Richard had arranged six visits to customers for me, two on Thursday, three on Friday and one on Monday afternoon just before catching my flight to Singapore. He had got all the girls to come into the office on Saturday for a day's training session but had arranged something special for me on Sunday. All he would tell me was to wear jeans and T-shirt and be prepared to get a bit wet, so it would be a good idea to put my camera in a polythene bag. Lulu, Stella and Jane were going to take me out for the day and look after me. I couldn't wait!

Sunday came and the girls collected me from my hotel. They told me that we were going to Pagsanjan Falls, which was about a one and a half hour drive out of town. Lulu had borrowed a company car and was going to be our driver for the day. It looked so funny because all the girls were at least six inches shorter than me and Lulu could barely see over the steering wheel. Once out of the city onto the country roads there were numerous side stalls selling Buko Pie, a Filipino style coconut pie made from fresh tender young coconuts combined with a creamy filling and enclosed in a flaky pie crust. We were going to sample some of these on the way back.

Still not knowing what to expect, we arrived at a riverside location where there were some long, wooden, dug-out canoes on the beach with their paddlers touting for business. Lulu selected one, which was hauled into the river. One paddler got in first, sitting right up in the bow. Then Lulu got in followed by me and then Jane. There was not much room in the canoe so I had to put my legs around Lulu and Jane had to put her legs around me so that we were tightly wedged in. The canoe was dragged further into the water and the second paddler jumped in, wedging himself into the back. Off we went up river with several other canoes, equally loaded with passengers, paddling along in convoy. At first the scenery along the banks was quite flat with coconut palms growing in profusion. As we rounded a bend I was amazed to see what appeared to be a Japanese P. O. W. camp complete with World War II gun boat moored alongside a jetty. There were wooden huts made out of palm tree trunks and several lookout towers with a bamboo cabin precariously perched on top of a bamboo scaffold. The girls explained that this had been a film set for a war movie and had been retained as a tourist attraction. It felt quite eerie…

Round the next bend we were heading for some rapids, which I thought at first sight we were never going to get through. There was a small gap in the rocks on one side, which the paddlers aimed for. With a loud thud and a jolt we hit the rocky bottom and were told to sit tight. The two paddlers jumped out and man-handled the canoe over the rocks, quickly jumping back in as the canoe re-floated in the calmer waters on the other side. The current was getting noticeably stronger as we progressed up river and now the banks were becoming steeper. We passed through a steep gorge that eventually opened out into a lagoon. On one side of the rock face was a huge waterfall crashing down in front of a cave. Ropes had been strategically placed across the lagoon with small buoys keeping them afloat. The paddlers took hold of a rope and hauled us towards the mouth of the cave.

'I'm going to get wet here,' I thought, making sure that my camera was now safely inside the polythene bag. With sheer brute strength our two paddlers hauled us against the current and into the cave, just missing the full force of the waterfall at one side but near enough to get soaked by the spray. The noise of the waterfall was intensified by the echo in the cave and was deafening.

We sat in the cave for a while, looking at the colony of bats roosting in the roof above us. Coming out was a lot easier as the current was now in our favour and with a few strokes of the paddles, we were clear of the waterfall and heading for a beach area to get out and stretch our legs. While we stood watching, a group of ten guys arrived and quickly changed into swimming trunks. A log raft was dragged out from behind a rock and all ten guys clambered on board, sitting down cross-legged on poles, which were lashed together with ropes. Three paddlers, also in trunks, got on the rickety raft, and taking hold of the ropes slowly dragged the raft towards the waterfall. This was the "adrenaline rush" ride and not for the faint hearted. As they neared the waterfall, the raft bounced around in the strong currents and flexed with every up and down movement. They were going to go right through the waterfall! You could see the sinews straining on the arms of the three pullers as they fought against the torrent of water, crashing down from the rocks above. You could hear the shouts and gasps of the occupants as the water cascaded over them making breathing difficult. Another couple of pulls and the raft was through, much to the relief of its passengers. They paused for a while in the cave and then had to face the return journey. This was not so bad for the pullers as again the current was in their favour but the weight of the water crashing down on them made the raft flex violently again as it passed through.

Our return to base was much more relaxed, with the wooden canoe picking up quite a speed in the current. Back past the prisoner of war camp and the coconut palm lined sloping banks. I could barely move my legs as the canoe was beached but I had dried out a bit, as much as the humidity would allow.

'Wow,' I said to the girls. 'That was incredible. Thank you so much for bringing me here.'

We found the car and started the journey back. Lulu selected one of the side street vendors and we pulled in for Buko pie. I have to say it was delicious, very creamy and fresh tasting with a lovely pastry case.

Back at the hotel I barely had time to get out of my damp clothes when Richard rang to say he would pick me up in 30 minutes and we would go out for the evening.

He took me to a nightclub where they had a good cabaret according to him. We sat and drank some beers with snacks watching the acts with enjoyment. Then came the strippers. As if sitting between the legs of two lovely girls, with their soft suntanned skin pressed to mine wasn't enough to rouse my passions. Now I had a series of equally gorgeous females parading naked in front of me. There was one particular girl who had some European features and I thought was too beautiful to be doing this. I commented to Richard how lovely she was and he agreed. A few more beers and Richard went off to pay the bill. On his way back to our table I could see in the dim light that he had a girl on his arm.

'Graham,' he said. 'This is Jacqueline and she is yours for the night.'

I was gobsmacked. Jacqueline was the gorgeous stripper that I had commented on, now fully clothed and Richard had paid for her.

'I can't,' I protested. 'I'm getting engaged soon.'

'Of course you can. You are not properly engaged yet and anyway, if it's paid for there is no problem!'

I did feel slightly awkward as Richard dropped Jacqueline and I off at my hotel.

'I'll pick you up at 8:00am tomorrow morning. You've got some training to do with the girls. Don't be late,' he said with a grin.

Monday was really crammed full. Richard was getting his money's worth out of me. The morning was taken up with a training session for all 20 of his girls followed by a quick lunch. Then I was whisked off to visit a new customer, a paint manufacturing company, who wanted to measure droplet sizes of paint coming out of a spray gun.

'Have we got enough time?' I asked Richard.

'Sure we have. The company is quite near the airport and your flight doesn't leave until 3:30pm.'

I spent 30 minutes with his customer and thought that I could solve his problem. He needed proof that our analyser would work so I suggested that he gave me some samples of paint droplets on a glass slide and I would look at them when I got home.

Satisfied with the outcome of this visit, Richard whisked me off to the airport, with only minutes to spare before the Singapore airlines check-in desk closed.

'There,' he said. 'Told you we would make it.'

I arrived at Changi Airport in Singapore totally exhausted. Fortunately Changi is probably the best organised airport in the world as everything works smoothly and on time. By the time I reached baggage reclaim, my case was already there and outside the terminal there were plenty of taxis. I was soon in the Orchard Hotel again and ready for some relaxation. I decided not to go out but to have a few beers and a leisurely meal in the hotel and do my favourite thing- people watching in the Atrium.

After a while the disco in the corner of the bar started up so I repositioned myself a little nearer so I could enjoy the music. After a few popular songs the DJ played Elton John's "Nikita" which gave me goose bumps. The words described exactly my situation, a love affair with someone behind the "Wall". If my story has intrigued you so far may I suggest that you listen to this song and you too might feel the same emotions, as the words and music are spot on.

181

Oh I saw you by the wall

Ten of your tin soldiers in a row

With eyes that looked like ice on fire

The human heart a captive in the snow

Oh Nikita you will never know

Anything about my home

I'll never know how good it feels to hold you

Nikita I need you so

Oh Nikita on the other side

Of any given line in time

Counting ten tin soldiers in a row

Oh no Nikita you will never know

Do you ever dream of me

Do you ever see the letters that I write

When you look up through the wire

Nikita do you count the stars at night

And if there ever comes a time

Guns and gates no longer hold you in

And if you're free to make a choice

Just look towards the West and find a friend

The tears welled up as I listened to this and when it finished I just had to go back to my room and try to telephone Lena. As before, I got straight through. It was difficult to talk in detail about anything as we both realised we were being listened to. I could tell from the tone of her voice that she had something to say but daren't on the tapped phone line. I would have to wait for another two weeks before I would see her again and find out what she wanted to say. She had received one of my postcards but by now I must have sent at least 20.

I only had two and a half days in Singapore, visiting customers right up to my next departure time to Kuala Lumpur at 5:45pm. Then another two days in Kuala Lumpur where I visited five customers and spent my last evening with my distributor at a cultural show. No girls involved at this one!

Saturday called for another early start to fly from Kuala Lumpur to Jakarta in Indonesia where I had never been before. I had a completely free weekend doing touristy things such as visiting a scorpion farm and I did pamper myself with a massage.

On Monday morning I caught a Garuda Airlines internal flight to Surabaya where I had to install some newly delivered equipment. The plane was just about ready to take off when the captain came on the PA system. *'Ladies and gentlemen, we have a slight imbalance in the plane before take-off so could I ask all the passengers in first class to go to the back of the plane and take their seats there until we are airborne.'*

The very disgruntled first class passengers made their way to the back of the aircraft and the flight crew started to do their safety demo. Unfortunately the captain forgot to say, *'cabin crew please take your seats for take-off,'* and put the aircraft into full thrust. All the poor little air hostesses ran uncontrollably down the aisle and ended up in a heap next to the rear-seated first class passengers. I couldn't believe it! But I did subsequently learn that Garuda did not have such a good safety record! I only had the one visit to do in Surabaya and the next day I had an even more exhausting flight schedule. Surabaya to Jakarta, Jakarta to Singapore, Singapore to Hong Kong, followed by Hong Kong to Shanghai. In Shanghai I had three days to support my agents at an exhibition.

The only thing I would like to share with you from my Shanghai visit was a culinary experience I will never forget. I was told that this was the season for a special fish, which swims up the Yellow River. It was a special breed of carp and was called Yin Yang Fish on the menu, a regional speciality and often referred to as the "dead and alive fish". Little did I know what was coming next. The fish was scaled and gutted while it was still alive, leaving the head intact. This fish exhibited an unusual trait that even when decapitated, its head stayed "alive" for some time with its eyes rolling, mouth opening and gills flapping for many minutes. The head was wrapped in wet paper towel and its body lowered into hot oil. It was served on a plate with its head still alive and the idea was to eat it's body before the head "died." I was disgusted but custom dictated that as an honoured guest, I had to eat the food put in front of me, as refusal was an insult to my hosts. I don't know how I managed it but I did. The poor creature was watching me eat it!

I don't wish to bore you, dear reader with lots of flight times but I did need to make you aware of the extremely tight deadlines I had to adhere to and how I changed from one set of cultures and customs to a completely different one, sometimes within 24 hours. On the Saturday I took the Cathay Pacific flight from Shanghai to Hong Kong and then their onward flight to Gatwick, arriving on Sunday morning. After an overnight stay in a hotel in Gatwick I transferred to Heathrow for the morning British Airways flight to Moscow. In order to achieve this I had to make sure that I had all the appropriate visas in my two passports before setting off three weeks ago.

One of the things I had to be particularly careful of when travelling with two passports was entering and leaving a country using the same passport. You can imagine the problems it might have caused if I entered on one and exited on the other. Effectively I would have been recorded as entering one country and never leaving, or leaving a country with no record of having entered it.

Chapter 27

Moscow, Sri Lanka, Australia and Singapore

L ena was in high spirits when I arrived. She couldn't wait to tell me that she had received a letter from her father and he would like to see her. As soon as the weather got a bit better she would go to see him with Uncle Slava. It would involve a long train journey of over 800 miles and a couple of overnight stops somewhere. She didn't know how the meeting would go as she had never known him and Lena felt very bad about him having left her Mum to bring her up own her own. Anyway she would have Uncle Slava with her to mediate if necessary, but didn't want to upset him in case he refused to write the letter giving her permission to marry a foreigner.

Not much happened that week. We enjoyed each other's company when I was not working and even managed a trip to the Russ Restaurant one evening - Lena getting us through the Ring of Steel using her domestic passport. She hated the "System" and told me that she had been expelled from the "Young Communists" for failure to conform. Lena did however drop one bombshell. She had recently been offered a scholarship at the prestigious Moscow State Tchaikovsky Conservatory. This was where all the great Soviet pianists had trained and places there were highly prized.

She had turned it down!

After considering everything that was going on in her life, she realised that this offer was possibly a ploy to make her stay in the USSR and ditch me. A very clever trick, which looked like a fantastic opportunity but would tie her into the Conservatory for years.

'I turned it down for you,' she said very emotionally. 'I love you and want to be with you and this offer would have stopped that.' If this really was the case, the gauntlet had been thrown down in the start of a campaign to stop our relationship.

I left Moscow this time feeling a bit nervous. What else would be thrown at Lena to try to stop us seeing each other? It must have been a quandary for the "System" as they desperately wanted the products I was selling and didn't want to exclude me from travelling to Moscow but still needed to stop our illicit relationship.

Back at home I had a mound of paperwork to deal with for the purchase of the flat. Fortunately I was back in the UK for four weeks, something I hadn't done for a long time. A survey needed to be carried out before the mortgage company would finalise their offer. My solicitor had written to me asking for confirmation of my agreement with my ex wife that I would leave her the family house in its entirety. She was also asking for all the utility bills to be paid for a two-year period plus her credit card. She knew that I was desperate to get the Decree Absolute and was asking for as much as possible. The solicitor thought that this was completely unreasonable and went back with a counter offer of one year on the utility bills and six months on the credit card, with a cap on it so that she couldn't go mad and max out on it every month. I had to get this sorted out as soon as possible as I would be away for over a month.

Fortunately it was all agreed before I left on the 16th of April, bound for Colombo - Sri Lanka. I can't remember why but I had to go via Singapore, which seemed strange as you fly past Sri Lanka to come back again. Unfortunately at Changi airport the plane taking us to Sri Lanka had developed a mechanical fault and we had to be bussed off to the Amara Hotel for an unexpected overnight stop. Never mind, it was Saturday and I didn't have any appointments until Monday morning.

My jobs in Sri Lanka were to install some equipment in the University's Radiology Department and to give a lecture at the Atomic Energy Authority on Tuesday afternoon. All was going well until partway through my lecture. I was interrupted by a very worried official who said, 'sorry to interrupt you Mr Hunter but something terrible has happened and you must return to your hotel immediately. A car is waiting for you outside. Please could you gather up your things and come with me straight away.'

'What on earth could have happened to instigate this action?' I thought. My driver sped off and I must say that the roads seem remarkably empty.

'A bomb has gone off sir, and the military have effected an immediate curfew, shutting the city down completely.'

As I approached my hotel I could see a group of people standing by the main door and a pile of wooden planks heaped up on the floor.

'Please Mr Hunter come inside quickly. You are the last guest back in and now we have to board up the doors and windows. We are confined to the hotel until further notice.'

I was aghast at this comment and went straight to the reception desk to get more information. And eighty-pound bomb had been detonated in the central bus garage when it was heaving with people. 113 people had been killed and it had left a 10 foot crater in the ground. The Tamil Tigers had claimed responsibility and the military feared armed repercussions and hostage-taking.

'But I have a flight to Singapore and Brisbane in the morning. What can I do?' I pleaded.

'I am not sure if the airport is still operational but the road into it is certainly closed,' said the receptionist. 'I will try to find out and let you know. Please try to relax and keep calm. The rooftop pool is open and drinks are on the house at the moment so why don't you go up there.'

I think that this was done in order to get guests off the ground floor as it was now dark with all the windows and doors boarded up. I must admit I did feel nervous but free drinks by the pool did sound good and definitely needed.

After a couple of hours the receptionist came up to find me.

'Mr Hunter, the airport is still functioning on a limited basis and your flight to Singapore is still on. They want to get tourists off the island as soon as possible. Please can you be ready to check out in the morning and someone will pick you up.'

I ate a hearty breakfast in the morning, not knowing what was going to happen and when I might be able to eat again. I sat myself down in reception and waited. Eventually someone arrived outside the boarded-up door and the boards were quickly taken down.

'Mr Hunter, your ride to the airport (note: not taxi) is waiting outside.

I gathered up my bags and went over to the door. Waiting outside for me was an armoured personnel carrier with gun turret and an army jeep with two rifle-toting soldiers in the back seat. My luggage was bundled into the back of the Jeep and I took the front seat. It was a scary drive through the city. The roads were empty and there was a tank on every major road junction. My jeep kept very close to the armed vehicle in front as we made our way up the main road to the airport. The perimeter road of the airport looked like a tank car park and it was apparent that they were expecting trouble. I could see a Singapore Airlines plane in the airport and hoped that it was mine. My cortege was allowed through the barrier and I was dropped off at the passenger terminal.

Yes, it was my plane and the ground staff were anxious to get it airborne as soon as possible so I was hurried through to the departure lounge with minimal fuss. We were soon on our way and the captain came on the public address system with comforting words and assured us that we were fine and would arrive in Singapore on time. I heaved a sigh of relief as the tension began to leave my body.

My next flight was an overnighter to Brisbane where I had two days' work to do, installing equipment at the Commonwealth Scientific and Industrial Research Organisation, CSIRO. As in South Africa, different sales people had been allocated to look after me at each location I visited, and Roger was my contact for Brisbane. I had the weekend free before flying on to Sydney and

Roger really did me proud. On Saturday we had a walk in a rainforest followed by a barbecue at his parents' house and a tea party back at his home.

I was interested to observe the barbecue culture, as it was very sexist. The men gathered round the barbecue swilling ice-cold beers while the ladies prepared the salads. It was not done to go and talk to the ladies or for the ladies to come near the fire pit. I have mentioned before that I couldn't get on with swilling ice cold Fosters from a bottle as it was far too cold for comfort. Most people had a pool and Roger's parents were no exception. The sign by the pool made me laugh. "Dear guest. Welcome to our 'ool. As you will see there is no P in it. Please keep it that way!" Obviously the ice cold beers had caught some swimmers short on occasions.

On Sunday we drove up the Gold Coast and visited a bird sanctuary followed by another barbecue in the evening and more ice cold beer swilling. I have to say that I was made to feel very welcome in a family environment, which, as an inveterate traveller, was far more enjoyable than spending time alone in a hotel.

My week in Sydney was taken up with helping set up an exhibition and manning the stand for three days, which kept me busy and made the time fly by. As it happened, the brother of my Uncle (by marriage) had emigrated to Australia years ago and although I had never met him and his wife, I had contacted them before my visit and had been invited to spend the weekend with them, near the Blue Mountains. Naturally I jumped at this invitation and they kindly came to pick me up after the exhibition had closed. At their house I had an experience that was new to me. I was offered a gin and tonic and asked to get the lemons.

'Where from?' I asked.

'From the garden of course,' came the reply.

They had a lemon tree in full fruit and I picked my own. You may find this silly but I thought it was fantastic.

The following week was the usual rush from city to city by plane. Sydney to Melbourne, Melbourne to Adelaide and Adelaide to Perth where I spent a few days in what was described as the city that was further away from any other city in the world. It did feel kind of remote. Then Perth to Singapore and back to my favourite Orchard Hotel on Saturday.

My week in Singapore was going to be very different as I was doing a major scientific exhibition and my new colleague at work who had recently been appointed to look after Western Europe as an export area, had been given the treat of coming out to help me. He had heard some of my stories and was keen to experience some things for himself. I met him at Changi airport and briefed him on the week ahead in the taxi.

Our distributor had done most of the work in organising the exhibition so it was down to Sean and me to set up all the equipment. This didn't take too long on Sunday morning leaving the rest of the day for me to show Sean around. I remember my first time here and tried to make it just as interesting and exciting for him as I first found it. We had a Singapore Sling in Raffles Hotel, lunch in the Hawker Food Centre plus a Durian fruit. Then we had a stroll up Orchard Road so he could experience all the persistent salesman trying to sell him watches and handbags, and persuade him to have a suit made - and then we came to the massage parlour.

'Fancy a massage Sean?' I asked.

'Why not,' he replied and we went in. The lady greeted me as one of her regulars. I introduced her to Sean saying that it was his first time here and could she find a nice girl for him.

'I got just the girl for you today. Come with me gentlemen,' and led us up the corridor.

'You will go in here,' she said to Sean, opening the door for him. I had not told him exactly what to expect, as I wanted him to have the same experience as I did the first time.

'Enjoy,' I said to him as he closed the door to his room.

I was put in the next-door room and although they were soundproof, I could just imagine what he was going through.

After our 45 minute session, Sean emerged looking very pleased with himself.

'That was lovely,' he said with a grin on his face.

The week went well at the exhibition and in the evenings I introduced Sean to more culinary delights at the Seafood Centre and the Banana Leaf restaurant. We packed up the exhibition on Friday afternoon, leaving Saturday as a free day before flying home on Sunday. I had never been to Singapore zoo, which boasted the largest captive population of Orang-Utans in the world. They were advertising an "Orang-Utan experience" so we decided to give it a go.

The "experience" was to have tea with an Orang-Utan and be able to be close up with one. Tea was a coconut, which the Orang-Utan drank the milk from while Sean and I were seated by her side. After she had finished, she put the coconut down and then put her arms around the both of us and gave us a hug. It was the most amazing experience and I will never forget looking into her eyes and seeing an intelligent animal looking back into mine. I would have liked to have known what she was thinking. It was a very humbling feeling and I treasure it to this day.

It made a nice change to have a colleague accompany me on the long haul flight back to Gatwick, arriving at 6:25 in the morning. I got back home to find a pile of mail including one letter to say that my Decree Nisi had been issued and another giving me an appointment to go to the County Court on Wednesday, just two days away, to finalise some details. I had only just got back in time to meet this appointment. In another envelope was an appointment on Thursday to collect my Decree Absolute. I was elated. Things had started happening.

Chapter 28

Moscow, May 1987

A s soon as I knew that I was getting my Decree Absolute on Thursday I telephoned the local Registrar's Office for an appointment first thing on Friday morning. I needed to apply for a "Certificate of No Impediment to Marriage Pursuant to the Marriage With Foreigners Act 1906" which would be needed when we booked our wedding date.

Before I left for my previous trip this month I had done some research on how long it took to get documents translated and legalized through the Foreign and Commonwealth Office. I was informed that it was normally around three weeks. Not wanting any further delays I wondered whether I could get some help from my contacts in Moscow, so I contacted the lady I dealt with in the Trade Section of the British Embassy in Moscow. She confirmed that she could get it done within three days of receipt of my documents and if I sent them to the FCO with an explanatory letter, they would put my documents in the diplomatic postbag. I could then pick them up from the Embassy during one of my frequent visits to Moscow. I needed my passport and all stamps on all pages translated plus my divorce certificate and the certificate of non-impediment. I also needed a letter from the British Embassy giving their permission for the wedding to take place.

I had booked a City Break to Moscow for the last weekend in May just in case there was anything we could do with our documents. Unfortunately we weren't quite there yet so were resigned to the fact that we could just spend the weekend together enjoying the fine Moscow weather at that time. We walked hand-in-hand round of the parks and amusement grounds that Muscovites flock to in good weather, learning a lot more about each other.

Lena told me that she was travelling to Yalta at the end of the week to visit her father, hoping to get his written permission for her to marry me. She was naturally very nervous about this as she had never seen him before but she would have Uncle Slava with her for support. I would be back in Moscow the following week and hopefully we would have good news.

Suddenly as we were walking along a wide Boulevard a large black Zil came screeching up behind us, mounted the pavement and stopped us in our tracks. Two "heavies" got out and walked over to us in a very threatening manner. They started to talk to Lena very aggressively but I could not understand what they were saying. Lena turned to me and told me to get my UK passport out of my pocket and tell them that I was a UK citizen here on business and to stop bothering us. I wasn't prepared for this but did as she said. I waived my passport at them and said, 'I am a British citizen here on official business so stop bothering us and go away.'

One of the "heavies" took my passport and spent some time scrutinizing it. My heart was pounding, not knowing what he was going to do but eventually he returned it to me, got into the car and drove off.

'What was all that about?' I said to Lena.

'They were KGB "heavies" trying to put us off our relationship as it is not acceptable under Communist rules.'

It had really given me a scare and I couldn't stop shaking.

'Let's go back to my flat now and stay off the streets for a while. I was expecting something like this might happen,' said Lena, equally as shaken as me.

The following morning I went back to my hotel to change and it was then that I found the letter from Mr Pankratov under my door (as described in chapter 10) which added to my concern about someone knowing exactly where I was all of the time. I did not regard Mr Pankatrov as a threat as he seemed to be helping me with my business in Moscow. I found it hard to believe that on the one hand I was being encouraged to do business in Moscow whilst at the same time being scared off having a relationship with a Muscovite.

I went to the meeting with Professor Rubin that Mr Pankratov had organized for the Monday and came away very pleased that there could be a lot more new business for me. Although I was working on a holiday, I had no trouble with this as I was being paid to visit Moscow frequently, which enabled me to see my fiancée.

I returned home on the Tuesday and sent off a letter to the FCO enclosing my documents for translation and explaining that I was travelling to Moscow the following week so could they get them out to the Embassy as soon as possible.

I waited until Sunday before trying to telephone Lena but her mother answered and told me that she was not home yet. I felt sick with worry, not being able to talk to Lena and find out how she had got on. My next trip was on Thursday and I was hoping that I could go to the Embassy to pick up my translations and report that we now had all the necessary documents to apply for a wedding licence. I waited until Tuesday and rang again. She was home. I could tell from the tone of her voice that it must have gone well but she would not discuss it on the phone. I would have to wait until Thursday to see her and find out how the visit went. At least it sounded positive, which relieved my nervous tension a bit.

Thursday came all too slowly for me but eventually I got there and rushed round to Lena's flat. She had met her father, who wasn't at all like she expected and told him about our relationship and the fact that we wanted to get married. He was actually very happy for her and hoped that she might find happiness in the West, *if* she could get out. Of course he wrote the letter giving his permission but it had taken longer than expected as they had to find an official to witness the letter and put an endorsing stamp on it.

We were both elated with this good news, realizing that another obstacle had been overcome but we still had a way to go yet. I had an appointment the following morning with Dr Dolganov again and had to get back to my hotel that evening to prepare for it. As soon as I could after my meeting I found a public phone (not bugged) and telephoned the Embassy to check on my documents. Yes, they had arrived and would be ready for collection on Monday morning. This left the weekend for us to spend more time together but in the knowledge that we were getting nearer to our goal.

On Monday morning we both went to the British Embassy but Lena was not allowed in and had to wait outside on the street. My documents had all been translated and certified and I showed Miss W the letter from Lena's father.

After reading it (in Russian) she said, 'Oh dear. I can see a problem...'

My heart sank. 'What problem?'

'There is a difference in the spelling of your first name in Cyrillic and this won't be accepted by the Russian authorities. There is no Russian name equivalent to Graham so it is translated literally as it sounds. In our documents we have used Грэам but Lena's father has used Ггэхзм. Both sound very similar but look different.'

I couldn't believe it! To get so far and be beaten by a simple spelling error. It wasn't possible for Lena to go and get another letter from her father and all my documents had been translated and legalized and could not be changed. I was gutted.

'Is there anything we can do about it?' I asked.

'I know,' said Miss W. 'I could write a letter explaining the difference and say that either translation of your name is acceptable. I could do it on Embassy headed paper and put an official stamp on it - the Russians like stamps!'

'Oh please,' I said.

Miss W could sense the desperation in my voice and confirmed that she would do it immediately if I could wait for about 30 minutes. Of course I agreed but thought of poor Lena waiting outside on the street, not knowing why I was taking so long. Miss W returned holding a lovely looking document on official paper with big stamp over her signature.

'That should do it. If you have any problems please let me know.'

When I got outside Lena was desperate with worry.

'What kept you so long?' she said.

I explained what had been done and hopefully everything was now in order. With a sense of relief we made our way back to the flat. My emotions had just been on a rollercoaster ride and I felt totally drained. I was leaving Moscow following day and had no room for errors. Now we had to plan for the next obstacle to overcome - applying for the marriage licence.

Chapter 29

The Wedding Licence

Although I always found ways of enjoying my work behind the Iron Curtain, I was excited to be returning home from Moscow as I was due to exchange contracts on my flat and moving in. I had booked two weeks holiday, a rare luxury for me, as I knew how much work had to be done to clean up after the previous cigar smoking occupant. I had no furniture as I had been lodging with my parents for some time and would have to go to a house clearance shop to get some second-hand items such as a bed and chairs. My thought was that when Lena came over, she could enjoy the experience of furnishing her new home from scratch.

The other very important thing to do during my holiday was to go to the Russian Embassy to apply for my wedding application Visa. This was a very special and hard to get Visa, and what proved to be the most difficult hurdle that we had to overcome. Lena and I both knew that this type of Visa was only valid for five days but the procedure to get the wedding license took six days. This was their way of stopping all but the most intrepid from marrying a foreigner.

Moving in day came with no problems particularly as I had very little to move in. My first thing was to go out and buy a mass of cleaning materials and ladder and set to on getting the nicotine stains off the walls and ceilings. What a disgusting job it was. It must have taken the best part of a week before I could even consider putting a coat of paint on. Before I took my holiday, I had a phone call in the office from Bob in South Africa. He had got Lena's ring made and was very pleased with it. He then asked if it would be convenient for Kieren to come to the UK for training during the second week of July and as per our deal, stay with me instead of paying for a hotel in exchange for getting the ring made with my sapphire. There was still a restriction on South African nationals taking currency out of the country so our little arrangement was a perfect solution. This had put a little more emphasis on the time I had to get my flat into a habitable condition and entertain an overseas visitor.

I took a day out from my decorating schedule to go to the Russian Embassy in London to apply for my next Visa. I made sure I took all my documents with me to prove that I was ready to apply for my wedding licence. As before it was a good idea to get to the Embassy very early to make sure that you would be seen before they shut. The lady I saw was very brusque with me, probably because she disapproved of a Russian marrying a foreigner, or maybe because someone was being given the slimmest of chances of permanently getting out of the USSR. Nevertheless it was approved and I got my five-day visa. Now I had to book a flight on the specific dates. I gave Lenin a wink and a smile as I left the Embassy. You know, just for luck.

I got a flight on Thursday, 30th July, returning on Monday 3rd of August which gave me Friday as the only working day to get our application in and then go to the Palace of Marriages to get a date - but only if we got the licence granted first. It was a big gamble to take but had to be done.

Back at my flat I invited some friends for a "decorating party". They would help me do some painting and in return I would keep them topped up with food and wine. This worked well and enabled me to get some second hand furniture delivered before Kieren was due to arrive.

On the day of Kieren's arrival I drove to Heathrow to meet him and thought that during the journey back to my flat I could brief him on my temporary furnishings and that it was not the same as staying in a hotel. Of course he didn't mind and like me preferred to the company of a local to being alone in a hotel. He waited until we got back to my flat before he took out the ring and gave it to me. It was beautiful and I was so pleased with it. I was sure that Lena would love it too, particularly as it was made specifically for her from gems obtained from countries I had worked in.

I must admit that during the four days that Kieren was with me my mind often wandered from work to wondering how we would get on with the wedding license application. I had to wait another 2½ weeks before I went back to Moscow. During that time I made several phone calls to Lena and although we couldn't talk openly on the phone as we knew we were being listened to, she reminded me to bring a good supply of duty-free items for presents. She didn't mention the word bribe but I knew from our discussions during my last visit exactly what they were for. She also said that she would make the arrangements for our two visits on the Friday.

Thursday eventually came and I loaded myself up with Duty Frees at Heathrow before getting on the flight. After checking in to my hotel I rearranged all my goodies into separate carrier bags, which were quite heavy. I thought that it would be best to take a taxi rather than fight with the crowds on public transport. Down at the taxi rank I had no difficulty in finding a willing driver as I am sure the boldly labelled duty-free carrier bags may have given them an idea of what I was carrying and what they might get paid with. It was a very hot day and the sweat was pouring off my forehead as I staggered into Lena's flat with all my bags. We had an appointment at 11:00am the following morning in the Soviet Registry Office, which was housed in the Ministry of Internal Affairs building, a huge Stalinist "wedding cake" style building so typical of the Moscow skyline. The Palace of Marriages had also agreed to see us whenever we could get there in the afternoon.

We knew we would have to bribe the Registrar to give us the licence but in a way that would not get him into trouble. The plan was that we would put a bottle of whisky and 200 Marlboro cigarettes in a plain carrier bag and put this carrier bag into another, in which we would put an equally heavy object such as a portable umbrella. You'll see why in a moment.

I needed to look smart for these two meetings so had to go back to my hotel in the morning to change into a suit. Lena got the taxi driver to wait for me while she sat with him. Suited and booted I checked over my documents again, put the ring in my pocket, took a deep breath and made my way back down to the taxi. My heart was already racing and my mouth was dry so I was glad I had remembered to put a supply of peppermints in my suit pocket. We pulled up outside the Ministry building feeling intimidated by the sheer size of this skyscraper. We made our way up the steps to the huge bronze front door. As usual there was a thug on guard at the door who looked us up and down as we entered. He had obviously clocked the carrier bag but could not see the contents. We were told that the Registrar was on the 12th floor so up we went in the lift. Lena gave me my last instructions on how we were going to do this as the doors opened and there we were...

No turning back now.

The Registrar had a huge desk with the usual picture of Lenin looking down on him from behind his seat. We got out all our documents, spreading them neatly on his desk. He scrutinised them all and made copious notes in a big file before starting to fill out a form, which I could see was headed *Wedding Licence* in Russian.

After blotting the ink dry he said to Lena that we would have to come back next Tuesday to pick up the licence once it had been authorised. Lena explained to him that because of my five day Visa, I had to go home on Monday and would not be able to collect it. His answer was emphatic. '*It will be ready on Tuesday.*' She then started pleading with him for help whilst he maintained his immovable stance. At this point Lena looked at me then looked down at the carrier bag and looked the Registrar straight in the eye. He nodded without making it sound. I very carefully removed the inner carrier bag containing the whisky and cigarettes and passed it over his desk. Very quickly he opened his bottom drawer and put the contents in it. He then took a rubber stamp and pad and without a sound being made, inked the stamp and gently placed it on our licence with a rocking motion. He blotted the ink dry and handed it over to Lena saying, 'I am sorry but if your fiancé's Visa is not long enough to complete this business I cannot help you. Goodbye.' (Obviously all this conversation was in Russian, which Lena translated for me afterwards). His office was definitely bugged and he needed to make sure that our little transaction had not been picked up. We walked out of his office still carrying the second carrier bag with the umbrella in it. The lift descended very quickly making my ears pop on the way down. The thug on the door looked us up and down again and seemed satisfied that we were still carrying the same carrier bag as we came in with so let us out of the door. Outside we were jubilant. We had beaten the system and got our wedding licence despite all the odds being stacked against us.

Next stop Palace of Marriages

The Palace of Marriages was not as grand as the name sounded but nevertheless was quite impressive. Our taxi driver pulled up under the huge canopy and I asked him if he would wait for us, putting two 20 rouble notes on the dashboard. This still surprised me that he would be waiting and not make off with the 40 roubles, never to be seen again. Our reception at the Palace of Marriages was much more pleasant and friendly. In another large office we spread out all our documents on the desk including our newly acquired licence. The lady got out a large diary and offered us 12:45pm on Tuesday, 8 September, just 5 ½ weeks away. I couldn't believe it. We now had a definite date that would be when we would be married.

Outside in the foyer we sat for a while, contemplating what we had just achieved. I thought that this would be a good moment to get Lena's ring out and asked for her hand. This rather took her by surprise and was overwhelmed with her emotions.

'Now we are properly engaged to be married,' I said with a tear in my eyes as well.

After admiring it for a while she took it off again and put it back in the box.

'Aren't you going to wear it?' I asked her.

"No not yet. I will use this ring to get married with and not until then will I feel that we have really accomplished our goal. Now I need to get you a ring. Let's go home now. The shops are open tomorrow and we can get it then.'

Back at the flat Lena gave her Mum the good news of what we had achieved and telephoned Genya and Elena to tell them and invite them round for a celebratory drink that evening. We put a couple of bottles of Russian champagne in the fridge and a bottle of vodka in the freezer in preparation.

Genya and Elena were delighted for us and sipped at the cool champagne. Genya had always had a wish to travel as I had mentioned before and I believed that he was a little bit jealous that Lena was one step closer to being able to get out of the USSR. During the animated discussions Genya and Elena said, 'what are we going to wear to your wedding? We haven't got any new clothes.'

'I could get you some if you like,' I blurted out, obviously feeling mellowed by the effects of the champagne. 'I am going to the Far East again in two weeks time and could get a suit made for you if I took your measurements.'

'Yes please,' said Genya.' Could you get me some black shoes and a tie as well.'

'I know,' said Lena. 'If Genya goes to see Aunty Valya tomorrow, she is a tailor and could take your measurements accurately.'

'That's a good idea. Now what about Elena's dress?'

Elena was less demanding and said that she was a size 14 and would leave the choice of dress to me.

'I need a best man,' I said, 'and I know the only person that this can be - Terry. As it happened, coincidence or not, 8th September was in the week that Terry and I had already organised attendance at another exhibition Sokolniki Park and we both would have visas organised. I would have to wait until I got home to ask Terry but I am sure that he could take time out to officiate for us. It all seemed to be falling into place.

Saying goodbye at the airport was even more difficult this time, as I knew I had to wait 5½ weeks until my return and hoped that nothing nasty would happen to Lena in that time. I was also missing her birthday on Wednesday, the day I was flying out to Kuala Lumpur. Never mind, we had so much to look forward to but still further challenges after the wedding.

Back at home I did something I have never done before in my life and that was to go to buy two ladies' dresses without the ladies being present. The lady in the wedding gown shop was very helpful and extremely interested in my story. Lena was a size 8 so there were many choices of dress to be made. The one dress that caught my eye had a tulip bottom and a plunging low back line. The lady in the shop was good enough to say that should anything go wrong with my arrangements, as long as the dress had not been opened, she would take it back for a refund. I very much hoped that I would not have to take up this offer. She helped me choose a little hat to go with it and I left with wishes of good luck and a smile on my face.

Next up was a regular ladies' clothes shop to find a dress for Elena. This was nowhere near as difficult and I chose a brown dress, which I thought would go nicely with her hair colour. Genya's suit would be next but I would have to get that made on my next visit to Hong Kong.

I was getting so excited as I could see something was happening now after all these months of waiting.

Chapter 30

Kuala Lumpur, Hong Kong and Korea

I was booked on a flight to Kuala Lumpur on my favourite airline, Cathay Pacific out of Gatwick airport. I enjoyed flying on this airline and was always looked after well. As the jumbo jet took off and started to climb, I felt a twang of pain in one of my teeth, which increased as the plane gained altitude. By the time that we had reached 30,000 feet it felt like someone was hammering a 6 inch nail through my head. I was in agony. After levelling off it seemed to go away so I could enjoy the flight. As we approached Kuala Lumpur airport and started descending, the pain came back again with a vengeance. I didn't know what was causing it but realised that I would have to see a dentist as soon as possible. After touchdown it improved a bit but didn't completely go away.

I was staying at the Pan Pacific Hotel in Kuala Lumpur and on arrival, asked the receptionist if there were any dentists nearby. She didn't think there were, so I bought a supply of painkillers to help with the pain. I was staying for six days in Kuala Lumpur and each night the pain got worse until on night five I couldn't stand it any more and telephoned reception to get the hotel doctor out to me. Within 30 minutes he arrived and confirmed that I needed a dentist as soon as possible.

'Come with me,' he said, 'and I will drive you round town to where I think there might be an all-night dentist.'

Bearing in mind it was now past midnight, we drove round Kuala Lumpur for about half an hour but couldn't find a dentist that was open. We returned to the hotel where he loaded me up with stronger painkillers. The following morning I telephoned my agents in Hong Kong who were meeting me at Kai Tak airport and told them of my predicament. They agreed that they would make an appointment for me with a dentist near to the airport.

I was dreading my flight to Hong Kong as I knew the pain would return as soon as we took off.

It did.

Painkillers were not touching it now so I resorted to several brandies from the trolley. They didn't work either. As we levelled off the pain decreased little bit but didn't go away.

'I've just got the descent to bear now,' I thought and hopefully I should soon be at the dentist.

The pressurisation cycle in the plane was obviously doing something to exacerbate whatever was going on in my mouth. Down we came into Kai Tak with me pushing hard on my cheek to try to alleviate the pain. As good as gold my agents were there waiting for me and whisked me off in their car. Within 30 minutes of landing I was sitting in the dentist's chair.

How efficient was that?

Dr Leung had a good look in my mouth and took an X-ray, which confirmed that I had got an abscess in my jawbone just below one of the roots of a molar tooth.

'You need a root canal treatment to release the pus from the abscess and let it drain. We can get started straightaway if you have the time.'

'Oh please,' I said almost begging him to start. 'I can't bear the pain any longer.'

With that he picked up his drill and started drilling. The pain was intense and after he had "scraped me off the ceiling," he said, 'ah you need an anaesthetic. Chinese people don't like anaesthetics and are rewarded with the relief of their pain when the pressure in the abscess is released and all the pus comes out!'

'But I'm not bloody Chinese,' I said in a very irritated tone. 'Give me an anaesthetic please. NOW!

As the anaesthetic began to work I felt pain free for the first time in seven days. It was lovely. Dr Leung got to work with a variety of different drills and probes and eventually said with some humour, 'there she blows,' as the pus squirted into my mouth. The smell and taste where disgusting.

'It's a good job we caught it in time,' he said. 'It could have got very nasty and was obviously made worse by the pressure changes when flying.' This is now explains why the pain had been worsening both on take off and landing.

He packed the hole in my tooth with some cotton wool and told me that I needed to come back for the next three days to flush it out and make sure it was completely clean before filling it. He gave me some more painkillers and antibiotics and asked me to come back at 2:30pm for each of the following three days.

It felt as if all my problems had been lifted as I walked out of his surgery. A bit numb but no pain. Now I could enjoy the delights of Hong Kong.

I got up early the next morning and went along to a nearby tailor. I gave him Genya's measurements which, Auntie Valya had taken and had myself properly measured by one of his fitters. He asked me to come back the following day for a fitting and any adjustments that might be required. As I was now officially engaged to Lena I thought it inappropriate to see Loli so I decided not to let her know I was here. It seemed strange not to, but my life was changing dramatically from now on.

My agents kept me busy for the next three days between trips to the dentist, who now knew to give me an anaesthetic as soon as I walked into the surgery. On the final visit he filled the hole with a new type of filling material that had not yet reached the NHS in the UK as it was very expensive. My total bill for the four day treatment course came to US$2040 - good job I had Health insurance cover through my company. On my last day in Hong Kong I returned to my tailor's shop and picked up all the suits. Mine fitted me perfectly and I was delighted with the quality.

My next stop was Seoul and I must confess I was a bit nervous about the flight, hoping that Dr Leung had done a good job and it would not hurt again on take off. Much to my relief it didn't so I celebrated with a few drinks from the trolley.

Mr Im met me at Kimpo airport and during the drive to my hotel I told him about my recent escapades in Moscow and that I was now officially engaged to be married next month.

'Great news,' he said. 'Let's go out tonight to celebrate and get a couple of girls.'

'Woh, hold on,' I said. 'I am now engaged to be married I must be faithful to my fiancée.'

'Oh don't worry about that. You are in Korea now and nobody will know.'

'No I can't,' I said. 'Sorry to be a spoilsport but that's how we do things.'

'Okay then. We'll have a few drinks and then I'll take you to the Manhattan sauna and bathhouse. We can have a massage and you can choose the level of service you like.'

'Suits me,' I said.

After a good steam and soak in the hot tub, I went for an exfoliative scrub and massage with a male masseuse, just to be on the safe side. Boy was he rough but thorough. When I was lying on my back, he took great delight in piling up all the dead skin he had removed from my belly to show me just how much had come off.

One new experience I had on this trip was an Express Bus ride from Seoul to Daejon and back to see one customer. Apparently this was the quickest and easiest way to travel to Daejon and allowed me to see some of the countryside.

Back at home I didn't have much time to prepare for the big day. I had got Elena's dress for the wedding but needed to buy Genya's shoes (size 11 - he was a big guy). Terry was delighted to have been asked to be best man and had done all of the organising for the forthcoming exhibition so that I had very little to do work wise. He was to be the only other Brit at our wedding, all the other guests would be Lena's relatives and friends.

My colleagues in the office were still worried for me and kept asking if I was positive I knew what I was doing. I am sure they had my best interests in mind but it did irritate me.

Chapter 31

The Wedding, September 1987

Packing my bags for this next trip to Moscow was quite a challenge. As well as all my clothes both for work and the wedding I had my Lena's wedding dress and hat that could not be squashed too much, Genya's suit and shoes, Elena's dress, six pairs of ladies tights and a little skirt for Ksenya, Lena's niece now two years old. I was taking a bit of a risk as Lena would not have seen the wedding dress that I chose and if it didn't fit or she didn't like it I didn't know what I would do. There was also the customs officer at Sheremetyevo Airport to get past so I strategically placed some Marlboro cigarettes and ballpoint pens around my cases.

I don't know how many times I checked my passport, Visa, tickets and papers but now it was time to go. It was early Sunday morning so the traffic on the motorway to Heathrow was not too bad. All my bags had checked in okay and were just on the limit of being overweight. I was really going to struggle at Sheremetyevo but at least I had got a one rouble note in my wallet to hire a baggage trolley when I arrived. The customs officer on duty was unusually in good humour and gratefully accepted a packet of cigarettes from me and even wished me good luck.

At the check-in desk of the Mezhdunarodnaya Hotel I had to explain to them that I was getting married on Tuesday and needed my passport and visa back as soon as possible, duly stamped with the hotel stamp to prove my residency here.

'I'll do my best but I can't guarantee it,' said the lady receptionist.

'I can't get married without it so please do your best,' I said as politely as possible so as not to rub her the wrong way. There was still time for things to go wrong so I'd better play it safe.

I quickly sorted out my luggage and repacked a case with all the goodies I needed to take to Lena. It made sense to use a taxi again as it would have been a struggle with a suitcase on the Metro, and very conspicuous.

When I got to Lena's flat, Genya and Elena were already there. They were all like children at Christmas, waiting excitedly to see what Santa has brought them. Lena loved the wedding dress and rushed up the hall to try it on. Fortunately it was a perfect fit and the tulip styled bottom really suited her. Genya had now got his suit on and was parading up and down the hall like a model on the catwalk. It must have been the first time he had owned a made-to-measure suit.

My choice of colour of dress for Elena was excellent as it complimented the colour of her hair and eyes. She too walked around with a look on her face like the cat that had just licked the cream. Lena's Auntie Valya, the tailor, had also been busy sewing dresses for herself, Galina, and the third sister Lyuba. Everyone was happy and looking forward to the wedding day.

On Monday Aunty Valya had been set the task of finding a restaurant that could accommodate a wedding party of twelve. I thought that this was leaving it a bit late but apparently this was how they did it. Forward planning was not an option in a Communist country as you never knew what the next day might bring. We traipsed round numerous restaurants with a negative answer in each. Auntie Valya was getting annoyed and her tough streak was now beginning to show. We made our way to our last hopeful - Prague Restaurant. I could sense from the tone of the conversation that things were not going well.

'So what is your problem?' said Aunty Valya with a very discontented tone to her voice.

'First problem is that we have a funeral party to cater for and if you came you would have to share a salon with the mourners.'

'Second problem - we have no tomatoes!'

'So if we brought our own tomatoes and were prepared to share a salon with the funeral mourners then there would be no problem!'

'Da'

'Then we will book it now thank you. Twelve people for a wedding lunch tomorrow at around 3:00pm and we will bring the tomatoes! Done!'

Although I was hearing this I just couldn't believe the negotiation that I had just witnessed. Aunty Valya was happy with her efforts and we set off back to the flat, feeling very pleased with ourselves.

Back at the flat Babushka and Dedushka had arrived for a pre-wedding drink. Babushka, although nearly 80, was still working full time as a trusted cashier in a department store and was always an early riser. She was given the task of going to the vegetable market first thing in the morning before the wedding to buy tomatoes and some cucumbers, just in case! Salad vegetables were normally in good supply at this time of year as the peasant farmers from the Southern Republics would bring their produce to the big City for sale at a better price.

Dedushka presented Lena and me with a wedding gift. Two parcels, neatly wrapped with brown paper and string and quite heavy for their size. Lena opened them with glee to find two sets of six wineglasses. Not just any wineglasses but glasses that Dedushka, an employee of the Kremlin, had "obtained" from his employer. They were very obviously hand made with a fine twisted stem of clear glass and three lions' paws supporting a cobalt blue glass bowl, topped with gold foil. Absolutely exquisite.

'How on earth am I going to get these home,' I thought to myself whilst still admiring their beauty.

Another present was waiting for us in the hallway from the Aunties and Uncles, an 8' x 6' Persian carpet. Now I was really concerned. How could I possibly get that back home with me as excess baggage? Genya and Elena had also brought a present, a large patterned, earthenware vase and saucer. I could see me having to use my exhibition transport company to help me out here.

The merrymaking went on well into the evening, the last guests leaving as the last bottle of champagne was drained. Being a bit old-fashioned I had decided that I had better go back to my hotel to spend the night and besides, I needed to pick up my passport and visa and get changed into my wedding suit. The lady in reception recognized me as I tried to creep in and gaily waived my passport at me.

'Here is your passport Mr Hunter. You might need it!'

I collapsed into bed but couldn't sleep. So many "what ifs?" kept going through my head.

'What if there was another mistake in the documents?'

'What if they don't accept the spelling correction by the Embassy?'

'What if Babushka can't get any tomatoes?!'

I must have dozed off at some point but woke with the start when that bloody chicken in the foyer started crowing at 6:00am. I quickly bathed and got dressed in my smart new suit and shirt with turned down corners on the collar and bright bow tie.

I went down for an early breakfast, hoping that not too many people would see me, but I stuck out like a sore thumb. Quickly I went back to my room for a last minute check that I had got everything and then out to find my taxi. The local custom at Moscow weddings was for the bride and groom to go and pay their respects to Lenin in his mausoleum in Red Square and I hoped that this had not been arranged for us.

Babushka was already at the flat, beaming like a Cheshire cat. She had got two kilos of tomatoes and six cucumbers in grubby carrier bag. It was her wish that Lena and I should have a church blessing before the wedding so I had to go along with this, albeit grudgingly. Religion was all but banned in the height of Communism and it had only recently been tolerated. Their local church, St Nicholas in Khamovniki, was a beautiful building painted in green and white with the classic golden cupolas on the roof. Inside the walls were lined with religious icons and the air heavy with the smell of incense burning. All around, little old grey haired ladies dressed in peasant clothing with what looked like their husbands' socks on, rolled down to the ankles in Nora Batty style, were beavering away polishing brass ornaments or sweeping the floor or removing burnt out candle stubs from the votive candle stand. All of them frantically crossed themselves each time they got near the altar. The priest greeted us, a Rasputin lookalike if ever I saw one. He said a few words, sprinkled us with holy water and swished his incense burner around a few times. Putting his hand on our foreheads in turn he uttered something in a chanting style and shook our hands. Babushka was satisfied.

It was only a short walk back to the flat but I still felt so conspicuous dressed in my wedding suit. Lena changed into her wedding dress and was helped with her make up by her Maid of Honour, her best friend Nina. Soon the wedding car arrived, a Chaika, (Russian for seagull) which was a large stretch limo. It was appropriately decorated with ribbons and flowers and really looked the part. Lena, Nina and I got in but before we could go to the Palace of Marriages we had to go to pick Terry up from the hotel. He was waiting for us outside as arranged so off we went across the City. People in the streets stopped and waved as the wedding car passed them by. I felt like royalty (Not that I am royalist!).

Now I was getting really nervous. My palms were sweating and my mouth dry. Lena had been tutoring me in what to expect and what I had to say. My Russian was still not good enough to keep up with a conversation, let alone repeat wedding vows but Lena assured me that I only had to listen and say "Da" (Yes) three times. She would prompt me each time I needed to say it.

The first thing we had to do on arrival was to give in all our documents, which were collected up by an official. All our guests had arrived and we were ushered into a large room with a string quartet playing quietly in the background. Lena and I approached the lady registrar behind a big table, accompanied by Nina and Terry at our sides. All the other guests seated themselves behind us. The registrar picked up what looked like a large clear plastic magic wand and started to prod at the documents, which had been laid out on the table in front of us. She spoke in clear, precise Russian. She paused for a moment and I got a sharp dig in the ribs.

'Da,' I said with a loud voice.

More wand waving and prodding and then a pause.

Second sharp dig in the ribs.

'Da,' I said again clearly.

A third session of wand waving and prodding but then this time I didn't need a prompt.

'Da,' I said again as soon as she paused.

After a few more words everybody clapped.

Wow! Was that it? Was I really married now? In Moscow in the height of Communism with no guarantee of getting my new wife out. It felt surreal.

We all retired to the back where we signed the register and our newly prepared wedding certificates were given to us. Out in the foyer I had to lend my camera to various people to take some photographs for us. The official photographer only took a couple of photos and told us that they would be ready in about 6 to 8 weeks!

The Chaika was waiting for us under the canopy outside to take us to the Prague Restaurant but this time we had to squash Babushka in as well with her carrier bag of tomatoes, which she had grasped tightly on her lap all the way through the wedding ceremony. She had to be first out of the car at the restaurant to get the tomatoes to the kitchen and quickly rejoin the wedding group. (You may at this point be thinking that this must all be a made up story but I can assure you it is all true. I have the pictures to prove it).

Fortunately we did not go via Lenin's Mausoleum but straight to the restaurant where Lena and I formally greeted our guests. We were shown to our table, which was laid out in one long line, alongside the funeral party, which was already in full swing. Not much mourning going on but plenty of vodka swilling!

Lena and I were seated in the middle of one of the long sides with Nina and Terry seated next to us. Lena started the speeches, which she did very eloquently although I couldn't understand everything she said. Then came my turn. I had to do it in English with periodic pauses for Lena to translate for me. Then came Nina and Terry's turn for a few words and then the feasting began.

I have to confess that I don't remember too many details now, partly because the time flashed by so quickly and partly due to the amnesic effects of Russian champagne and vodka. What I do remember clearly is being turfed out of the restaurant at about 7:00pm into the warm sunlight of a fine Moscow summer evening. Now we had to find a taxi, our Chaika having long gone. What must we have looked like, a bride and groom walking the streets of Moscow trying to flag a cab down. Eventually a private car stopped for us and agreed to take us home for a packet of Marlboro cigarettes. Fortunately I had one left in my suit pocket. We all regrouped back at the flat and the drinking continued until the small hours of the morning.

I awoke the following morning, next to my new bride and I still couldn't believe that this was real. The sun was shining, the crows making a devil of a noise outside the bedroom window and my now mother-in-law bashing the living daylights out of some piece of chicken in the kitchen. She was preparing my wedding breakfast and what a breakfast it was. Not only fried chicken but caviar with black bread, osetrina, a selection of cold meats and tea.

I was not required on the exhibition stand in the morning as we had to go to the Embassy with our marriage certificates to register the ceremony. This time Lena would be allowed in as my wife and she needed to know the people there, as she would be a regular visitor over the coming months.

When we arrived at the Embassy, Lena was noticeably nervous. The guards outside the Embassy were of course Russian and we had to show our passports and wedding documents to gain access. Lena had her domestic Russian passport, which naturally the guards questioned and had to telephone inside to seek permission to let her in, which they did. Once inside, Lena was under the protection of Her Majesty's Government but back outside, the Russian guards now knew what Lena was doing and who knows what contacts they had. The Embassy took photocopies of our documents and made Lena feel at ease. They showed her where to come when she was ready to apply for a UK entry permit, but this could only happen after she was given an Exit Visa from the USSR and this would be the next hurdle. Since Mr Gorbachev started his program of Glasnost and Perestroika things had eased a little in the Soviet Union but Communism still reigned supreme and an Exit Visa was something that was very difficult to get. Indeed the very fact that you were applying for one immediately branded you as a traitor for wanting to leave the Motherland. Life could be made very difficult for Lena in Moscow from now on.

We took the Metro back to Lena's flat and I had to leave her to go to Sokolniki Park. I was greeted warmly by the few Brits who were attending the exhibition (we all knew each other as it was like a club). They all wanted to share in my wedding celebrations so it was decided that we would organize a second party at the Russ Restaurant on Friday evening. Vladimir organized the booking for us and also organized sufficient taxi drivers who were willing and able to get us through the Ring of Steel.

I went to find our lorry driver in the lorry park and explained to him that I had some wedding presents that I needed help with to get them back to the UK. He agreed that I could pack the wine glasses and vase in the packing case with our kitchen equipment but he couldn't hide the rolled up carpet, leaving me with that problem. I telephoned the British Airways Moscow Office to explain my problem and they confirmed that if I rolled it tightly and bound it securely they could take it on the plane as oversized luggage like they would do with skis. Funnily enough, Persian carpets were not on the list of banned articles from being exported out of the USSR so I shouldn't have a problem with Russian customs.

The evening at the Russ Restaurant was packed with fun and alcohol. Fellow diners, realizing what our celebration was about, came over to our table to congratulate us and raise a toast. Finally it was time to go and a sense of sadness and foreboding came over me. I realized that the following day I was flying back to the UK, leaving my new wife in Moscow and not knowing if I would ever see her again. If the authorities really had it in for her, she could disappear! I held her close to me in the taxi, cherishing every last moment I had with her.

In the morning we rolled up the carpet and covered it as best we could with the limited packing material available. I went back to my hotel to pack my bags and Lena arranged to come and pick me up with the carpet and travel with me to the airport. The journey went far too quickly and hating goodbyes, Lena bundled me, my luggage and the carpet out of the taxi and after one farewell embrace, went off in the taxi without looking back. I could have sobbed my heart out but somehow managed to keep calm in order to get through customs.

The customs officer dealing with me was remarkably good humoured. I explained that I had just got married and the carpet was a wedding present. No problem. He let me through without even wanting a tip. The checking in staff at the British Airways desk were also helpful and told me to retrieve the carpet in Heathrow at the oversized luggage window after I had got my bags off the carousel.

I sat on the plane, long faced and miserable, so much so that the passenger sitting next to me asked if I was alright. I told him what I had just done and almost brought him to tears as well. I turned back and continued my inward sorrow.

At Heathrow my carpet arrived intact and I made my way to the Something to Declare channel as I could not disguise the fact that I had a roll of carpet over my shoulder.

'Good evening sir,' said the customs officer as I plonked the carpet down on the table in front of him.

'What flight have you come in on and what have you to declare?'

I thought of saying, 'this bloody carpet, isn't it obvious?' but restrained myself.

'I have just got married in Moscow and had to leave my bride behind.

This carpet was a wedding present…'

'May I see your documents to prove this please sir.'

I handed over my passport and wedding certificate for him to inspect.

'So you are telling me that you have one used carpet which is a wedding present?'

'No, it's new,' I insisted.

'I'm sure sir that you told me it was used. There is no import duty payable on a *USED* carpet,' he said stressing the word used.

I got the message. 'Yes I believe it has been used for some while.'

'Thank you sir. Off you go. Have a nice evening.'

What a nice guy I thought as I repositioned the carpet on my shoulder and made my way out, ignoring all the funny looks I was getting.

Chapter 32

First time in Japan

When I got back home after the excitement of the wedding, my moods became very gloomy. I had now got a new wife but had to leave her in Moscow, not knowing when or indeed if I would see her again. She now had the task of getting her documents organised and applying for an Exit Visa, something that was rarely granted. We had noted that another summit meeting between President Reagan and President Gorbachev was due to take place in Washington in October and Gorbachev had already met Reagan several times including one meeting in the Oval Office in August. It had been rumoured that Gorbachev was going to issue some more Exit Visas in a show of goodwill prior to the Washington Summit on 12th October so Lena made sure that she was in the queue.

She telephoned me on 6th October with the very good news that her application had been accepted. Again we couldn't talk in much detail but she did tell me that she now had to apply for an International Passport and once issued she would have to give up her Domestic Passport and forfeit the right to live in Moscow. This was going to be very dangerous for her as the KGB would have their eyes on her and regard her as a traitor. It was my intention to go to Moscow around Christmas time if everything was in order by then and to take my parents with me. We would then all leave Moscow together and accompany Lena back to her new home making something of a celebration about it.

I was off again on a four-day trip to Budapest. It felt very strange that I was back behind the Iron Curtain but in a different country to Lena and not being able to contact her. There was only one weekend between this trip and another twenty-seven day visit to Hong Kong and other Far East countries, so I spent my time doing some more decorating in my flat. It did help to keep my mind occupied on other things and besides that I had to have it looking half decent if I was to "collect" Lena at Christmas time.

I only had an overnight in Hong Kong giving me a chance for a catch up meeting with my agents before flying off to Tokyo. I was really looking forward to this visit as it would be my first time in Japan. Boy, was I on a steep learning curve, getting to grips with local cultures and customs and how to behave in business meetings. I had appointed the company Shimadzu to sell our products in Japan and they were attending a large exhibition, Bio'87, to showcase our products. I had already done some research and had some special business cards printed which had my details in Japanese on the reverse. Apparently there were two small changes I had to make as well as getting an accurate translation. Firstly as a manager, I had to have rounded corners on the cards. Secondly as I was to be the dedicated trainer, advisor and point of contact for everything, I had to have gold edges around the card. These two details would let the recipient of my card know my status and how deeply to bow when greeting me.

As an aside story here I had been told by one of my Embassy contacts that he once had a big problem with the translation of his card into Chinese. His diplomatic title was First Secretary, Department of Trade and Industry and not knowing any better it had been translated into Principle Typist!

The next thing I had to learn was how to greet and be greeted by a business contact. As you can see from the above paragraph, a lot of importance was put on the giving and receiving of a business card. It had to be handed to the recipient by holding it in two hands with the printing the right way up to be read. This would be similarly accepted with a two-handed grip, studied then a bow given commensurate with the status of the giver. The card was then placed on the table in front of you so that you could see it during the whole business meeting. No way should you take it one-handed and put it straight into your top pocket. This was taken as dismissive and was an insult.

Mr Hamazaki or Hamazaki-san as I had to call him, had been assigned to me as the Product Manager. After meeting me at the airport and taking me to my hotel, he took me out for the evening to sample some delights of Japanese cuisine. Japanese beer and whisky were fine but my favourite by far was sake, served warm. Individual plates of food were served but the two that were most memorable on this occasion were roast sparrows and chicken gizzards!

We had a very busy couple of days on the exhibition stand and after it closed on the Friday all the lads went out for a meal together. They chose a Tepanyaki restaurant where we could all sit around a central food preparation area and watch the Tepanyaki chef perform acrobatics with his knives. The central area was sunk into the floor so that the diners when seated on the floor could still be level with the service area. He had a sheath on his belt, which housed a couple of knives. He would whip them out, toss them in the air and catch them by the handles before chopping up the food. When finished he would juggle with them, toss them in the air again and with a final flip, rehouse them in the sheath. Heaven knows what damage the ultra sharp knives would have done to his hands if he had caught them the wrong way round. Cooking the food was also a juggling act, flipping the food around the hot griddle and then onto a plate.

He would serve us all in turn, moving round the cooking area in acrobatic movements as he flipped our food onto our individual plates.

By now I was a dab hand with chopsticks which always impressed. I could demonstrate my prowess by picking up an individual grain of rice or pea or, if available, a whole quail's egg.

As I was staying over at the weekend and there was no work to do, Hamazaki-san had organised some social activities for me. One of his hobbies was ornate writing and there was a meeting of his club in a paper factory on Saturday. It was about a one hour drive out of Tokyo and he was to follow a car driven by the writing Master and a couple of his lady pupils. After about half an hour of driving suddenly the Master's car veered off the road, ran down a drive and crashed into someone's house. For some reason he had blacked out and lost control of the car. All the occupants were quite badly injured and before long a couple of ambulances arrived noisily. Hamazaki-san was so embarrassed that I had had to witness this horrible accident and told me that he would have to go to the hospital with the Master as it was his duty to look after this venerated man. He got a taxi for me to take me to the nearest station and gave me strict instructions on what train to catch back to Tokyo and what station to get off at for my hotel. He would contact me later at the hotel when he was able to leave the Master.

I was a little nervous travelling on my own for the first time in Japan. Although the signs had English written below the Japanese, it was still very confusing but Hamazaki-san's instructions worked well. The railway system was very regimented with marked spaces on the platform where the doors of the carriages would open. Passengers getting on the train waited in an orderly fashion on the sides of the opening to allow the passengers to get off before rushing in, in advance of the doors closing. In busy times they had an official "pusher" on the platform who would push the last passengers in to allow the doors to close.

Tokyo is very short of space so everything is either very crowded or very small or both. My hotel room was no exception. Once inside I could touch two of the walls simultaneously while standing in the middle of the room. It was a bit longer in the other direction with a small shower cubicle and toilet. Never mind. It was only for sleeping and washing so it would suffice. Hamazaki-san eventually called me late afternoon. The Master and the two ladies had face and head injuries but were not life-threatening. They would have to be kept in hospital for a few days and Hamazaki-san kept apologising as he felt he had let me down and that I might have lost confidence in him, which would never do in Japanese culture. I assured him that it was an accident and not his fault and I certainly had not lost faith in him. He said he would have to leave me to my own devices for the evening and that he would pick me up in the morning so could I check out and be ready by 8:00am.

'No problem,' I said. 'See you then.'

So I now had to fend for myself in an unfamiliar city with the language and writing that I could not understand. I was getting quite hungry so I thought I would go out for an early supper and there were plenty of restaurants around the hotel. I didn't have to worry about not being able to read the menus as the Japanese had a really neat solution to the problem. Everything on the menu was recreated in a very lifelike plastic model on plates in the windows of the restaurants, all neatly numbered. All I had to do was to look around and see what I fancied. I could then go into the restaurant and ask for the appropriate number. Easy! One thing I still struggled with was where and when to take your shoes off so as not to walk on floor space designated for sitting on.

I had chosen a one-pot noodle dish, which was brought to me with chopsticks. This was going to be interesting! How do I cope with the liquid using chopsticks? I looked around the restaurant to see how others were coping. It looked like it was okay to pick up the bowl once the noodles and other solids had been eaten, and to drink the liquid as if from a cup. What horrified me was the noise that the Japanese diners made during this process. It seemed that the slurping noises were compulsory and the louder the better to show your appreciation. I struggled with this as it brought back memories of mealtimes as a child, getting a clip round the ear for eating noisily. I just couldn't purposely slurp so drank mine quietly. It's amazing how some things can become so engrained in your psyche that they cannot be changed easily.

I took a leisurely stroll back to the hotel, passing lots of shops with brightly illuminated fronts, mainly selling electronic products and games. I passed one greengrocer with very neatly displayed produce in the window. The apples looked as if they had all been polished and I really fancied one. It was fairly easy to buy one, using hand signals and pointing to the one I wanted but I was horrified by the price. £3 for one apple. 'It had better be good,' I thought.

It was Sunday, another non-working day and Hamazaki-san had planned something else for me. We were going to take the Bullet Train from Tokyo to Kyoto, a ride of about 2¼ hours at high speed and spend the afternoon in Kyoto before going on to Osaka, where Shimadzu had an office. We took a taxi to the main station but I did find it a struggle carrying my suitcase with 27 days' supply of clothing in it, around the crowded platforms. We found our train, which fortunately was not too full so I managed to find somewhere to put my luggage. Hamazaki-san suggested that we sat on the right side of the train, as that would be where we would get the best views. Off we went, travelling slowly at first through the crowded suburbs of Tokyo but once in the open countryside the driver opened the throttle. There was a digital speedometer above the door between the carriages and it soon increased to 120 miles an hour. Wow, were we moving!

Hamazaki-san had very good English and we chatted easily. At one point he said, 'keep looking out of the window. You will soon be able to see Mount Fuji.'

I could. It was an amazing view of the iconic volcano, its crater capped with snow. Clouds shrouded the lower slopes where the snowline ended. It was one of those images that you would always see in books and magazines on Japan but seeing it for myself was an exhilarating experience.

When the train pulled into Kyoto station the first thing we had to do was to find a left luggage locker for our cases so we could go round the city unhindered. Kyoto is famous for its cherry blossom in spring but we were now in October. Nevertheless Hamazaki-san had chosen to take me to see some ornamental gardens, which would look beautiful in their autumn plumage. The gardens were huge with several temples and many ornamental fishponds stocked with the most beautiful koi carp. Apparently there was to be a traditional wedding in one of the buildings in the garden and Hamazaki-san asked me if I would like to see it.

'Of course I would. Let's go.'

We found the building quite easily as there was already a crowd beginning to gather around it. The actual ceremony had already taken place in one of the temples but now the bride and groom were going to participate in the tea ceremony. The single story building had paper partition walls which were drawn back to reveal a platform on which the bride took centre stage, kneeling on the floor to perform the complex stages of making tea and offering it to her husband. The costumes they wore were stunningly colourful but looked very awkward to wear. The bride's face was made up Geisha style with white cheeks and bright red lips. She very carefully put the green tea in the pot and added the water. The pot then had to be stirred with a whisk for a defined number of turns before pouring it into a handleless cup. The cup was then rotated on the table by another set number of rotations before she offered it to her husband, both hands grasping the cup and her head bowed in obeisance to her man. How they managed to come up with such an ornate and complicated way of making a cup of tea beats me but it was lovely to watch.

After we had completed our tour of the gardens we made our way back to the station, retrieved our luggage and caught the train to Osaka where I would be staying for the next three nights.

The next three days were mainly taken up with training their sales force but we did get one customer visit in to the University Hospital. I also managed to get a telephone call to Lena who was still waiting for her International Passport to be issued and was feeling very anxious.

For a change, I was taken out to dinner one evening by the chief engineer Iwasaki-san, who took me to a karaoke restaurant. Despite constant requests for me to sing I declined, leaving this to my host who had quite a good voice. The food was interesting to say the least, half the time not knowing what I was eating. There was one dish that I enjoyed but wished I hadn't after Iwasaki-san told me it was whale's tongue.

Next up Taiwan. I had an early morning flight from Osaka to Taipei where Alex was waiting for me. I only had one working day in Taipei, when we visited the Military Medical Research Institute and the University Medical School, plus on Saturday morning a meeting with the Managing Director of Alex's company. The rest of the weekend was free and Alex, being the perfect host, took me on some more sightseeing tours plus of course a visit to the barber shop. Well, I had to get my haircut somewhere!

The whole of Monday was spent travelling. Taipei to Hong Kong to Jakarta. I overnighted in the Sari Pacific hotel, near to the airport as I had an early flight in the morning on the Garuda Airline Surabaya shuttle. After my previous experience on Garuda I was a little nervous about this flight but it went off without any problem. It was quiet in Surabaya so apart from work, nothing much happened.

Saturday was another day of travelling. The Surabaya shuttle back to Jakarta then a Thai Airlines flight to Bangkok, which arrived around 10:00pm. I was exhausted after all this travelling and was only too glad to check into the Dusit Thani hotel and collapse into my bed. Theera met me on Sunday and looked after me all day, briefing me on the week ahead. We worked hard, visiting many customers and relaxed hard in the evenings in various bars plus a couple of regular massages to relieve the tensions of the day.

The following Sunday I flew back to Hong Kong where I met up with my Managing Director, Dennis, who was flying out to help me with an exhibition in Seoul after a few days in Hong Kong. We were both booked into the Excelsior hotel which was situated in Causeway Bay with fabulous views over the harbour to Kowloon. This visit I had telephoned Loli to tell her I was coming and arranged to meet her at 9:30pm for dinner.

I was dreading this meeting...

I had to tell about my marriage to Lena and that I probably wouldn't see her again. I left Dennis in the hotel and caught a taxi over to Kowloon to our favourite Japanese restaurant. I felt that I needed to have this meeting as Loli had played a very important part in my life for the past two years and I couldn't just disappear without an explanation. I remembered what her sister had said to me during her visit to London and I really didn't want to hurt her feelings. We had had an unusual friendship - not that of a Bunny Girl and her client but that more akin to two lovers of different ethnic origins. Loli put on a brave face and congratulated me on my marriage. She had hoped that our relationship might have gone further but it was obvious that she couldn't survive in the UK and I was not likely to move to Hong Kong permanently so it hadn't happened. I felt so sad as we parted after dinner and with one final embrace, she put me into a taxi, the correct one for going back to Hong Kong Island. A beautiful phase of my life had just ended. I often wonder what happened to her and what she might be doing in later life. I still have my little black book with all my names, addresses and phone numbers and so many memories came flooding back as I referred to it during the writing of this book.

At breakfast the next morning Dennis noticed my melancholy and tried to cheer me up. After I had returned to the hotel last night I had telephoned Lena who told me that she had got her International Passport and was going to the British Embassy to apply for an Entry Visa. However she was now getting threatening phone calls from the KGB and midnight knocks on the door, which she chose not to answer as she knew who it would be. Life was getting dangerous for her and I worried for her safety. The pressure was on. We were joined for breakfast by one of our Hong Kong agents so I had to snap out of it and concentrate on business matters.

We had appointments to see the British Trade Commissioner and a freight forwarder plus a couple of customer visits before leaving on Cathay Pacific to Seoul on Wednesday. We had booked a stand at Korinstrument '87 which was supported financially by the Department of Trade and Industry. We had to comply with their conditions in order to claim the funding hence Dennis was with me to help out. We were booked into the Seoul Hilton which was very familiar to me. We would be staying there for eight days to do this three-day exhibition and some more customer visits.

One evening after we had finished dinner in the hotel with our distributors, Mr Im had gone off to the toilet and when he came back, he came straight over to me and said, 'Graham there is someone downstairs who would like to see you.' My heart skipped a beat on hearing this. I knew who it would be – Ko He-Rang.

I made my apologies to my fellow diners and with a pounding heart, made my way down to the disco in the basement. Sure enough He-Rang was sitting on the side-line with some of her mates who I had met in her flat. She turned to look at me and gave me the look that said she was going to tell me off.

'Where have you been? Why haven't you come to stay with me? I have missed you. I thought we were good friends.'

'Oh dear,' I thought. 'I have to tell her and I know it's going to upset her.' It had been many months since I saw her last and what I hadn't realised was the seriousness with which she took our relationship. I had moved in with her on previous visits and she had expected this to continue. I held her hand and took a deep breath.

'You remember that I told you that as well as having a girlfriend in Hong Kong, I also had a girlfriend in Moscow. Well, two months ago I married her and I am now trying to get her out of the USSR but with great difficulty.

She remained silent for a while, taking in what I had just told her.

'Does that mean we won't see each other any more?'

'I'm afraid so,' I said with a lump in my throat.

She paused again for a while, released my hand, got up, gave me a peck on the cheek and walked out of the disco. That was the last time I saw her. This visit was really turning into an emotional rollercoaster and boy was I feeling it. The rest of the week passed without incident and I was glad to have Dennis as travelling companion on the way back to Gatwick. As usual my itinerary was jam packed full and I only had two weeks at home before I had to return to Bangkok and Seoul to install the equipment I had sold on previous visits. Each sale I made included an installation and training charge to pay for my return visit, which was how I managed to travel so much and why my diary was constantly full.

Chapter 33

Loy Krathong

When I got home the first thing I did was to call Lena. She had now got her British Entry Visa and had all the documents necessary to come to the UK. However she told me that the threatening phone calls were increasing and she was getting more and more concerned.

'I've got less than two weeks away this month, which I can't get out of but I will be back in the UK on 14th December. I will arrange to come out to Moscow before Christmas with my parents to collect you and help you through all the formalities.'

'Please come quickly. Things are getting very difficult here.'

The race was now on. I still had to do a lot of work on my flat and with any luck Lena would be joining me in a few weeks' time. I needed it to look nice when she arrived. My moods improved dramatically as I now knew that the end of our torturous journey was in sight but I still had another Far East trip to do. This time I was going to Khon Kaen University Hospital up in the north of Thailand where I imagined I would not be able to call Moscow from. I left Gatwick on 5th December and spent Sunday in Bangkok. As it happened the 5th December was a full moon, the start of Loy Krathong. This was an amazing festival of lights where people made little boats out of banana leaves, put a candle on them and set them alight before releasing them on the river. As the little boat floated away, the tradition was to make a wish for something you wanted in the following year. Theera and the guys took me to a restaurant by the river for an evening meal where hundreds of people were gathered along the riverbank, releasing their little banana leaf boats. The river was alight with hundreds of little candles burning brightly as they floated down in the current. After we had finished our meal Theera purchased a little boat for me and escorted me down some steps to the river's edge. I lit the candle and launched my boat, making a wish as it floated off.

'I wished that Lena could safely get out of the USSR and join me in the UK as soon as possible.'

I stood for a while at the water's edge and watched my boat until it became indistinguishable from the hundreds of others. Being a scientist I didn't believe in things like this but I would hedge my bets as I had nothing to lose from it.

On Monday morning Theera and I took an internal flight to Khon Kaen where we were staying for three nights. I was to install some equipment in the University's Anatomy Laboratory, which was right next to the dissection room. I recognised the smell immediately and couldn't resist having a peak in. There were 12 post-mortem tables each with bodies on in various stages of dissection. Not a sight for the faint hearted.

That evening Theera took me to a little restaurant that was used by the locals. Knowing that I would try anything he ordered a speciality dish for me. *Cows' appendix soup with baby birds*! A large steaming bowl arrived at the table in which was a clear, light brown liquid with what looked like macaroni in the bottom. These were the cows' appendices. A small bowl was placed next to it with three small eggs. The waiter proceeded to crack the eggs and drop the contents into the hot liquid. I was horrified to see that the contents of the eggs were little live chicks that were just about to hatch. The poor little things drowned in the hot liquid and were quickly cooked at the same time. I then had to eat the whole baby bird, beak, feet, feathers and all. I was allowed to pick up the bowl to drink soup and then pick out the appendices and eat them. I can't say I enjoyed it but it was an interesting taste and texture.

The following day I had to train their technicians in the use of the equipment I had just installed and after a full day, a group of us went out for supper. The Thais are lovely people, very friendly and hospitable and always wanting to please. We had a lovely evening and I was ready for my bed when I got back to the hotel. For some reason I decided that I would call my parents just to let them know I was okay and to see if they had any news. My mother answered and after the initial exchange of niceties she said, 'I've got someone here who wants to talk to you.'

After a short pause another female voice came on the phone.

'Hello Graham,' said a voice with a very noticeable accent. It was Lena.

I was staggered.

'What are you doing there? How did you get there? When did you arrive?' I had a multitude of questions to ask.

Lena briefly explained that the KGB threats had been getting unbearable so she decided to do a runner. She had telephoned my parents, who she had never met before, to say that she was getting a flight on the next day, the same day that I had flown to Bangkok, and to ask them to meet her at Heathrow on Sunday the sixth, the day that I had launched my little boat and made my wish. She had only packed one suitcase and took a taxi to the airport early on Sunday before it got light so that she might not be seen by anyone watching her flat. She had said goodbye to her mother not knowing when or if she would see her again. At Sheremetyevo she was treated quite rudely by the airport staff and the Aeroflot crew, which had upset her considerably. At Heathrow when she saw the passport control officer she broke down in tears and was escorted off to a side room for a private interview. She was so distraught that they put out an announcement in the arrival lounge for "Mr and Mrs Hunter meeting Lena Hunter from Moscow, please come to the airport information desk." My parents not being world travellers were taken aback by this announcement but made their way to the information desk. They were escorted behind the scenes to the private interview room that Lena was seated in. Bearing in mind they had never met her before and only seen photographs, it was not the most auspicious of first meetings. However once all the formalities had been completed she was allowed out and went with my parents to their car.

She sat quietly in the car, all the new sights, smells and sounds were overwhelming for her. On arrival at my parents' house she wandered around looking at everything and trying to take it all in. Having been used to living in Moscow, a very big city with roads 16 lanes across, the leafy suburbs of south London seemed like a country village to her. There were neighbours next door who could see you over the fence into your garden! Oh yes – a garden. Something that flat dwelling Muscovites would not have. And the neighbours talked to you. She clammed up at first as the Russian attitude was not to trust anyone until they earned your trust. My poor parents didn't know how to cope with this and did not understand different countries' cultures and customs.

The phone went dead. I had lost the connection. I cannot describe my feelings exactly but imagine that I was halfway round the world with another country to visit for nearly a week and my new wife had just escaped from the clutches of Communism and was now in my parents' house. How I wished I could get the next flight home.

On Wednesday we flew back to Bangkok and I spent the night in the airport hotel as I had an early flight to Seoul via Taipei. Mr Im met me and I couldn't stop talking about my recent activities and the fact that Lena got out of the USSR. I don't think he could fully understand the magnitude of the hurdles we had overcome but nevertheless congratulated me. The next few days dragged, as all I could think about was Lena at home.

At last I was descending into Gatwick and would soon be at my parents' house. I picked up my car from the long-stay car park and tried to drive carefully but I couldn't help but go faster than I should have. I pulled up outside my parents' house and rushed in. There was Lena standing in the hallway waiting for me. I just couldn't believe it. We had taken on the Communist system and won. We embraced for a long time with tears streaming in both of our eyes. Mum and Dad had stayed in the background just letting us savour the moment. I was lost for words and couldn't speak for some time. Eventually I started asking her all of the questions I needed answers to but she was still shell-shocked from the experience and didn't want to relive the last few days just yet.

'Give me some time and I will tell you,' she said wiping the tears from her cheeks.

I couldn't let go of her and held her close as we walked up the hall and into the living room. I took the big reclining armchair and got Lena to sit on my lap. Mum made a cup of tea for all of us and some home-made fruitcake.

'Lena certainly likes her tea,' said Mum.

'Ya chaiovnika,' said Lena which I tried to translate for Mum. It was difficult to translate exactly but it meant that she was a tea lover. Lena's English was fine but some of her pronunciations had confused my parents. Maybe it was because I was used to listening to English spoken with a Russian accent that I had no trouble understanding her but I learned later that she had been getting very frustrated with not being understood the first time she said something. I assured her that soon she would and that they would come to understand her with time. She would only be speaking English from now on. I stopped to think about this for a while. It must be quite a shock to only be able to speak your second language and there would be times when her vocabulary wouldn't be sufficient for some conversations. There was no one she could talk to for clarification in Russian and would have to make do with dictionaries.

When I eventually got back to the real world I realised it was Monday, a working day, and my office would be expecting me back. I telephoned them to explain what had happened and asked for the rest of the week off at short notice. They couldn't refuse, as I was technically owed more days off than I could possibly take before the end of the leave year.

I thought that it would be prudent to stay with Mum and Dad for a few days as they had a large shopping centre only ten minutes walk away. Lena had arrived with only one suitcase of clothes and toiletries. She had left almost everything of a personal nature behind, as all she wanted was to get out of the Soviet Union. She would have to build a new life with me and that would start by going shopping for some clothes tomorrow.

It felt so strange sleeping with Lena in my old childhood bedroom and having to push two single beds together. It was exquisite to snuggle up together as we had been through a lot to get to this stage and were determined to enjoy every moment of our new lives. Before going to sleep Lena said to me, 'if we are going shopping tomorrow we will need to get up early.'

'Why?' I asked quizzically.

'We need to be in the front of the queue!'

I had to laugh and replied there are no queues and no shortages. We can go shopping any time and there will always be goods for sale. She couldn't get her head around that just yet.

'Just wait until tomorrow and you will see.'

Chapter 34

Lena's first experience in UK

As it was so near to Christmas I decided that it would be better to stay with my parents and go to our town after Boxing Day. That way it would get Lena used to some of our ways of life before taking her to her new home. We went shopping for new clothes and our first trip to the shopping centre was disastrous. As it was Christmas there were decorations and lights everywhere and lots of vibrant window displays. Lena was overwhelmed. Lots of goods on sale and no queues! We looked in some clothes shops but within 30 minutes Lena had a panic attack.

'Take me out of here now. I have a terrible headache and want to go home.'

We walked back to my parents' house in silence. She was shocked at what she had just seen and needed time to take it all in. She had seen some pictures in glossy magazines that some of her friends back in Moscow had "acquired" but seeing it for real was too much. We sat for a while with a reviving cup of tea while I explained to her that she would have to get used to the fact that we had no shortages of products and our purchases were only limited by the money that we earned.

'I will need to earn money as soon as possible,' she said having recovered her senses after Mum's tea and cake.

'What will I be able to do for a job?'

'Well you have a good degree in Hydrometeorology so we'll start looking for jobs in which this will be relevant. How are your computer skills?'

'The computers in Moscow were very basic and the keyboards were in Cyrillic. I will need to learn how to use a UK keyboard.'

After lunch we had another try at going shopping for clothes and this time came back with some. 'There is a lot she's going to have to learn,' I thought to myself. 'I am going to have to be very patient with her and not rush things.'

Christmas came and we had several invitations to visit my parents' neighbours for drinks. Lena was always very quiet at first. People would ask me, 'would Lena like a drink?

'Please ask her - she does speak English.'

This happened so many times that it started to annoy me until I realised that no-one had ever met a Russian who had escaped from the USSR and did not know how to react to her. She was something of a novelty to everyone. Eventually she started to join in the conversations until someone asked her how she got out of the Soviet Union.

'I don't want to talk about that now,' she would say abruptly as it was obviously something that was so bad that she was not ready to recall it yet.

The time came for me to take her to her new home. We packed our bags, said our goodbyes and set off. Lena was very quiet during the 1½ hour journey, gazing out of the window to take in all of the scenery. The first shock she had came only a few minutes into the drive. My parents' house was only a short walk from Richmond Park and it was a useful shortcut to drive through it. Inside the park were several herds of both red and fallow deer, originally put there by King Henry VIII for his hunting pleasure. She was overwhelmed yet again.

'Aren't we in London?' she asked.

'Yes we are but there are several Royal Parks in London. This one used to be my playground when I was a small boy.'

We continued, mostly in silence, while Lena tried to take in everything that she was seeing. There were the occasional questions but I did not push her to make conversation only giving her the answers when required.

As we got near to our town, which has a population of about 15,000 and set in the rolling arable fields of East Anglia, I started to give her more details about where we were going to live.

'Only 15,000 people. That's a village!'

To understand her reaction you must put yourself in her shoes. She had only lived in a city where everybody lived in flats. There were no houses with gardens and the roads through the city were anything up to sixteen lanes wide, eight on each side of a dual carriageway. The population of Moscow was approximately 12.5 million. In her eyes this was a village.

We arrived at our flat and went up the three flights of stairs where I ceremoniously carried her over the threshold.

'What, no lift?' was her first comment. 'All the flats in Moscow have lifts.'

'Yes but this is only three floors with five flats in all. There is no need for one.'

Once inside she wandered round in silence, taking time to go out onto both balconies to take in the views over the rooftops to the fields beyond.

'It's not very well furnished here.'

'Yes I know but I wanted you to take part in choosing the furniture and fittings.'

'When can we do that?'

'As soon as you like. I have money put aside to pay for it.'

We unloaded our bags and put the food that my mother had given us into the fridge.

'We will have to go food shopping tomorrow then we'll have a walk around town to get you acclimatised.'

Our first night in our new home was divine. I still couldn't believe it as we snuggled up together. It had taken over two years from our first meeting in the Russ Restaurant to get to this point but sheer guts and determination had got us through.

On the first working day after the Christmas and New Year holidays I took Lena into the office with me to introduce her to my colleagues. They were all enamoured with her and Simon, who had met her before in Moscow said, 'you are so lucky to have such a pretty young wife.'

I snapped back at him. 'That was not luck. That was sheer guts and determination. If I had listened to you I would have given up over a year ago!'

Dennis came out of his office to greet her, having met her on one of his trips with me to Moscow. I think he understood what I had been through as he had travelled with me quite extensively over the past couple of years and had shared a few "experiences" with me. I asked him if it was okay to have a few more days off as I needed to get Lena used to her new surroundings before leaving her on my next overseas trip. It was ironic that my next trip at the end of January was to Moscow but she would not be there this time.

We wandered around the town arm in arm and very close together. I bought several newspapers both local and national in order to start looking for a job for her. We also called in to the doctors' surgery and the dentist to get her registered. She could only take so much in a day and soon wanted to get back to the safety of the flat. As luck would have it (I hate that word luck) a local lady was advertising private typing lessons in her house so I gave her a call. I explained Lena's background and her needs and she was very happy to take her on. She could start her off on weekly evening sessions starting at 7:00pm and could do the following week. 'Well that's a good start,' I thought.

The TV fascinated Lena, having been restricted to only approved channels in Moscow with no adverts and lots of official doctrine. She flipped through them all trying to take in something from every channel.

'Are all the goods they are advertising available in the shops?'

'Yes. They are all competing with each other to try to persuade you to buy their products.'

Although I had spent a lot of time in Moscow living with a real family. I was still taken by surprise at the little things we take for granted that Lena had not seen before and was fascinated by them. There was even more for her to get acclimatised to than I realised.

Lots of my friends and colleagues wanted to meet her and we had an invitation to lunch with one friend and to dinner with another. As usual my friends did not know how to talk to Lena and still asked me questions instead.

'Lena does speak good English so please do ask her,' I would say. During dinner Lena had spotted something on the sideboard that had intrigued her but hadn't had the courage to ask about it. She whispered to me, 'what's in that big box on the sideboard with the wire on the front?'

I asked Mel for her and the answer was that it was his daughter's pet rat!

"Would you like to see it Lena?'

His daughter went over to the cage, opened the front and returned to her seat at the dinner table. She called to the rat who came out of its cage, down the sideboard, across the floor and climbed up her leg. It then made itself comfortable on her shoulder as she continued to eat her dinner. You couldn't have imagined the look on Lena's face. She asked if she could touch it, which she did gingerly, having never seen a white rat before let alone known anyone who kept one as a pet.

Dinner proceded with Lena keeping a watchful eye on the rat, which was still sitting comfortably on the daughter's shoulder.

On the way home she was full of questions about what she had seen that evening but one very interesting one was,

'Why do people treat me as if I'm an exhibit at the zoo?'

I explained that firstly she was probably the first Russian to take up residence in this area. Secondly the only thing British people knew about Russians is what they saw on the television like the Mayday parade through Red Square and the reporting on the Chernobyl disaster. There had also been a lot of coverage on the Georgi Markov assassination on the streets of London back in September 1978 when the KGB had allegedly been implicated. So the fact that she had escaped the clutches of the KGB made her something very special.

She sat very quietly for a while taking all this in.

At the weekend we went into London for a day to take in some of the sights. We did Tower Bridge and the Tower of London first as these were iconic images of London. Lena stood on the spot transfixed. I remember what I felt when I first stood in Red Square and I imagined this is what she would be experiencing right now. We made our way to the underground station and took a train to Knightsbridge. Again some major differences for her to take in. We had to wait more than 10 minutes for a train but in Moscow they were every two minutes. The fare in Moscow was the equivalent of 3p for travelling any number of stops but I had paid pounds for a short distance.

We made our way to Harrods where she was particularly keen to visit the Food Hall. Passing by the fish counter, caviar caught her eye as she recognised the blue tins that her mother bought in Moscow.

'How much are those tins,' she asked pointing to the blue tins of Beluga caviar.

'£250 each,' I replied.

'What,' she shrieked. 'We pay five roubles in Moscow.'

Five roubles would be five pounds at normal exchange rates but 50p at black market rates.

I could see she was getting quite agitated and asked if she was okay.

'No I'm not. I'm getting a sick headache. Can we go home now please?'

Lena explained that as a child her mother used to spoon feed her caviar from the tin as a vitamin supplement as opposed to the cod-liver oil that I used to be given.

The following week I had to go into the office and leave Lena alone for the first time. I was a little nervous but it had to be done. I had left her with some money and she assured me that she would spend her time wandering round the town and reading some newspapers. She was gradually gaining in confidence as the days progressed and had made friends with shopkeepers whose shops she had called into regularly. She discovered the lovely delicatessen where she had been staggered by the choice of meats and cheeses available and had spent some time chatting to the proprietor everyday. She had found that once he had finished hand carving a big leg of ham, he sold the bone plus whatever chunks of meat were left on it for £1. She had been making herself ham sandwiches every lunchtime and saving the bones for me to make pea and ham soup with.

In the office I was making arrangements for my next trip to Moscow on 25th January but discovered that I also had to go to Israel on 16th February for 9 days and I could take Lena with me if I wanted to. Of course I jumped at this possibility and started looking at what I needed to do. Lena would have to travel on her Russian passport and would have no problem getting into Israel but needed to apply for a re-entry visa to get back into the UK. A bit of a hassle but no problem. We had time to do it.

Everything was happening so quickly now and we had so much to do. I drove her to her first typing lesson and showed her how to get there on her own the following week when I was in Moscow. She came out very excited and told me that the tutor could also teach her shorthand writing and she would like to do that as well as it could be useful in the future. I had got my Russian Visa and tickets organised and helped Lena to apply for her re-entry visa at the Home Office. My secretary was tasked with getting me a return flight to Tel Aviv on 16th February and liaising with our distributors out there on venues and accommodation and advising them that my wife would be travelling with me. I also had a meeting with Terry to discuss the next Moscow visit and took Lena with me. It was the first time they had both met outside of the Soviet Union and Terry was delighted to see her again. He too had thought that it would have been very difficult to get her out but we had succeeded and he was impressed.

My trip to Moscow felt very strange. A complete reversal of roles. I was behind the Iron Curtain and Lena was back in the UK. Naturally I went to visit Galina several times to keep her informed on how Lena was doing. My spoken Russian by now was getting quite good but I still made lots of silly mistakes as I had learnt it by listening to Lena and her mother talking together. My usual mistake was to make all the nouns feminine and it sounded to others as if I was talking as female. There were two memorable mistakes that I made when talking to a group of Russians. We were discussing rose gardens in the UK and they had asked me how we kept our gardens looking so good and productive. I wanted to say that we put some cow manure onto the soil and dug it in. Unfortunately the Russian words for cow and Queen were quite similar and I ended up saying that we put the Queen's shit on our gardens. This resulted in a lot of laughter. 'No wonder your gardens looks so good,' came the reply. My other mistake was that the word for rain was dozhdik and for a hedgehog, yozhik. I would frequently mix the two and refer to the weather as it is "hedgehogging heavily today!"

Lena and I had arranged that on one of my evenings with her mother she would telephone me. The phone rang at the agreed time and Galina answered. After a chat with her daughter she passed the phone to me. It felt so surreal. She was getting on fine back at home and was practising her English. She had found a course being run in Peterborough College for English as a foreign language in April and she wanted to go to. I explained that she would have to travel by train but it was possible. We could work out the details and enrol her when I got back home.

Back at my hotel that guy on camera duty behind the bed head must have found it strange that I was sleeping in my bed every night. The new buzzwords on the streets were now Perestroika and Glasnost since the very successful Reagan - Gorbachev summit last year. People liked Gorbachev as did Margaret Thatcher who had said, 'This is a man I can work with.' You could sense that changes were coming....

When I got back home Lena was very excited that our trip to Israel was coming up soon and very pleased with herself that she had spent five days on her own without any mishaps. She had found her way to her typing and shorthand course and had spent the week in a combination of finding her way around town and reading lots of material in English. I too was very pleased with her and could see her confidence growing.

My secretary had booked us on an El-Al flight to Tel Aviv. I had never been to Israel before or flown on El-Al so I was quite excited too. A new country to visit with a new wife. Checking into our flights involved a security procedure that I had never experienced before. We had to queue up to have all of our bags searched followed by a grilling by a customs officer on where we were travelling to and why. Then the customs officers changed over and we had a second grilling, asking the same questions and then the two guys shared our answers to see that they agreed.

We were booked into the Sharon Hotel in Hertzalya, about a fifty minute taxi ride from Ben Gurion airport. It was right on the beach, our room having a fabulous sea view. Lena was in heaven, spending a lot of time on our balcony taking in the ambience. There was a message for me at reception saying that we would be picked up at 9:00am. I would be taken to the office of our new distributor while the wife of my colleague would look after Lena for the day. We would then meet up in the evening for a meal with another salesman and his wife.

They all loved Lena. What I hadn't realised was that a lot of Russian Jews had escaped from the USSR to Israel and all were welcomed. Although Lena was not Jewish she was Russian and was now being treated as a real person, not as an exhibit in a zoo. They were used to Russians and she was lapping up all the attention.

Friday morning was my last customer visit for that week and our hosts had arranged to take us to Nazareth and Caesarea for the afternoon. We were really spoilt by their generous hospitality and enjoyed their expert commentary on all the sites we visited. They explained that as Saturday was the Sabbath, they would not be able to look after us and suggested that we took the tour to the Dead Sea and Masada for the day. They advised us on appropriate clothing to wear for the desert and to take our swimming costumes and a towel.

Back in the hotel that evening the receptionist helped me book the tour and we would be picked up from the hotel at 7:00am the next morning. It cost US$37 each for the whole day which I thought was very reasonable. It was a 90km coach ride through the desert and passing by Jerusalem. Once there we had a lot of different things to do which we did our best to pack into the time allocated. We had a mud bath, floated on our backs in the Dead Sea whilst reading a newspaper and went for a camel ride. We then took the cable car up to Masada where we had a guided tour round this ancient site. By the time we had to return to the coach we were exhausted and very hungry as we had only eaten a couple of Sharon fruit during the day but had drunk a large amount of water in the arid desert conditions. Back at the hotel we gorged ourselves on the lovely food and fruit and then collapsed in our room, tired but very happy after an amazing day. Lena couldn't stop chattering about our experiences. You can imagine that having lived her whole life in a huge city that was covered in snow for at least four months of the year, what a unique experience this has been.

Sunday, Monday and Tuesday were working days with the same arrangements as before. One of the wives would look after Lena while I was doing customer visits. We spent eight nights in all in Hertzalya, the whole trip being very successful business wise and very enjoyable during leisure time.

'Where can we travel to next?' Lena asked on the flight home. 'Can I come on more business trips with you?'

Chapter 35

Far East & Home, March 1988

After our very successful visit to Israel I had eight days in the UK before setting off on a sixteen day trip to the Far East again. I would have loved to have taken Lena with me but it just was not possible on this occasion. I promised her that one day I would take her to the Far East but it was far too difficult to organise at the moment. Whilst I was footloose and fancy free I had no problem with my extensive travel plans but now I had my lovely new wife and I felt terrible having to leave her for such a long time at such a dramatic phase of her life. She was becoming more confident with her new way of life every day and she assured me that she would be okay in my absence. I left her with sufficient cash to last for the duration of my travels and promised that I would telephone her every other day if I could. I gave her my detailed itinerary before I set off for Gatwick again.

I took the British Airways flight to Kuala Lumpur leaving at 3:35pm and arriving at 4:15pm the next day. There were only a couple of customer visits to do with nothing of interest to report here and then went on to Singapore for two days. I was in my favourite Orchard Hotel where I spent two evenings watching the world go by in the foyer after two busy days with my distributor. I must confess I did ask the DJ in the disco to play Elton John's "Nikita" on both nights just to remind me how far I had come in the last two years. It brought a tear to my eyes on both playings. I rang Lena and she was fine, reminding me that I needed to bring a nice present home for her.

Next Singapore Airlines to Taipei and then Cathay Pacific to Seoul, staying in the Manhattan hotel. The next day we were taking an Express Bus to ChongJu and staying over night there in the Woo Sin Hotel. This was a bit of a dive and lived up to its name. I do have a little habit which is when seated in upholstered chairs or sofas in a public seating area, I run my hands around the gap between the arms and the seat as frequently you can find money there which has dropped out of somebody's pocket. Seated in a leather sofa in the rather seedy bar, I ran my fingers round the edges. Bingo. I found some coins. Motivated by my success I continue round the back and to my horror came across a syringe and needle. Fortunately it didn't prick me but I soon stopped and withdrew my hand. The Express Bus back to Seoul the next day where I spent one more night in the Manhattan Hotel before leaving by Japan Airlines for Osaka.

Sunday was spent going round to Kyoto again which was quite different in spring to autumn but equally as pretty with the cherry blossom coming out. I found some lovely silk blouses, which were quite reasonable by Japanese prices so I bought a few for Lena. One customer visit in Kyoto then on the Bullet Train again to Tokyo. I had three nights in the Star Hotel which was one of those tourist hotels with rooms barely 8' x 8' square and very cramped. Hamazaki-san was my companion again and as I had got to know him quite well he invited me round to his house for an evening meal with his wife. This was a great honour. You have to know a Japanese person very well before you get invited into their home.

Hamazaki-san's house was very modest and small as are most Japanese homes due to the lack of space. At the front door I was greeted by his wife with a very low bow, normally reserved for very important people. At the door I duly took off my shoes and put on the guest's slippers. There was a central square living room with nothing but a table in the middle and mats around it to sit on. The wooden floors were highly polished and very slippery. There were several doors off this room but no evidence of any stairs. I was invited to sit on the floor on one side of the square, low table and found it very uncomfortable. Hamazaki-san's wife served us food and drink, which was extremely delicious but I wasn't sure what I was eating. They explained that due to the shortage of space the central room doubled up as their living room, dining room and bedroom..

At one point during the meal I needed to pee so asked where the toilet was. It was one of the doors off this room and had several pairs of slippers lined up outside it. The procedure was to change out of your living room slippers and into your toilet slippers before entering the tiny bathroom. After relieving myself I came out of the toilet and walked straight over to the table. Oh my goodness what a faux pas I had made. I had walked back to the dining table with the toilet slippers on. Immediately Hamazaki-san's wife got a bucket and mop and started to wash the floor with disinfectant. I was so apologetic as I did not realise the seriousness of what I had done but all was forgiven and we completed the evening without any more faux pas. Hamazaki-san put me in a taxi with instructions in Japanese to the driver on which hotel to take me back to.

On Thursday I caught the Cathay Pacific flight back to Hong Kong, spent Friday doing a couple of customer visits and caught the night flight back to Gatwick. Unfortunately Gatwick was fog bound and we were diverted to Heathrow. This was very inconvenient as my car was at Gatwick. Eventually I got back home to a very excited wife who couldn't wait to see what presents I had brought back for her. She had been to two typing/shorthand lessons and was picking it up very quickly. She showed me the language course that she wanted to do at Peterborough College, which I thought would be perfect for her. Her English was already very good but this course would familiarise her with the vagaries of our language and spelling anomalies. It was an intensive course requiring Lena to attend every day for several weeks and she would have to travel by train to get there, another skill that she would have to learn.

Bearing in mind I had only got back to the UK on Saturday I had to drive back to Gatwick on Sunday to pick up Alex from Taipei who was staying for three days on product training on a new instrument we had recently developed. We put him up in a local hotel and Lena joined me in the evenings when we entertained him. He wasn't staying long enough for me to return the hospitality that he had given me in Taipei but we did invite him to our flat to show him how we lived.

We enrolled Lena on the course and after studying the train timetable we started to plan her travel. She needed to be in Peterborough at 9:00am but as there was no direct line she would have to travel to Cambridge first and then change. The station at Saffron Walden was about a five minute drive from our flat and there was a shuttle bus service at peak times which linked in with certain train departures. So providing she caught the shuttle bus just near to our flat at 7:45am she could make it on time. While I was in the UK I would drive to the station but she would have to use public transport when I was overseas.

In April I had one week in Poland and one in Hungary so Lena had to use the shuttle bus on these occasions. She loved the course and purchased a lot of reference books to help her. One book I remember that she found very useful was called "Ship or sheep", which had a collection of words and sayings that if pronounced even slightly incorrectly, had a totally different meaning, a bit like me with the Russian words for rain and hedgehog. Towards the end of the course the tutor asked her to a meeting in her office with the Mayor of Peterborough. Peterborough was twinned with Vinnitsa in the Ukraine and a twin town visit had been organised for the end of April. He needed a Russian interpreter and asked the language school in the college if they knew of anyone suitable. Lena has been put forward as a potential candidate, knowing how well she had got on during the course. She was delighted to have been asked and immediately accepted the role. This only gave her a couple of days notice but this didn't worry her at all, in fact she relished the challenge. On the day of the visit she dressed up smartly and took her usual train to Peterborough. Arriving home that evening I was anxious to know how she had got on.

'It went off fine,' she said with a very matter-of-fact voice, and that was all I could get out of her.

Two days later she got a letter from the Twinning Officer in Peterborough City Council and I give the contents of the letter exactly below.

"The Mayor, the Chairman and members of the Twinning Subcommittee have asked me to thank you for so kindly giving up so much of your time to act as an interpreter during the Civic visit from Vinnitsa. Without this help the visit would not have been a success and your skill and expertise was admired by all concerned.

Apart from the hard work, I do hope that you were able to enjoy participating in the visit. The visit was a great success and our guests enjoyed all the aspects of the visit. The success of this visit was due in no small part to your own personal contribution."

I was delighted for Lena to have received such a letter, which could now be used as a reference for her. Her language skills had developed so much that she was now able to do simultaneous interpreting i.e. Russian in her ear and English out of her mouth as they spoke and vice versa. I think that this was a turning point for her and boosted her confidence no end.

Our job search continued for a few weeks when one day we found an engineering company in Cambridge advertising for someone with knowledge of hydro meteorology to work on a project on the flood defences on the River Severn. Bingo. This job specification could have been written for Lena. She applied for the job and got it.

One of my concerns for Lena was that she held a Russian passport and only had "leave to remain in the UK". This meant that if she wanted to travel overseas she would have to get a re-entry Visa every time, which was not guaranteed, and an entry visa into every country we wanted to visit. I needed to get British citizenship for her as soon as possible. I thought that the wife of a British citizen would automatically qualify for citizenship but I was wrong. I was advised to write a letter to Douglas Hurd MP who was then the Under-Secretary of State at the Home Office. In my letter I mentioned that currently Lena had a Russian passport but could not return to Russia for fear of reprisals from the KGB and did not have permanent residency status in the UK effectively making her Stateless. I got a reply from him, which basically said that to apply for UK citizenship you had to have been resident in the UK for three years so she would not be eligible for this until December 1990. This was very disappointing for us and we were resigned to the fact that she could not travel very much with me until we got a UK passport for her.

The months flew by, what with Lena in full time employment and me travelling, albeit on a reduced scale. She joined the local Sports Centre and learnt to swim plus a lot of other keep fit activities. Life was looking good. One day while I was flicking through the job section of the daily Telegraph I saw an advert from a company manufacturing computer terminals who wanted someone with sales experience in Eastern Europe to get them into this new market which was now opening up due to Mikael Gorbachev's policies of Glasnost and Perestroika. It offered a better salary than my current one and would only involve travel behind the Iron Curtain so no more long haul flights. It appealed to me so I put in an application and guess what, I was offered the job. After a lot of discussion with Lena, I accepted it.

The company knew absolutely nothing about the market and thought that if IBM had a presence in Russia then so could they. My brief was to go out there as soon as possible to research the market and even to look for a joint manufacturing opportunity. Wow. A totally carte blanche job description in virgin territory in which I had a lot of experience. Never mind that it was not a medical product, they wanted my knowledge of doing business in the USSR. I started on 16 September 1988.

Chapter 36

1988 & 1989

The first couple of months with my new company were spent doing product familiarisation and market research and finding out who I should contact in the USSR. To start with there would be the official Import/Export companies responsible for placing orders. They would be able to tell me who wanted to buy and had money to do so. Armed with sufficient product knowledge and a list of Impex companies I made my first trip to Moscow in late November. My first breakthrough was to discover that the State Post and Telegraph Office were in the market for a large number of computer terminals and were more than happy to talk to me. I had to bear in mind the Export Licensing Regulations which limited me to what I could sell but the good thing was that once new technology came in, I could sell off all the older, previous generation technology to them. This pleased my company no end as they could clear out old stock. It would take quite a while to seal the deal but I had made a start. I also found out that a good exhibition for me to attend was "Electronorgtechnica" which would be held in February as part of the British-Soviet Month and was supported by the Department of Trade and Industry. This was perfect timing giving me enough preparation and shipping time to participate. The Import/Export companies connected with this exhibition were "Elorgintech" and "Minchimprom". I was absolutely delighted with the results from my first visit to Moscow in my new role.

Back at home, Christmas was coming and Lena was much more prepared for the shopping indulgences that this period brought. However now that she was working another new experience for her was the office party! Her office had a party with a difference. Being an engineering company, they held an annual Lego building competition on the afternoon prior to the party and Lena had been selected for one of the four competing teams. She had never seen Lego bricks before. The four teams were given a large box full of Lego parts and given three hours to design and make something. Their efforts would be judged and the winner announced at the party. She really got stuck into the spirit of the competition once she had familiarised herself with how Lego bricks worked. When she came home from the party she was dumbfounded at peoples' behaviour once they had had a few drinks. There were the usual office party dramas including arguments and sexual innuendos culminating in couples disappearing together for who knows what. This would never have happened in Moscow.

1989 began with a bang. Having got a free hand to do whatever was necessary to get the business, I started using Lena to prepare documents in

Russian for me. We bought an IBM golf ball typewriter and I managed to acquire a golf ball with Cyrillic font on it. A rare find. We had to re-label the English keys with the Cyrillic alphabet and although Lena had become proficient in touch typing in English she now had to relearn in Russian. She had already displayed her expertise at simultaneous interpreting and it did not take her long to master the keyboard. She could flip between English and Russian and back again in an instant. She could also make telephone calls to Russia, which were becoming easier to do with direct dialling now being allowed. It was fairly obvious that these calls were still monitored as you could often hear the whirring and clicking noises in the background. We organised mailshots, something unheard of before in the Soviet Union, to advertise our presence at the forthcoming exhibition in Moscow on the 21st to 24th of February.

One day I got a surprise phone call from a man called Simon who announced himself as the head of the Russian section at the BBC World Service. He had obviously got my contact details from the British Soviet Trade Organisation. He invited me to come to Bush House in London to do an interview about my business with Russia. I told him about my Russian wife, which was also very interesting to him and asked her to come along as well as it would make the interview more personal.

As you can imagine Lena was over the moon at the possibility of doing an interview on BBC radio, which would be broadcast to Russia. It was almost like being able to thumb her nose at the "System" which tried so hard to prevent her from leaving the USSR. The interview went well and Lena and Simon hit it off. He invited us to dinner at his house where he could learn more about our story. As a BBC employee he often got complimentary tickets to many of the London shows but usually at short notice. He asked if we would be interested in any of them that he was unable to attend. Of course Lena jumped at this opportunity and over the course of the next couple of years, Simon would often call saying, 'I've got two tickets to a ballet in the Barbican for tomorrow night. Do you want them?"

Naturally she wanted them and we ended up going to a lot of different productions, all free of charge. It did involve a lot of last minute reorganisation of our plans so that we could get into London by 7:00pm after work.

All my exhibition items had successfully been packed and shipped off to Moscow by truck. I was told that I could take one of the company's technical specialists with me to help with all the issues I could not handle and he was excited at this prospect. I had given Mike a good idea of what to expect in Moscow and to dress appropriately for the sub zero temperatures in February. He was still a bit sceptical about some of my stories but nevertheless took my guidance. We were booked into the Mezhdunarodnaya Hotel which was always impressive to a newcomer to Moscow. He had heard me talk about the large chicken in the foyer but now he could see it for himself, which added some credibility to my stories. He did stay very close to me all the time once he realised that not being able to read or speak Russian would preclude him from any activities on his own. One evening I told Mike that I wanted to visit Lena's Mum and would leave him alone in the hotel if he was happy with this. Chatting with him in his room before I left, I asked if it was okay and what he was going to do.

'I have some technical stuff to read which will keep me occupied but it would be nice if I could meet some of these gorgeous women you have spoken about.'

'Seriously? You would like a lovely Russian girl for the evening? Well you could go down to the hard-currency bar and see what's going on but whatever you do, do not leave the hotel. I will see you at breakfast at 7:30am in the morning.'

With that I left his room and made my way round to see Galina.

I was down to breakfast before Mike and when he did arrive he was very bleary eyed and tired.

'Good morning,' I said cheerily

'You bastard,' he replied.' You set me up.'

'What are you on about?' I said quizzically

'After you went last evening I settled down to read some of my stuff and there was a knock on the door. It was a gorgeous woman.'

'I understand that you would like some company tonight,' she said seductively.

'How could I refuse?' Mike said.

'Honestly I didn't set you up but it just goes to prove what I said about being listened to in your room. You are the new boy this time and they wanted to know a bit more about you. What did you talk about?'

'Well she did ask me some questions about my work and she was quite interested in my home life.'

'I hope you told her that you weren't married.'

'I think I did but I can't remember now.'

'That's good if you did because that is one potential weak spot out of the way. At least they can't send photos of you to your wife.'

Mike went white. 'Do you mean they were..... watching me?'

'Of course they were, from the camera behind the mirror at the head end of your bed.'

'She didn't leave until about 3:00am this morning and fucked me three times.'

'Well I hope you enjoyed it. Welcome to the club!'

'She left me her phone number and said I should call her next time I was in Moscow.'

Mike devoured his breakfast and went back for more. He would eat anything and never uttered a complaint about the unusual breakfast fare.

The exhibition went very well and this time I had Tanya again as my interpreter who remembered me well. I had a pile of leads to follow-up including two potential joint manufacturing partners, one in Pskov and the other in Vilnius.

On my return Simon invited Lena and me for another BBC interview on how well the exhibition had gone. I also had to give a report to the Department of Trade and Industry in order to claim my subsidised funding.

March was soon upon us and my diary was filling up alarmingly. I had been invited to attend the meeting of the Eastern European Working Party focusing on Bulgaria as a new market. I had also been contacted by the Soviet Trade Delegation in Highgate to discuss further business opportunities. On top of all this I had promised Lena a long weekend in Paris at the end of March and had to organise her French visa and UK re-entry visa. This rekindled my worries about not getting UK citizenship yet and the problems with travelling on Russian passport.

I was a member of the Saffron Walden Business Breakfast Club and a fellow member was Sir Alan Haselhurst MP who was Deputy Speaker in the House of Commons at that time and our local Member of Parliament. I had spoken to him previously about Lena's issues and he asked me to come to see him officially in his monthly constituency surgery which I did. He said he would write to Douglas Hurd himself to see if anything could be done to expedite matters.

I was encouraged by Sir Alan's offer of help which made me think that once this trip to Paris was over we might be able to get a UK passport for Lena and put a stop to all the travelling difficulties.

As it happens our trip to Paris was fantastic. The only frightening bit was when we left the UK and Lena's "Leave to remain in the UK" stamp in her passport was cancelled. I had booked a hotel in the centre of Paris and I bought some tickets for the Moulin Rouge show and dinner. We visited the Eiffel Tower, Montmartre and went to the Louvre to see the Mona Lisa. The Moulin Rouge required evening wear so we dressed up in our finery and took the Metro to the theatre. We were ushered to a table quite near to the stage, which I thought was fantastic to get such close-up view of the acts. Dinner was served and various acts performed on stage right in front of us. Just as desserts were served, the stage was transformed into a giant aquarium as the next act was a crocodile wrestler.

'This is going to be interesting,' I thought.

Out came the wrestler, muscles rippling as he showed off his physique in his scanty swimwear. Two handlers entered the stage carrying a huge crocodile and released him into the aquarium. The intrepid wrestler jumped into the aquarium and proceeded to grapple with the giant reptile, sending waves of water over the top of the tank and all over us and our dessert. We were soaked. Now I knew why the stage side seats were cheaper, not more expensive as I had imagined. The waiters came up to us with towels, offering their sincere apologies and plying us with complimentary cognacs, which we gratefully accepted.

After a lovely four days in Paris we flew back to the UK and I began to feel apprehensive about Lena again. At the Border Control I went one way and got straight through with my UK passport but Lena had to join a longer queue and I lost sight of her. After what seemed to me as an interminable time she eventually appeared smiling, waving her passport at me to show that she had got her "Leave to remain in the UK" granted again. Phew, I could do without all that attention again.

In April I had one visit to Sofia, Bulgaria and one visit to Moscow. Since Mikhael Gorbachev had come to power things were beginning to relax a bit in Moscow. Lena and I thought that this might be a good time to try to get her mother to come and visit us. In order to get a UK entry Visa I had to write a letter of invitation, addressed to the Consular Section of the British Embassy stating that I had the financial means to support her during her stay and then got the letter countersigned by a solicitor to confirm that he knew me and that the statements in the letter were correct. I had prepared this letter before my trip to Moscow and was able to deliver it personally to the Embassy, giving it to the staff who I was familiar with. They would telephone Galina when it was approved and invite her to the Embassy with her International passport, which had been issued with a lot less fuss than Lena's. As far as we were concerned everything had gone smoothly. Galina arrived at Heathrow on Friday, 5th May. This was the first time she had flown and also the first time she had left Moscow. She emerged from the arrivals hall, wide-eyed and shell-shocked at the sights that greeted her. After the dimly lit Sheremetyevo Airport and the cake tins in the ceiling, the bright lights of Heathrow with goods on sale everywhere must have made her think that she had died and gone to heaven! I stood back while Lena rushed over to greet her Mum and waited until the floods of tears stopped before I went to greet her as well. She told Lena that although she had got her International Russian passport and exit visa, she too had had threatening phone calls from the KGB saying what would happen to Babushka, her mother, if she didn't return to Moscow within four weeks.

Lena was able to take some time off work to show her mother around and at the weekends I joined them for some longer trips outs. We did the usual sights of London where Lena made the point taking her to Harrods Food Hall in order to show her the tins of caviar. She nearly fainted in the shop and we had to take her out quickly, also suffering the same panic attack and headaches that Lena first got.

It must be hard for you, dear reader, to understand this swell of emotion as we are used to a capitalist economy. If you had been deprived all your life and fed the Communist doctrine that everything you needed was supplied by the State, it was like the sudden realisation that the Socialist dogma was false and there was a better life to be had in the West.

She had been brainwashed with lies but now the truth was blatantly obvious.

Galina's visit flew by and during those four weeks I received my first big order from Moscow much to the delight of my company, proving that it had been a worthwhile gamble to employ me. The order was to equip the State Post and Telegraph office with hundreds of computer terminals. I had a lot of work to do with all the paperwork involved especially with the Letter of Credit and terms of delivery. I was suddenly the blue-eyed boy in the company as this was one of the largest orders they had received. To top it all I received another order from Bulgaria and a request to send three of their engineers to our factory for training.

The magnitude of this order made the company realise that the size of the potential markets in Eastern Europe justified their ambitions to set up a joint manufacturing venture somewhere in Russia. I was given the go-ahead to follow-up the leads I had got from the recent exhibition and to arrange a trip to visit potential joint venture companies, taking the Technical Director with me. Wow, what a responsibility. That excited me tremendously.

We took Galina back to Heathrow on 5th June with the inevitable tearful goodbyes. We reassured her that she could come again next year but in the meantime I would be visiting Moscow a lot more frequently and would always go to see her.

Chapter 37

Vilnius & Pskov, August 1989

From the beginning of June I had been working intensively on organising visits to two companies that had expressed an interest in a Joint Manufacturing Cooperation, one in Vilnius, Lithuania and the other in Pskov in the far west of Russia, only 20km east of the border with Estonia. Both required special visas to travel outside of Moscow and both involved long overnight train journeys. To cap it all I had been asked to take the Technical Director with me on the Pskov trip as this seemed the most promising.

But first I had to go to Vilnius on my own, the first time I had travelled outside of Moscow other than to the Russ Restaurant. This was going to be a real challenge as I had to take an overnight train from Moscow which left at 19:19pm but my flight to Sheremetyevo Airport only landed at 15:40pm. I had less than four hours to clear customs and get a taxi to the Bellaruski Vokzal. I would be met at the station in Vilnius but I had to get there first. I was a little nervous but glad that I had a reasonable command of the Russian language and alphabet and was sure that my invisible KGB minder would not let me go wrong! I managed to get to the station on time and found my way to the right platform. I was sure that someone was following me as it was too much of a coincidence to see the same person in the crowd so many times. For once I was pleased to have a tail. The sleeper compartment on the overnight train had four bunk beds per compartment, two on each side, with little curtains that drew across the side of the bed to afford some degree of privacy, as you never knew who you might be sharing with. As it happens I had one fellow passenger, a Russian businessman from Moscow, who just happened to speak English.

Coincidence - I think not.

It was not the face I had seen in the crowd but I wouldn't put it past them to have me tailed all the way as not many foreigners got the opportunity to travel outside of Moscow. We chatted for a bit and he offered to share his sandwiches with me which I accepted as I had no food with me.

There was a stove at the end of each carriage where a very stern looking grey-haired lady boiled a huge kettle and kept a brew of tea on the go all the time. There were very few toilets and my nearest one was two carriages down the train.

'I better not drink too much,' I thought as I didn't want to go wandering down the corridor in the night.

We pulled into Vilnius Station a little after 9:00am where my hosts were waiting for me. I only had one night in Vilnius before getting the overnight train back to Moscow so it was really going to be a whistle stop visit. This company manufactured small electronic goods and I hoped to see if they might be suitable partners for a joint manufacturing arrangement. I was taken round the factory which seemed adequate but there were too many things that they could not make that we would need to ship over to them. It could work but wasn't an ideal arrangement.

One of the specialities of the city was "black ice cream". I'm not sure what was in it but I had to try some. It was tasty enough and very welcome on the hot August day. They accompanied me to dinner and then back to my hotel. We agreed that we would have further discussions in the morning.

After sleeping on it I came to the conclusion that this was not the right partner for us and worked on ways that I could tell them politely. It wasn't too difficult as they had picked up my vibes during the tour but thanked me for giving him the opportunity to present their company to me.

On the night train back to Moscow I had the compartment to myself, which felt a bit eerie in the middle of the night. It reminded me of the film Dr Zhivago but the only difference being there was no snow outside. I had remembered to take some extra food from the breakfast table for on the long journey back to Moscow. I had one day and one night in Moscow with a couple of meetings organised plus of course a visit to Lena's Mum. She wanted to hear all the news since her visit in June and I had remembered to take some photographs for her

My meetings went well and I managed to find time to pop into the British Embassy to give them an update on my activities. I also told them that I would be back in two weeks time with the Technical Director to do another factory visit but this time in Pskov. They were impressed with my achievements so far and admired my stamina in making so many visits to the USSR. Good old British Airways got me back home on the Friday, albeit a bit late, but I had the weekend to recover before starting preparations for the next visit.

Shimon the Technical Director was both pleased and nervous at the prospects of our visit to Pskov. He was Jewish and travelled on his Israeli passport, something he thought that the Russian authorities would not like. I assured him that if he was granted this special visa then it proved that they wanted him to visit and nothing bad would happen to him. I would look after him so he needn't worry about dealing with the Russian language and signage. I took both his and my passports and visa applications to the Russian Embassy and had to leave them for special consideration. Lo and behold a few days later they arrived in the post, duly accompanied by the separate Visas. As a collector of stamps in my passports I was always disappointed that there were never any Russian stamps. It was always done on a separate piece of paper, slotted into the passport and removed on exit. Maybe it was a blessing as I was getting through a passport every two years, filling it completely with entry and exit stamps from all the other countries I visited. Looking back now, I must have travelled to Moscow over 40 times and will probably have a big file on me by both the Russian and British agencies.

Shimon was somewhat relieved that he had been granted a Russian Visa and I set to on briefing him how to behave in Russia and to always take his lead from me. I explained that he would be the new boy and might get special attention. His hotel room would definitely be bugged and we had to agree that any private discussions about our negotiations should take place in the open air, away from any hidden microphones. I don't think he actually believed what I was telling him but I certainly did get the ideal opportunity to prove it to him during our travels.

Shimon had high-level meetings with his fellow directors and was given a brief on what they wanted him to achieve. We packed everything we thought we might need and much to Shimon's surprise I took a quantity of company headed paper, carbon paper and my trusty portable typewriter plus of course a company stamp which Shimon was authorised to use and sign against.

The big day came and on Saturday 26th of August we met up at Heathrow Airport to take the British Airways flight to Moscow. Although I used to use Aeroflot as well because of the large bottles of champagne and the safe landings in the snow, I didn't want to put Shimon through this experience on his first visit hence the British Airways flight. As usual the captain came on the PA system announcing that we were now entering Russian airspace at which point I gave Shimon a nudge.

'No going back now,' I said teasingly

I described the procedure at Sheremetyevo Airport again and ensured that he was in the queue in front of me. I pointed up to the ceiling and asked him, 'so what do they remind you of then?'

'They look like non-stick cake tins,' he replied, with the recollection that I had described this to him some weeks ago.

'See I told you so. Now for the ten minutes facing the steely blue/grey eyes behind the slot in the passport kiosk.'

I could see Shimon was visibly nervous as he stood in front of the dimly lit kiosk. Bonk bonk went the sound of the stamp on his visa and through he went. I had given him strict instructions not to move away from the other side of the gates that he had just gone through and ignore any approaches from anyone. I soon followed and we made our by way to baggage retrieval. As usual the taxi driver found us adding to Shimon's sense of nervousness as he could now see that all my briefings were coming true.

We were booked into the Mezhdunarodnaya Hotel, which pleased me. Once inside the hotel you could be anywhere in the world except for the unique clock in the foyer with the equally large cockerel perched on the top. I told him not to get lulled into a false sense of security as his room would be bugged and a large mirror behind the bed would have a concealed camera behind the one-way glass. We only had one night here giving me time to collect railway tickets for our overnight trip to Pskov.

Our train left from Leningradski Vokzal and I had no problem finding a taxi to take us there. It was a huge building situated on Komsomolskaya Square and served the Northwest of Russia and beyond to the Baltic Republics. It was fairly easy to find the train but I soon became aware of someone who was following us. It didn't surprise me as not many foreigners were allowed to travel out of Moscow and I presumed that they needed to make sure I was going to where I said I was going. I chose not to tell Shimon at this point, as I did not want to add to his anxiety. As I mentioned previously, sleeping cabins on long-distance trains had four bunks and you never knew who you might be sharing with. Fortunately for us we had the cabin to ourselves, which was relief as the only privacy available was the little curtain that drew along the length of the bed. The tea lady was on duty at the end of the carriage with her large kettle of boiling water making the tea, which was the only refreshment available on the train. She came across as not really wanting to be there and very grudgingly served us with tea. I was not sure whether our tail was also on the train and if he was I didn't see him.

We pulled into Pskov station in the morning, after a non-eventful night, cramped in very narrow bunk beds. We were met on the platform by welcoming party comprising of some of the senior staff from the company we were visiting plus some dignitary officials from the city. We were really being given the red carpet treatment. They suggested that they took us to our hotel first where we could freshen up and then they would show us around the city.

Our hotel was adequate but had a pervading smell of "Breath of Lenin" soap. The bathrooms had bath plugs, which I wondered whether it was just for our benefit. After a quick wash and change I met Shimon back in reception where our hosts were waiting for us. Although it was Monday, a working day, they were first going to take us to the old monastery which was inhabited by an ancient order of monks. It was a beautiful building with golden cupolas glinting in the August sunshine. We were taken round the Abbey by a monk, dressed in his robes with a large sash round his waist, in Friar Tuck style. He could speak English very well and proved to be a very good guide. The best bit for me was the crypt where all the dead monks were interred. The monastery was built on the site of some natural caves and these caves provided very good environment for storing bodies. Coffins were piled high against the walls of the cave in a higgledy-piggledy fashion and looked very unstable. Our guide explained that he too would be interred in the crypt one day and they believed that their bodies would be preserved in a lifelike form inside the coffin, the atmosphere in the crypt stopping them from decaying until they were resurrected in the second coming of Jesus.

'Aren't you tempted to open one of the coffins to see if the bodies are preserved?' I asked the monk.

'Oh no we don't need to. We have faith that our bodies will remain in perfect condition indefinitely.'

My pathology background would not allow me to think that this was possible as the bodies had not been treated with any preservatives and the natural bacteria in the intestines would have soon putrefied the corpse. I did not want to upset our friendly monk so I kept my thoughts to myself.

Next we were taken to a small jetty on the river where a small river cruiser boat was waiting for us. This boat was owned by the company and used for entertaining purposes. The plan was to cruise up the river and past the company's premises and its other land assets! The bar was well stocked and various nibbles were put out for us. As we sailed past the factory and offices, which were enormous, they explained that they liked to look after their workers and as such had a farm next-door where they reared and slaughtered pigs and chickens for their use in the staff canteen. A cooked lunch was supplied to all their employees in the middle of the day. They also had an orchard with apple and pear trees. which if not eaten were turned into juice again for the use of staff. I couldn't believe I was in the USSR as this was so different to life in Moscow. The boat turned around and we made our way back past the factory but then docked a bit further down the river where a barbecue had been prepared for us. Poor Shimon was very tempted with the very aromatic pork but restrained himself. The food was plentiful and periodically new people would come and join us. Some spoke English but some needed an interpreter. I was just about managing to hold a basic conversation in Russian, much to their admiration. After a very tiring day we were eventually taken back to our hotel and would be picked up in the morning at 8:30am for a trip to the factory.

Back in Shimon's room we sat for a while discussing the events of the day, which I hoped were being listened to. Shimon said how much he had enjoyed the day and it wasn't anything like he had expected and he thought that they were nice bunch of people who he could work with.

'I'm so looking forward to seeing their production facilities and just hope that they have everything required to meet our specifications,' said Shimon.

'All good stuff for the record,' I thought as I left for bed.

In the morning we met for breakfast and it was the usual unusual offerings. Hard-boiled eggs, cold fish, beetroot, black bread and apple juice. Shimon was not impressed with this and ate very little, preferring to have several cups of coffee instead. Our hosts picked us up promptly at 8:30am and off we went to the factory.

This company that I had chosen to see manufactured televisions, not too dissimilar to computer terminals so on paper was the favourite of the two. We had formal greetings from the bosses of the company and then started our tour.

The manufacturing shop floor was spacious with approximately 50 staff sitting at electronics benches, soldering printed circuit boards and assembling complete units. Everything was manual with no visible automated processes. They explained that there was no such thing as unemployment in the USSR, so there were plenty of people available to do manual labour. Shimon paid particular attention to the soldering skills of the mainly female workforce, asking to inspect their work at various stages of assembly and frequently expressing his approval. Next we moved onto the moulding shop where all the cases for TVs were made.

'So do you make absolutely everything for the televisions here on site? Haven't you considered getting some items produced for you elsewhere by specialist moulding companies?' asked Shimon.

'Yes we make absolutely everything here with the exception of a few of the electronic components,' was the reply.

Shimon was visibly impressed with this, having got used to farming out lots of component manufacturing back at home and relying on just-in-time deliveries. Everything here was done on-site.

We moved on to testing and quality control of final products where Shimon particularly wanted to see what test equipment they had. It was all very old-fashioned but adequate for the job.

Next came packaging and dispatch. This was a real eye opener for both of us. Out in the back was a lumberyard where two guys were employed to make the wooden packing cases and pallets used for shipping. Not only that but there was a small metalworking shop where one guy was employed to make the nails for the packing case assembly.

'Do you supply other companies with these packaging materials?'

'No, we only make what we need.'

'So what happens if the nail maker can make more nails then you need? Couldn't you sell your excess to another local company?'

'No, he would have a rest for a while.....' came the surprising answer.

'And the packing cases too?'

'Correct. We only make enough for our own production needs. We are told at the beginning of the year how many televisions we need to make and if we finish them early then we can all have a rest.'

It really took us by surprise. The thought of production workers sitting around doing nothing because they had finished their quota. I whispered to Shimon that I would explain about a Command Economy later back at the hotel.

Lunchtime came and we were taken to the staff canteen where a special table had been laid out for us. There were bottles of Georgian red wine and Russian champagne on the table with the offer of Kvass as well. I suggested that Shimon should at least try Kvass but it was an acquired taste. I quite liked it but Shimon thought it was horrible and politely refused any more.

Plates of food were brought out from the kitchen, piled high with mashed potato and cabbage. I hoped that they had not given us pork from the company's farm but no they hadn't, it was chicken. They had obviously paid attention to Shimon's Jewishness and not wished to put him in an awkward situation. Pudding was a bowlful of preserved cherries, again from the company's orchard and was quite delicious. I'm sure that there was a lot of alcohol used in the preservation and this added to their lovely taste.

The afternoon was taken up with a lot of discussions about how we saw a joint-venture working and what both parties wanted to get out of it. The potential market was huge as all of the Soviet bloc countries could be accessed via this company if production could be made big enough to cope with it. It certainly had spare capacity to be able to make a quick start. Eventually the discussions came to a logical closing point and the vodka was brought out for a toast. Poor Shimon, not being much of a drinker, did struggle with the concept of knocking the whole glass back in one, particularly as it was straight out of the freezer, but he made a sterling attempt.

We were taken back to our hotel and arranged to have another meeting in the morning. Before entering the hotel I reminded Shimon that if we were going to discuss the events of the day in his room, we would be listened to.

'I can't believe they would go to those lengths to spy on us,' he said.

'Please believe me... it happens. We should only say things that we want them to hear.'

Shimon reluctantly agreed, still maintaining his sense of disbelief. We sat and talked for a while, agreeing that the company certainly had the skill sets and infrastructure that we were looking for but there were a few points that he was not happy with that needed further discussion.

'What were the things you noticed during our visit today?' I asked.

'Well there was as overpowering smell of fresh paint as soon as we walked in.'

'Yes that's right. They had painted the whole factory to make a good impression for you.'

'What! They did it just because we were visiting?'

'Yep. That shows you how keen they are to get our business. What else did you notice?'

'All the ladies assembling printed circuit boards were wearing their earth wrist straps.' (This is essential in printed circuit board assembly to prevent any build up of static electricity from discharging onto the board and corrupting some of the components).

'Correct. They would have had a good pep talk before we arrived to make sure they were all abiding by the rules. What about the wooden package making shop and the nail maker?'

'I can't believe that each factory might have the same facilities but don't pool their resources for better economy.'

'Economy of scale is not the issue in Command Economy,' I began to explain. 'What happens is that each year a factory is given a quota to manufacture from Central Government. This has no bearing on actual need or cost, just a figure that the Government want to achieve. This could result in either over or under production with no penalty providing the company has made their quota within the year. If they finished early, all their workers could have a rest and this ensures there is no unemployment. If they under produce they are penalised.'

Shimon was gobsmacked but could see the potential for using up any of their spare time.

'So what have you enjoyed and what have you not enjoyed about your trip so far?'

'Well I have thoroughly enjoyed the hospitality we have been shown but as for Russian breakfasts - they are disgusting. I'd kill for a plate of fried eggs.'

Seizing the opportunity I said in a loud clear voice, 'seriously, what would you do for a plate of fried eggs?'

Flippantly Shimon replied, 'I would sign a contract tomorrow if it was possible.'

If I was right and we were being listened to, someone might have picked this up and acted on it.

After a good night's sleep we came down to breakfast and took our seats. Without being asked what we wanted, one of the waitresses came over to Shimon carrying a hot plate. What was on it but four fried eggs. Shimon went white with shock and nearly fell off his chair.

'There. I told you so. Now do you believe me? You'd better do something to keep your side of the bargain today!' Poor Shimon was speechless but still devoured his fried eggs with fervour, gradually recovering from the shock.

We were picked up again at 8:30am and driven to the factory for more discussions when Shimon raised his couple of concerns. I can't remember the exact details now but to Shimon they were important and involved having to supply some parts from the UK. The company could make them but expressed a preference for them to be supplied by us.

They ummed and aahed for a while but continued with their demands. We stood our ground and insisted that they should make everything locally. In the end there was a bit of an impasse so we agreed that we would go back to our hotel where I could type up the document described as a "Letter of Intent" which would sum up each sides' responsibilities if a final deal was struck.

It took me awhile to type this document on my portable typewriter with several carbon copies squashed into the roller, but I managed to produce the required number of readable copies. I called our hosts to say that the documents were ready and could they come and collect them before taking us to the station for our overnight train back to Moscow. They turned up fairly promptly and expressed some disappointment that we had still included our terms, not theirs but would take them back to the factory for consideration and if signed, bring them back to us before we left.

Shimon was getting a bit agitated about this and was thinking that he might be going home without an agreement being signed. We sat and chatted in his room while waiting for our car to the station and I scribbled on a piece of paper

Don't give in and don't say anything that might give them the upper hand. Take my lead in this conversation.

'It would be a great shame if we don't get this deal but we still have the other company to consider if they don't sign up,' I said in a loud clear voice, winking at Shimon who now knew that we were being listened to. 'That company I saw the other week in Vilnius might be worth revisiting,' I said but knowing that I had already ruled them out.

Our car arrived but no signed documents. Shimon looked so disappointed but outside the hotel I whispered, 'it's not over yet. Anything could still happen.'

Our train was waiting at the platform when we arrived and we were escorted to our carriage. Once inside we the opened the window wide to say our goodbyes before the train pulled out. To Shimon's surprise, one of our hosts came running up the platform waving some papers in his hand. He just made it to our carriage before the train started moving and thrust the paperwork through the window.

'We have considered your offer and accept your conditions. Here are the countersigned documents.'

With that the train started to move and I breathed sigh of relief .

'There you are Shimon, your signed Letter of Intent to take back to your co-directors. We did it.'

He was both amazed and pleased and congratulated me on how I had handled the visit.

'I couldn't have done it without you. Thank you so much not only getting the deal for us but for making my experience so memorable. I too will now have lots of stories to tell my family when I get back home. I'm sorry if I didn't believe you at first but you have shown me how we need experienced people like you to work out here.' This compliment really made me feel good as I had so enjoyed letting someone in on the secret world and goings on in the USSR.

Come September I was exhausted and organised a couple of days annual leave. On day one I had a call from my office to say that the Soviet Trade Delegation had called. Minister Smirnov was in the UK and wanted to meet me and to see the factory. Well of course I had to cancel my leave and go to this meeting. A Russian Government Minister asking to see me. It must be good.

I met Minister Smirnov at the station and we had an immediate rapport. No Special Branch this time, or at least I was not aware of any. He was a tall, well built man in his late 50s with whitish grey hair. As Minister for Trade he wanted to see what we did and get to know me. What an honour. The day went very well and included a tour round the factory and a good lunch in the Managing Director's favourite restaurant. This certainly scored some brownie points for me - I could attract the interest of the Russian Government Minister.

Chapter 38

The Wall came down

1989 was a momentous year in world history. After Mikhail Gorbachev's period of glasnost and perestroika and the actions of Solidarity in Poland, on 9 November, the Berlin Wall came down. For years a symbol of The Cold War and a divided Europe, it was now being attacked by a crowd of people armed with nothing but sledgehammers. Guards who would previously have shot dead anyone trying to cross the wall stood by helplessly and watched. Once the Wall was breached thousands of East Germans came flooding across into West Germany after years of isolation and deprivation. Tears of joy were openly displayed as once separated families now were reunited. The world had never seen such a momentous event and it was the subject of television coverage for weeks.

Lena sat and watched the television aghast. For the whole of her life she had been controlled by Communism and now it was in its death throes. People who previously had believed in the propaganda of Communism now realised that they had been living a lie. What on earth was going to happen now. Would all the people from countries behind the Wall now flooding into neighbouring Western European countries overload their ability to support them.

Once the Wall was breached between East and West Germany in Berlin, other borders were challenged all along the boundaries of Eastern European countries, with no resistance from the border guards at all. In Romania a revolution was led by the National Salvation Front and the once hated dictator, Nicolae Ceausescu was arrested and shot along with his wife. In Albania, probably the most isolated state in Eastern Europe, they didn't know that the Berlin Wall had come down due to the dearth of information available to them. It wasn't until early 1990 that the revolution started and a group of about 100 people demolished a statue of Joseph Stalin in Shkodra. After the execution of Ceausescu, their leader Ramiz Alia knew that he might be next if radical changes were not made in his country. He signed the Helsinki Agreement, which forced conformity to Western European human rights standards. Once reporters with their cameras got into these countries where they had never been allowed before, the world saw the austere conditions that their people had been forced to live under. Probably the most vivid and harrowing images were those of children in Romanian orphanages, which prompted a surge of applications from people offering to adopt them.

My thoughts turned to concerns that now the Wall was down and people were moving freely, how much longer could I work as an expert in

Eastern European trade if everyone could now begin to sell their goods freely.

Chapter 39

1991 – 1998

In April 1991 the European Bank for Reconstruction and Development was formed with the brief to fund projects in the newly emerging Eastern European countries, post-communism. Margaret Thatcher had fought hard to have it based in London rather than Paris but had to concede to having a French President, namely Jacques Attali, the former financial advisor to President Mitterrand. One of the Bank's rules was to hire foreign staff in the ratio of the country's shareholding in the Bank. Russia had a 20% stake, which meant that out of a staffing quota of one thousand, two hundred of them should be Russian. Lena saw the Bank's advert and immediately put in an application. An interview appointment came through very quickly and off she went to London, to a building right opposite Lloyd's of London in Leadenhall Street. She came home very excited as the interview has gone well and she had learnt that one of the Bank's major projects was to finance the rebuilding of the decrepit sewage system in St Petersburg, a project where her degree in hydro meteorology would be useful. Of course she got a job, working in the infrastructure team with a magnificent salary, which with her new diplomatic status, was paid tax-free. She was on cloud nine. Travelling would involve catching the 7:50am train from Audley End station to Liverpool Street where her office was only a short walk away. Lena was never one to hurry getting ready for work and it was always me who flapped around her, trying to hurry her up. We had timed the car journey from our flat to the station and with no traffic around we could do it in 4½ minutes. Lena would leave it until six minutes before the train was due with my blood pressure going up by the minute. More often than not we would arrive at the station just as the train was pulling in and she would casually get out of the car, kiss me goodbye and step straight onto the train.

'What's all the panic about?' she would say, as cool as a cucumber.

After a period of getting used to working in the Bank she found out that in the current level of staffing there were only four Russian speakers, three were Russian and one was a Russian speaking Polish lady. As you can imagine her language skills were in great demand especially when it came to technical documentation. She realised that to get further in the Bank some sort of financial qualification would be an advantage so she enrolled on a part-time course in accountancy, which would take several years to complete.

She had never had so much money before in her life and loved to go shopping at lunchtimes especially as she was very close to a lot of designer shops. She also discovered a Japanese restaurant and developed a great liking for Japanese food. She would often call me on a Friday afternoon and suggest that I drove into London that evening so we could both eat Japanese. It only took me 50 minutes as the traffic at that time was coming out of London and by the time we had finished our meal it had died down completely. The staff in the restaurant got to know Lena very well as a regular customer and would often say to us,

'We have got some fresh something or other in from Tokyo today and we are sure that you would like it. Can we prepare it for you?'

Of course the answer was always yes, without ever asking the price as she could afford it on her salary.

The Bank's Christmas parties were something else. They would take over the Dorchester or Grosvenor House Hotel in Park Lane and entertain the 1000 members of staff plus their partners to a lavish spread of food and drinks. There were ice sculptures on the tables, dripping their ice cold water onto carefully placed collection vessels. No expense was spared in giving the staff a good time.

1991 was a very good year for Lena in many ways. With the help of our Member of Parliament, Sir Alan Haselhurst, who wrote to Douglas Hurd, the then Home Secretary, on our behalf, Lena was granted British nationality and got her first British passport. This now allowed her to travel freely, and she disposed of her International Russian passport with great delight. This couldn't have been more timely as EBRD were holding their Annual General Meeting in St Petersburg and Lena was asked if she could attend. She was a little nervous at first but soon realised that with her diplomatic status and travelling for EBRD, there was nothing anybody could do to her in Russia.

The year passed very quickly and soon we were into 1992. On Friday, 10th April Lena had been working late and didn't get home until gone 8:00pm. I gave her supper and we sat down to relax in front of the television. The 10 o'clock news came on with a news flash that an IRA bomb had gone off in the Baltic Exchange, just round the corner from EBRD. The blast from the one ton bomb was so big that it is completely destroyed the Baltic Exchange and severely damaged surrounding buildings. At least three people were known to have died with many other casualties.

Lena gasped. 'I was only there just three hours ago. I could have been one of the casualties.'

On Saturday morning she got a telephone call from one of her colleagues who had gone into the Bank to assess the damage. He asked if Lena would come in as soon as possible to help with the clearing up and to salvage what they could. When Lena got to her office she was horrified to see the damage on her floor. In her seat, a jagged sheet of plate glass was embedded in the back. Had she have still been sitting there when the bomb went off, she would have been sliced in half.

The damage was so extensive, with all windows blown in, that they had to move to some temporary accommodation which was a mammoth task, especially trying to rescue all the important documents and files. For a week everyone went to work in jeans, not suits, as the work was dirty and dangerous.

Cutting a long story short, a new building was refurbished to house the Bank, conveniently for Lena, in an office block overlooking Liverpool Street station. This made it even easier for her to finely tune her journey home as she could see the platform from her window and as soon as her train had pulled into the terminus she would ring me to say what train she was catching and walked the few minutes into the station.

The other major event in Lena's life also happens in 1992. Boris Yeltsin, the new Russian leader, came to visit London and in particular wanted to meet Jacques Attali to talk about some big loans. Mr Attali, knowing Lena's linguistic skills and also being a bank employee (i.e. nondisclosure agreement already in place) asked her if she would be his interpreter during the State visit. She couldn't believe her luck. Imagine having come from a repressed Communist state where the KGB had hounded her for marrying me and now she was being asked to interpret for Russia's State leader and the President of a big European Bank.

On the big day she carefully chose her clothing for the meeting and made sure that she caught an earlier train in the morning. She was officially introduced to Mr Yeltsin right at the beginning of his visit, as she then had to start working immediately as a simultaneous interpreter. During the initial small talk Mr Yeltsin asked how many Russians worked in the bank. Knowing the answer herself, she carefully worded the question to Mr Attali.

'I am not sure,' said Mr Attali. 'How many do you think there are Lena?'

Knowing that there were only four she carefully worded the response to Mr Yeltsin.

'We're not quite sure of the exact figure Mr Yeltsin but there are quite a few!'

She told me later that she was busting a gut to say, 'there's only four,' but responded politically correctly.

With a French presidency, there was obviously a bias towards employing French staff and as it happened, there were more than the official ratio prescribed. Lena had coined her private Russian nickname for the Bank, a "Ligushatnik", which roughly translates into "*a green slimy place where frogs live.*"

1993 also had some memorable highlights for Lena. The foyer of the new EBRD building in Exchange Square was spacious and was an ideal venue for an exhibition. In conjunction with the mayor of St Petersburg, Jacques Attali had managed to organise an exhibition of "Sacred Art Treasures of the State Museum of the History of Religion in St Petersburg" and had personally invited Lena to meet the Mayor, Mr Anatoly Sobchak at the official opening.

Whilst Lena was enjoying the best times of her life, I on the other hand had a spell of bad luck. The company I had been working for and had made a significant amount of sales for in Eastern Europe was the subject of a takeover bid from a much larger company. At the staff meeting to announce the takeover we were all assured that our jobs were safe. Unfortunately that turned out not to be true and the new owners moved their own staff in, making me and a lot of others redundant. I was devastated, particularly as I had just been given honorary membership of the Institute of Export in recognition of my export achievements to Russia. To make it worse, I was going to lose my company car, a perk which I had enjoyed for many years. Our only saving grace was that Lena was earning a good salary, which would keep us going until I found another job.

I started sending my CV's out to various recruitment companies and applied for several export jobs advertised in the Daily Telegraph. I was invited to 3 interviews but because at the age of 42, I was declined as being too old. I argued that how do you get experience in the export market without getting older but to no avail. They all wanted younger people. In desperation I rang an old friend of mine in Denmark who I had known for many years. He was a brilliant engineer and bit of an inventor. He was as shocked as I was to hear my news. I asked him if he knew of anyone that could use my skills and experience. To my surprise he said, 'yes I do, me.' He had just invented a range of products for the emerging IVF market and was looking for someone to sell them for him in the UK, which being the birthplace of IVF was an important market to get into.

'Why don't you fly out to Copenhagen as soon as possible and come and stay with me for a few days when we can discuss what can be done? I will pay for your airfare.'

Having not had a paycheck for a few months I was only too grateful to accept his offer.

I couldn't believe my luck and after clearing it with Lena I booked flights for the next day. He had taken on a small factory on the outskirts of Copenhagen and had started making some of his new inventions. He had already contacted some of the big names in the UK who had all expressed an interest. I thought that it was beautifully made equipment, which is no less than I would have expected from him. We agreed on how we would cooperate and my friend also agreed to fund the purchase of a car for me and advanced me some money until I could start selling his products and make some profits for myself.

When I returned home Lena couldn't wait to hear how I had got on. (Mobile phones hadn't been invented then!) We decided that I could turn our spare bedroom into an office and use our garage as a warehouse.

Having now got her accountancy degree Lena was keen to advance her career and being in the finance sector in London, she got to know a few people who pointed her towards one of the trading banks who were recruiting. After a couple of interviews she was offered a job as a trainee on the trading floor whilst studying for exams to get her properly registered. The salary was again excellent but she now had to pay income tax. Life was now returning to normal again.

My new business really began to take off. I attended various international exhibitions, with Lena accompanying me whenever possible, and met lots of overseas companies also starting off in the new IVF market. I was approached by several of them who had heard that I was doing well in the UK and asked if I would like to represent them as well. This was now a serious business, not just me working from my spare bedroom and garage. I needed to expand and take on some staff. By chance I was introduced to a local Business Angel who was looking for more investment opportunities. I put my case to him and before I knew it he had raised some share capital for me and we set up a Limited Company. I needed more space to work from and found a local farmer who had converted some of his outbuildings into offices for rent. This suited me admirably as they were only 3 miles from my flat and easily accessible for deliveries. Lena was made a Director and took on the role of Company Secretary, which she could do easily, as well as carrying on with her regular job.

In January 1996 Lena passed her Securities and Futures Authority exams and became a Securities Representative on the trading floor, the first Russian to have done this in the UK and a female at that. It was at this point in her career then she realised that the "glass ceiling" operated in a male dominated environment. An intelligent female was a threat to the men and being attractive as well made it even worse. She was now finding it more difficult to progress up the career ladder and couldn't at first understand why until someone explained to her about the "glass ceiling". Not one to be beaten easily she found a more senior role in another trading bank who had headhunted her.

Sitting back and taking stock of our lives, things were looking pretty good. My company was doing very well and we had started up a manufacturing facility to make some of the specialist products required in IVF. Lena had a good job and we could afford nice holidays and to eat out regularly. She had always wanted to ride a horse and decided that now was the time to do it. There was a riding stable about 5 miles away from our flat so Lena enrolled for weekly riding lessons on a Saturday. Naturally she wanted all the kit that went with it so off we went to a saddlery shop and bought the works. She took to horse riding like a duck to water and was soon jumping over fences and gates, looking like a real professional and full of confidence.

Chapter 40

1998 - 2000

In the summer of 1998 we both attended an international exhibition in Gothenberg, Sweden and two months later Lena told me that she was pregnant. This was great news for both of us as she was now coming up to 37 years old and felt it was time to have a child. We did all the antenatal stuff but come October I started to worry about her behaviour. Initially I put it down to the female hormones in pregnancy. One Saturday she took the car into Cambridge and ended up coming home more than three hours later than expected.

'Where on earth have you been?' I asked her in very concerned tone of voice.

'Well I parked the car in one of the multi-storey car parks and then forgot where I had put it. I had to hire a taxi to drive round all the car parks until I found it. Sorry to have worried you. I'm okay.'

It was so out of character for Lena to forget anything but she seemed okay so I let it go, but not without some concern for her. Several days later I met her from work at the station and asked her how her day had gone.

'I've spent the day helping the police with their enquiries.'

'What!' I exclaimed.

'Oh don't worry about it. It was nothing and it's all sorted now.'

She wouldn't answer any more of my questions and told me to forget about it.

The next day I had an outpatient appointment to see the consultant surgeon who had operated on my shoulder earlier on in the year. Lena had taken a day off work to come with me. We were called into his consulting room but there was only one chair in front of his desk.

'I will ask the nurse to get another chair for you,' he said to Lena.

'Don't worry,' she said pushing the papers aside on one corner of his desk. 'I'll sit here,' and with that she hopped up onto his desk and sat there, swinging her legs and rifling through the pile of papers she had just moved.

I was flabbergasted and apologised to my surgeon but at the same time telling him that she was pregnant.

'That's alright,' he said with a smile. 'Pregnancy can do funny things to ladies. Let her sit there.'

When we got out I really let rip about her behaviour but she dismissed it as if nothing had happened which irritated me even more.

'That was no behaviour for a grown woman.'

That night we went to bed after the 10 o'clock News as usual but I was awoken with a start by Lena reaching out of bed and fumbling with something underneath.

'What's the matter?' I asked, thinking that she might have dropped her glasses on the floor.

'I'm looking for the apples,' she said in a very matter-of-fact voice.

'Wh…what?'

'Yes I'm sure I put some apples here the other day and I can't find them now.'

Now I was really getting worried about her behaviour and after comforting her and telling her to go back to sleep I decided I would telephone the GP in the morning as they did an emergency surgery on Saturday.

After explaining my worries to the receptionist who answered the phone she put me straight through to the duty doctor.

'This doesn't sound right. Bring her into me straightaway.'

Lena didn't want to go at first telling me to stop worrying and everything was alright. I insisted and we quickly walked the five minutes down the hill to the surgery.

In the surgery the doctor did all sorts of cognitive tests, reflexes, etc. and then sat down opposite us with a worried look on his face.

'I'm not happy with what I have found and I would like a second opinion. I'm going to ring the duty neurologist at Addenbrooke's Hospital and I would like you to take her in now.'

He picked up the phone and after explaining Lena's symptoms to the neurologist, he agreed that he would see her in immediately. A feeling of dread came over me… I could tell that the doctor was concerned.

At Addenbrooke's Hospital I took Lena straight up to the neuro surgery ward as agreed where they were waiting for her. After a lot more testing and questioning they wanted to do an MRI scan on her head.

'Why don't you go to the canteen and get cup of coffee and come back in an hour?'

My anxiety levels had reached a peak but I left Lena on the ward and went off for a coffee. All sorts of nasty thoughts were going through my head but I tried to dismiss them. Back on the ward Lena was now lying in bed with a hospital gown on, smiling away as usual. The doctor took me into the side room and sat me down saying, 'prepare yourself for the worst. The MRI scan has shown that your wife has a brain tumour in a region of the brain which is inoperable.'

I felt as if I had just been run over by a train. He went on to explain that the tumour was about the size of walnut and as a space-occupying lesion, had damaged the adjacent normal brain cells, which explained her behavioural changes.

'We would like to keep her in and do a biopsy on the tumour to see what type it is and whether chemotherapy is an option.'

'What, now?' I asked.

'Yes now,' he said. 'The sooner the better as we have to take into account that she is pregnant as well. Perhaps you had better go and see her now and explain what is going to happen....'

I tried to compose myself and put on a brave face as I went back into the ward.

'What? Have I got to stay in now? What about my job?'

'Don't worry about that. I will deal with it on Monday.'

'Are they going to operate on my brain?'

'Yes they are going to do the needle biopsy through a tiny hole in your skull to see what is going on in there.'

She went quiet for a while trying to take in what I had just told her.

Trying to lighten the situation a little I said, 'you know what? If I had to have brain surgery there are only two places that I would be happy with. One is this centre of excellence here in this Cambridge teaching hospital and the other would be in Belfast hospital.

'Why Belfast?' she asked.

'Well with all the IRA bombs that have been going off, they are well practised at dealing with serious head injuries.'

She lay there and thought a bit more about her dire situation. We sat in silence with me holding her hands tightly.

After a while another doctor came in and introduced himself.

'Good afternoon Mrs Hunter. I am Mr Murphy (made up name) and I am going to be doing your surgery today. Let's get you prepared and we can get it done this afternoon.'

After explaining the procedure to Lena he left us, advising me that I should go home and come back later. They would telephone me when she was out of surgery.

I turned to Lena and said, 'there, you have got the best of both of my options. A surgeon who has trained and worked in Belfast and is now a consultant here in Cambridge. You couldn't wish for better than that.'

I kissed her goodbye and made my way along the maze of corridors to the garden area outside where I sat on a bench and howled my eyes out. My whole world had just collapsed in on me.

My wife was going to die.

But what about our baby?

Not knowing who to talk to, I found a public phone box and telephoned my parents. Between sobs I managed to blurt out the terrible news. I returned to my solitary bench and tried to compose myself in order to drive home. I was in a daze, a very unreal feeling that I could not comprehend. Somehow I manage to get home and sat quietly drinking several cups of strong tea.

The phone rang at sometime in the early evening but I can't remember when. Lena was out of theatre and Mr Murphy wanted to see me on the ward as soon as possible. I rushed back into Cambridge and was greeted by Mr Murphy who took me aside before I could see Lena.

'We have done a needle biopsy but it was very difficult, the tumour being so deep in the brain. We sent it straight to the lab where they have given us a preliminary report that the cells we removed are all lymphocytes, which is more indicative of an inflammatory mass rather than a malignant tumour. We propose to treat her with a course of steroids, which hopefully will reduce the swelling and allow her to continue with the pregnancy. As far as work is concerned I can sign her off for a month initially and then see how it goes. We will need to do another MRI scan in a couple of weeks to see how the steroids are working. Once the swelling has reduced the neurological symptoms she has been exhibiting may improve but no guarantees as the brain has been damaged.'

I went into the ward to see Lena and there she was, sitting up smiling but with half of her hair shaved off. My immediate thought was, 'she's not going to like that,' as she was always so proud of her appearance and having half a head of hair would be disastrous. I explained what the surgeon had told me which she seemed to be taking in but was more keen to know when she could come home.

On Monday the full report came back from the lab confirming that the cell mass was all composed of lymphocytes so was certainly not a tumour of brain cell origin. They started Lena off on a course of steroids and let her home on Tuesday.

The first thing she wanted to do was to call her Mum in Moscow. I couldn't follow the conversation exactly but Mum was asking if I could write a letter of invitation so that she could get a UK visa to come and help me look after her. Naturally I agreed to do this and got the wheels in motion to get the paperwork prepared. By now Galina had been a regular annual visitor, which had been made so much easier after the collapse of Communism. I still had to get a letter endorsed by a solicitor confirming who I was and that I had the financial ability to support her during the day. This had to be accompanied by a copy of three months' worth of bank statements to prove my financial status.

I took Lena back for a second MRI scan which showed that the mass had shrunk considerably, adding weight to the original diagnosis. The steroids were reduced but they had already had a side effect on her - an enormous appetite. She had started to put weight on quite quickly. Her Mum didn't help as the Russian way of looking after a sick person was to feed them up. I did speak to Lena's employers who were very understanding but couldn't contemplate having her back in the high-pressure financial market until she had a clean bill of health.

We continued with our antenatal visits and little one seemed to be developing okay with no adverse effects from Lena's treatment. Her Mum stayed for a month and once she was reasonably happy with her daughter's improvement, went back to Moscow. However in December Lena's blood pressure started to go up, much to the concern of her obstetrician, a guy I knew very well professionally. He decided to hospitalise her, putting her on complete bed rest. Unfortunately the blood pressure would not come down with medication and proteins were detected in her urine, indicating full-blown case of pre-eclampsia, a dangerous condition for both mother and baby.

She was only 23 weeks into her pregnancy but there was no choice. To let it go on any longer would risk the lives of both mother and baby but a 17 week premature baby was extremely unlikely to survive. Addenbrooke's Hospital had a good history of saving severely premature babies so the decision was taken to do an emergency Caesarian section. Two hours later little Antonina was delivered, weighing in at just 500g – half the weight of a bag of sugar. She was rushed down to the Neonatal Intensive Care Unit where she was connected to a ventilator and a host of drips, cannulas, and electrodes and placed in an incubator. They had put a little woolly hat on her head to keep warm which reminded me of a knitted woolly cosy on boiled egg.

She was alive and fighting.

Her blood pressure was a bit low due to the medication that Lena had been on and her heart rate was a bit erratic. I was allowed in to see her and to hold her little hand through the door of the incubator. She was so tiny but next door to her was another premature baby who had been delivered at 21 weeks and was doing well. I was somewhat encouraged to talk to the Mum who had been there every day for the last two weeks. One of the nurses came up to me and said, 'I don't know what you are doing to her but keep doing it. She is responding to you and her vital signs are stabilising.'

I stayed as long as I could but I had to go back to see Lena after her surgery. She was a little confused as things had happened so quickly and her legs were still not working after the epidural.

'We've got a little daughter,' I said for want of something better to say but we already knew this from the ultrasound scans. I was exhausted and realised that I had been in hospital all day that only had one cup of coffee so I decided to go home and come back as soon as I could in the morning.

After a good night's sleep I went back to see Lena who was a lot perkier. The nurses suggested that we wheeled her down to the Neonatal Intensive Care Unit on her bed to get a first glimpse of her baby daughter. I got a porter to help me and between us we pushed Lena along the maze of corridors. The doors on NICU were obviously designed for such an eventuality as the bed passed through easily. We got her as close as we could to Antonina's incubator and let her hold her hand. I don't think that she could accept that this little thing was her baby as she hadn't been through a long enough pregnancy and hadn't given birth naturally. After about 10 minutes she asked to be taken back to the ward, which we did.

I was still having to work and needed to go back to my office but said that I would be back in the evening. When I got back to the ward, sister came to talk to me saying, 'your wife must have some clout.' She has had two VIP visitors this afternoon. One was Mr C – my shoulder surgeon who had been following her progress after the little episode in his consulting room some weeks back. He had taken the time to come up to the maternity unit to see Lena with some flowers and chocolates much to the surprise of the staff, knowing who he was. The second visit was another consultant gynaecologist friend of mine who worked in the London Hospital and happened to be in Cambridge. I was so pleased to hear this as I felt a sense of support, albeit from a distance.

I popped along to see Antonina again before going home for the night. At 6 o'clock in the morning I was awoken by the phone ringing. It was the duty doctor on the NICU.

'I am sorry to ring you so early Mr Hunter but Antonina has had a setback during the night and is seriously ill. Please could you come in as soon as possible.'

The adrenaline was pumping as I rushed to put my clothes on, jumped into my car and sped off to Cambridge. Parking was not too difficult at that early hour of the morning so I was soon in the NICU. The duty doctor took me into the side room and explained that Antonina's blood pressure had dropped in the night and she had been given some medication to counteract this. Due to her extreme prematurity, the blood vessels in her brain had not yet developed properly and one of them had ruptured, giving her a bleed on the brain. There was nothing they could do to cure this as unfortunately her brain had been irreparably damaged. It was unlikely that she would last another 24 hours but even if she did, she would end up as a cabbage. They suggested that I might like to spend a short while with her but the kindest thing to do would to be withdraw treatment and turn the life support machine off. She would not suffer as she was already in a coma.

My world had just collapsed in on me again. How much more of this could I take? I don't remember how much time I spent with Antonina with tears streaming uncontrollably down my cheeks but I eventually found the strength and courage to flip the switch on the ventilator and left the room. I was beside myself with grief and sat for some while in the quiet room with one of the ward sisters trying to comfort me. It suddenly hit me that I would now have to go and break the news to Lena so I tried desperately to stop crying and put on a brave face to walk back to maternity. I was met on the ward by one of the sisters who escorted me to their quiet room where I broke down again. I remember saying to her, 'I have just killed my little daughter,' between sobs.

'Of course you haven't,' she tried to reassure me. 'She wouldn't have lasted another day and all you have done is just helped her on her way.'

Eventually I composed myself and went to see Lena.

You have been crying,' she said. What has happened?'

'Our baby daughter has died. She had a brain haemorrhage.'

She went quiet for a while and then said, 'well I suppose it was never meant to happen.'

I don't think that she actually understood the situation. It could have been that the area of her brain that had been damaged was affecting her comprehension.

I was really struggling to keep my composure and realise that I now had to deal with the death of Antonina and to continue to care for Lena who had a potentially terminal condition. Although I am not religious, far from it, I suddenly thought that the hospital chaplain might help me so I asked Sister if she could arrange for me to meet him. He was in the hospital today so I went down to the chapel to see him.

'Please don't think that I'm being hard-hearted but I just can't handle the death of my baby daughter and to care for my terminally ill wife at the same time. Please could you help me by dealing with Antonina's death formalities. I just can't cope with both.'

He was very understanding as you would expect from a hospital chaplain and agreed to deal with the formalities of Antonina's death. Although I knew nothing about what he did, I was told sometime afterwards that he had arranged the registration of the birth and death and also attended her cremation at Cambridge crematorium. Following this he had scattered her ashes over the Field of Remembrance at the crematorium.

It was now only a few days until Christmas when I took Lena out of hospital and back home. Our town was illuminated with lots of Christmas lights and was full of happy looking people enjoying the festive season. I couldn't have felt more miserable. I already hated Christmas and current events only helped to increase my anti Christmas feelings. I tried to keep positive for the sake of Lena, who still didn't seem to have any visible emotions for what had just happened to her.

It was a good job that by now my business was a very successful and I had some lovely staff who somehow managed without me for awhile. After Christmas Lena had to go back for a checkup in the postnatal clinic and I found it heart breaking to have to wait in a room full of people with babies.

'What are we doing here?' asked Lena, confirming my thoughts that she had no idea of what she had been through. My friend, the obstetrician, was equally upset for us when he met us and struggled for words to try to help us. It was he who informed me about the chaplain's activities and asked if I wanted to visit the crematorium to which I responded with a definite NO. For me to continue to deal with the current situation I had to put any thoughts of Antonina out of my mind.

The weeks passed into the New Year but Lena was now a very different person. She had put on a lot of weight and her behaviour had become quite childish in a way. No longer the self-confident lady with a high profile job in the city but a child very dependent on me looking after her.

Some weeks later, and I can't recall how many, my worst fears were realised. Lena woke up in the middle of the night looking for apples under the bed. I immediately telephoned the hospital and was asked to bring her straight in. After all the familiar tests and another MRI scan it was confirmed that the tumour had returned and was bigger than before. Mr Murphy came to see us and said that he needed to do another brain biopsy to try to understand what the cell mass was. Lena was admitted immediately and the operation scheduled for the next day. She wasn't quite sure what was going on but I managed to keep calm and assured her that she was in good hands.

The biopsy was carried out and the report came back. Yet another whammy. It was a very rare primary cerebral lymphoma, a malignant tumour which had developed from a piece of normal lymph tissue making its way into her brain and becoming malignant. This is why the first biopsy appeared to show lymphocytes, normal white cells which are associated with inflammation or infection, but were now malignant. She was immediately put back on high doses of steroids to try to reduce the tumour while the plan of chemo and radiotherapy was put in place.

In order to accurately aim the radiotherapy beam, she had to have a full facemask made which would be used to secure her head to the table without any movement. I went with her to have the mask made. Her face was covered with something like cling film and two straws inserted in her nose. Her whole face was then covered with a gooey plastic material and she had to keep perfectly still while the plastic set, only being able to breathe through the two straws up her nose. She was amazingly brave and didn't move at all, only tightly gripping my hand for reassurance that I was there with her. Once it hardened the plastic was peeled off and several tabs attached to it which would be used to screw it down to the table thus totally immobilising her head during treatment.

As the days passed, Lena's appetite became insatiable and she ballooned. Once a petite size 8 she had now become an unrecognisable size 22. One day I had a telephone call whilst trying to do some work in my office. It was the hospital saying that Lena had gone missing off the ward and couldn't be found. The police had been called, as they were worried that she might have wandered out of the hospital in her dressing gown and they were now combing the streets of Cambridge looking for. I went rushing in to join the search, greeted by the ward staff who were so apologetic and embarrassed that they had lost her. After several hours she was found by a cleaner. She had made her way down to the hospital shop, stolen pockets full of food and shut herself in a broom cupboard on another ward whilst she gorged herself. I was so embarrassed by her behaviour and went down to the shop to offer to pay for what she had stolen. It was inconceivable that a once highly trusted member of a Bank and who had worked with Boris Yeltsin, had now resorted to shoplifting. I asked the ward staff if she could be locked in a private room if this was going to continue. They were not able to do this as it would require her to be Sectioned under the Mental Health Act and they did not want to do that. From that day onwards, for every day that she was in hospital, my first visit in the evening was to go to the shop and pay for everything that she had stolen that day.

I had telephoned Lena's mother and arranged for another letter of invitation to be sent to her. She arrived just at the time that Lena was going to start her chemotherapy, following her course of radiotherapy. She had been very brave during this therapy as it must have been very scary with only two straws to breathe through. The chemotherapy was so strong that it is completely knocked out her immune system and she had to be kept in a separate room with reverse barrier nursing procedures, fed with food which had been prepared under aseptic conditions. I didn't realise it at first but every time I took Galina into visit Lena she had been smuggling sandwiches in her coat pockets to feed her daughter up. Once I discovered this I had to go through the degrading procedure of searching her before I let her into the room. She didn't understand the consequences of feeding her daughter infected food while she had a non-existent immune system. At least now she was kept on the ward and couldn't escape to steal food. After several weeks of treatment she was allowed home under strict supervision so I was glad in a way that her mother was still staying with us.

I started to be able to spend more time at work until I got a phone call from Galina in a severe panic.

'Come quick. Come quick. Lena very ill. Blood everywhere.'

I dropped everything and sped home. It was only a ten minute drive but it seemed like an eternity. I rushed up the several flights of stairs to our flat, completely out of breath and my heart racing. She was unconscious on the floor with blood streaming out of her mouth. I managed to roll her over into the recovery position, the adrenalin surge helping me overcome her large body mass, and dialled 999. I explained to the operator that she had recently had brain surgery and was unconscious with blood coming out of her mouth. Within 10 minutes there was someone at the door, not an ambulance man but her GP who had been notified by the ambulance call centre and had rushed up from the surgery. After he completed his examination the ambulance crew arrived, not in a road ambulance but in the air ambulance helicopter which had landed on the school playing field near us. This was followed by the paramedics.

Lena was beginning to come round now. The GP's assessment was that she had had an epileptic fit and had bitten through her tongue, hence the copious bleeding from her mouth. She was taken to Addenbrooke's Hospital where she had her tongue stitched up. During the stitching she had another violent fit in A&E, so confirming the GP's diagnosis. This was brought on by the tumour either shrinking or growing and the surrounding brain tissue sending a series of erroneous electronic signals, which sparked off the fits. She was prescribed anti epileptic drugs and released to home under strict constant supervision orders.

Galina's visa was about to run out so we had to make a trip to the Home Office to ask for an extension. It was a good job we had Lena with us as we were able to prove that her ill health was the reason for the need for an extension. This was subsequently granted.

Lena had no more fits and began to stabilise although her appetite still matched her size 22 frame. Social Services had issued me with a bariatric lifting device in case she fell over again as I would be incapable of lifting her. Galina went back to Moscow and left us on our own for the first time in months.

One day, quite out of the blue, Lena said to me in a very nonchalant way,

'Did I have a child? What happened to it?'

This caught me completely unawares and I burst into tears. I tried to explain to her but she stopped me.

'I'm sorry, I didn't mean to upset you,' she said. 'I won't ask you again.'

I had always promised Lena a trip to the Far East and especially Singapore to have tea with an Orang Utan in the zoo. She had heard my stories about my visits and wanted to experience it for herself. I decided that as she was fairly stable health wise, although still with a voracious appetite, I would take her on a holiday and fulfil my longstanding promise. I booked a trip which covered four cities, namely Kuala Lumpur, Bangkok, Hong Kong and Singapore, spending a couple of days in each venue. She was so excited by this and couldn't wait to go. I soon realised as we were on the first flight that it wasn't going to be easy. She wanted food more frequently than it was served up and kept asking for more. The ladies on the Thai Airlines flight to Bangkok were very accommodating and kept finding things for her to eat.

In the hotel she got up at 4:00am, found her way down to the kitchen and chatted up the chef to feed her. One memorable event was at a cultural evening where there were some beautiful ladies dancing. Lena decided to get up and join them, much to my embarrassment. However the ladies weren't a bit phased, despite her strange appearance, still with no hair, and showed her how to dance Thai style. The audience loved this and gave her a round of applause. The next day we had a traditional Thai massage, which she loved and in the evening a trip on the river with dinner included. Unfortunately she couldn't wait for dinner to be served and went off to the kitchen to ask for her dinner now.

The next stop was Kuala Lumpur where we had a beachside hotel. On the beach was a man doing foot massages so guess who was first in the queue every morning. Yes, Lena.

I thought I was going to have a real problem when we arrived in Hong

Kong as the passport control officer didn't believe that it was Lena's passport because the photo was that of an attractive brunette of slim build and here was this very large lady with no hair. He called over one of his colleagues and they had a long discussion over her passport photo but it wasn't until I stepped up to the desk and explained about her illness that they let her through.

Whilst in Hong Kong we did the evocative Star Ferry crossing at night and amongst some of the daytime visits, I showed her the Peninsular Hotel where they had a fleet of twenty or so courtesy Rolls Royces. Apparently there were more Rolls Royces per capita of the population in Hong Kong than anywhere else in the world.

The last destination was Singapore which was the place she was most looking forward to. The zoo was on Sentosa Island, which involved crossing a busy sea lane by cable car. Because the cars had glass bottoms, you could get a good view of the large passenger ships passing underneath but with my acrophobia I had to keep my eyes shut while Lena was jumping around with excitement. We got to the zoo where the first thing we did was to buy tickets for the Orang Utan experience. Guess who was first up when they asked who would like to come up and cuddle an Orang Utan? Of course Lena was and she was over the moon with the experience, so much so she wouldn't stop hugging the creature and return to her seat. I am sure the animal understood her plight by the faces it was making at her. I felt very emotional as this was the one thing I had always promised her.

Back at home I noticed that Lena's mobility was getting worse to the extent that she struggled walking up the several flights of stairs to our flat. I decided that we needed to move on and buy a house that had a toilet on the ground floor. Our flat sold very quickly and luckily we found a suitable house just as fast. I had to stretch my finances to be able to afford the mortgage but this was the only way that I could look after Lena safely. It was fortunate that I still had the use of the mechanical hoist she fell over several times and could not get up on her own.

We spent Christmas in our new home followed by the Millennium 2000 celebrations but Lena's health was now beginning to deteriorate seriously. She appeared to be losing her appetite and also slurred her speech but what was actually causing this was the tumour starting to grow again and knocking out the area of her brain that controlled swallowing and speech.

Next her mobility deteriorated and she was unable to get up and down the stairs to bed. At this point I asked for help and got social services to supply a hospital bed that could be used to make a downstairs bedroom and also organised some daily visits from carers to help wash and dress her.

As the tumour progressed her ability to swallow and speak were almost non-existent. Her GP suggested that she should be admitted to a hospice to assess her and also to give me some respite. She was put on a drip to treat her now significant dehydration and to give her some nourishment. She was also given pain relief as she was showing symptoms of developing generalised pain. I could see that she was not happy in the hospice and wanted to be with me so I asked if I could take her home and what support I could get to help me. Knowing my medical background they said I could but would need to be taught how to put up her subcutaneous drips and operate the morphine pump. One of the nurses prepared a drip set-up tray and an orange for me to practice putting the butterfly needle in.

'I don't want that orange. Please would you demonstrate on me so I can understand what Lena might feel.'

I rolled up my sleeve and the nurse inserted the butterfly needle into an area of my arm that I could see. She also showed me how to flush out the lines and more importantly how to connect and operate the morphine pump. We timed it so that her latest drip was about to run out and as the injection site had "tissued out" a new site for injection was needed. They watched me as I inserted the needle and covered it with a sticky patch to keep it in place. The morphine pump was attached through a two way valve in the IV line. Satisfied with my ability to set up the drip and medication they arranged for her to come home by ambulance and to get a MacMillan nurse to come in at night so I could get some sleep and rest.

I managed to cope with the help of some carers who came in several times a day but I had difficulty knowing when she was in pain and where it was because she couldn't speak. I had an idea. We had a little fluffy toy pig (don't ask why) which I gave to Lena and explained that when she had pain she should squeeze the little pig where the pain was and I could give her a shot of morphine. This seemed to work. I was getting more and more tired and exhausted after several weeks of this regime and the MacMillan nurse suggested that Lena could go back to the hospice for a week so I could have a break. I reluctantly agreed to this and an ambulance was requested to transport her. I remember vividly the look on her face as I helped get her into the ambulance. It was almost as if she was having a last look at her home and saying goodbye. During the week she deteriorated rapidly and went into a coma.

Lena died in my arms at 1:20pm on Thursday, 9 November 2000, aged 39.

Printed in Great Britain
by Amazon

33423946R00159